Founders of Modern Political and Social Thought

MACHIAVELLI

Maurizio Viroli

OXFORD UNIVERSITY PRESS

1998

Oxford University Press, Great Clarendon Street, Oxford OX2 6DP
Oxford New York
Athens Auckland Bangkok Bogota Bombay Buenos Aires
Calcutta Cape Town Dar es Salaam Delhi Florence Hong Kong Istanbul
Karachi Kuala Lumpur Madras Madrid Melbourne Mexico City
Nairobi Paris Singapore Taipei Tokyo Toronto Warsaw
and associated companies in
Berlin Ibadan

Oxford is a registered trade mark of Oxford University Press

Published in the United States
by Oxford University Press Inc., New York

British Library Cataloguing in Publication Data
Data available

Library of Congress Cataloging in Publication Data

Viroli, Maurizio. Machiavelli/Maurizio Viroli. –
(Founders of modern political and social thought)
Includes bibliographical references and index.
1 Machiavelli, Niccolò, 1469–1527–Contributions in
political science. I. Title. II. Series.
JC143.M4V523 1998 320.1'092–dc21 97-51509

ISBN 0–19–878088–5 (hardback)
ISBN 0–19–878089–3 (pbk)

1 3 5 7 9 10 8 6 4 2

Typeset by J&L Composition Ltd, Filey, North Yorkshire
Printed in Great Britain on acid-free paper by
Biddles Ltd. Guildford and King's Lynn

To Amy Gutmann and George Kateb: friends.

Acknowledgements

This book has been written upon Tim Barton's and Mark Philp's injunction. Should it have some intellectual worth, they deserve the credit; should it not, I deserve the blame.

My single most onerous debt is to Quentin Skinner, to whom I owe the suggestion that I should explore Machiavelli's texts in the context of the tradition of classical rhetoric. If I have failed to do justice to his most valuable suggestion, I am the only one to be censured.

I also owe special thanks to Mrs Hilary Walford, whose severity has made possible the production of a decent manuscript and has demonstrated, once again, that Machiavelli was absolutely right in praising well-used cruelties.

Only the unique intellectual and congenial atmosphere of Princeton, however, has made the completion of this work possible. I therefore wish fondly to express my gratitude to the Department of Politics, and the University, and, more particularly, to two members of the noble congregation of Princeton's political theorists, to both of whom I owe so much that words are inept properly to explain my feelings. This book is dedicated to them.

Contents

Abbreviations

Arte della guerra	*Dell'arte della guerra*, in *Arte della guerra e scritti politici minori*, ed. Sergio Bertelli (Milan: Feltrinelli, 1961)
Discorsi	*Discorsi sopra la prima deca di Tito Livio*, in *Il Principe e Discorsi*, ed. Sergio Bertelli (Milan: Feltrinelli, 1983); references are to book and chapter
Discourses	Niccolò Machiavelli, *The Discourses*, ed. with an Introduction by Bernard Crick using the translation of Leslie J. Walker, SJ, with revisions by Brian Richardson (Harmondsworth: Penguin, 1970)
Discorso	*Discorso intorno alla nostra lingua*, ed. Paolo Trovato (Padua: Editrice Antenore, 1982)
FH	*Florentine Histories*, trans. and ed. Laura F. Banfield and Harvey C. Mansfield Jr. (Princeton: Princeton University Press, 1990)
Gilbert	*Machiavelli: The Chief Works and Others*, trans. and ed. Allan Gilbert (3 vols.; Durham, NC: Duke University Press, 1965)
Il Principe	*Il Principe*, in *Il Principe e Discorsi*, ed. Sergio Bertelli (Milan: Feltrinelli, 1983); references are to chapter
I primi scritti	*I primi scritti politici (1499–1512)*, ed. Jean-Jacques Marchand (Padua: Editrice Antenore, 1975)
Istorie	*Istorie fiorentine* (Florence: Le Monnier, 1990; reprint of 1857 edn.); references are to book and chapter
Il teatro	*Il teatro e tutti gli scritti letterari*, ed. Franco Gaeta (Milan: Feltrinelli, 1965)
La vita	*La vita di Castruccio Castracani da Lucca*, ed. Riekie Brakkee, Introduction and commentary by Paolo Trovato (Naples: Liguori, 1986)
Legazioni	*Legazioni e commissarie*, ed. Sergio Bertelli (3 vols.; Milan: Feltrinelli, 1964)
Lettere	*Lettere*, in *Opere di Niccolò Machiavelli*, iii, ed. Franco Gaeta (Turin: UTET, 1984)

MF	*Machiavelli and his Friends: Their Personal Correspondence*, ed. James B. Atkinson and David Sices (DeKalb, Ill.: Northern Illinois University Press, 1996)
The Prince	*The Prince*, ed. Quentin Skinner and Russell Price (Cambridge: Cambridge University Press, 1988)

Introduction

Niccolò Machiavelli was the restorer of the Roman conception of politics as civil wisdom—that is, the idea of politics as the wisdom of the citizen whose aim is to preserve the civil life—and the founder of the theory of modern republicanism based upon this conception. He was a founder, but in a very different sense from the usual meaning of the word, and most of the pompous titles which have been attributed to him should be put aside, beginning with the least justified of all, that of founder of the modern science of politics.

In his political writings he did not intend to found a science of politics, but to retrieve and refine the conception of political theory as an essentially rhetorical practice based upon historical knowledge and the ability to interpret actions, words, and gestures. He was a restorer, an interpreter, a narrator, and an orator. He laboured to restore and to add new beauty to Roman republican political wisdom, to understand the sense of political processes of his own times, and to tell stories to remind his contemporaries of the political ideals they had forgotten.

The interpretation of Machiavelli as a founder of the science of politics is wrong, no matter what meaning we attribute to the word 'scientific'. If scientific means 'empirical', in the sense of a method of studying political events through accurate collection and description of facts, the claim is incorrect, because, as I discuss in Chapter 2, Machiavelli did not collect or describe facts, but interpreted words, actions, gestures, and texts in order to give advice, make predictions and reconstruct stories *post factum*. If scientific stands for 'demonstrative', in the sense of the early Hobbes's conception of the science of politics and ethics as a deductive system based upon irrefutable definitions of names, there is nothing in Machiavelli even remotely similar.[1] If scientific stands for a Galilean method of inquiry based upon experiments, demonstrations, and generalizations, this model too is totally alien from Machiavelli's style of thinking. He never made experiments; at most he ventured in conjectural reasoning to predict possible outcomes of political situations. He never made generalizations based upon the review of a significant number of facts; at most he presented advice framed as general rules to make them more eloquent and reinforced his arguments by citing examples taken from ancient histories—that is, facts that had already been literally elaborated—or episodes selected from modern history that he himself interpreted, glossed, coloured, and amplified. One could respond that Machiavelli applied a scientific method to the study of politics in the sense that he refused to assign to superhuman causes political events and rather studied them as they were as opposed to 'as they should be': he was a scientist as opposed to a theologian or a moralist. The truth is that, as I explain in Chapter 1, he speaks not only of non-human entities intervening in political affairs, but also of occult natural powers and of heavens influencing human conduct, of portents, premonitions, and divinations, which is exactly the opposite of what is taken to be the mark of a genuine modern scientific approach.

To look at things as they are as opposed to as they should be is not at all an exclusive feature of the scientist of politics. Students of politics trying to interpret political reality also look at things as they are. The crucial distinction is how and from what distance one looks at things as they are. In the case of Machiavelli, he looked at political events from very close to, so as to be able to 'judge by their hands'[2]—that is, to understand the meaning of political actions, and the intentions of particular individuals, not to identify general and permanent laws. When he declared that his intention was to 'concentrate on the effective truth of the matter', as opposed to the imagination of it,[3] he was not issuing a manifesto of scientific realism, as has been endlessly repeated. Instead he was affirming that he intended to understand political reality by uncovering meanings that were not immediately visible but which could be identified, tentatively and provisionally, only by looking at things from very close to, by going under the surface and 'judging by their hands'.

In addition to the fact that his method of studying political reality was interpretive and historical rather than scientific, it is important to recognize that he wrote as an orator, as I try to clarify in Chapter 3. He wrote as a rhetorician, not just in the generic sense that he composed his works elegantly, but in the more precise sense that he wrote them according to the rules of classical rhetoric. He wrote to persuade, to delight, to move, to impel to act—hardly the goals of the scientist, but surely the goals that an orator intends to achieve. He pursues truth, but his truth is always a partisan truth; always a truth coloured, amplified, ornate, and interested; and at times it is not truth at all—a liberty which a scientist can never allow himself, but which an orator is surely permitted to take. Because he wrote as a rhetorician, and not as a scientist or a philosopher, he was able to compose *The Prince* to give advice to a prince on how to secure *his* state, and *The Discourses on Livy* to instruct his compatriots on how to order and govern a free republic. The great puzzle that has tormented so many interpreters is, in fact, no puzzle at all, if we read both works for what they are—namely, two exemplary texts of political rhetoric.

If these remarks on Machiavelli's method of investigation and writing are right, then the claim that we should regard him as one of the founders of the spirit of modernity must be reconsidered.[4] This claim belittles the important detail that Machiavelli's political theory is based upon the belief that ideas, languages, and modes of life which have been in the past alive in the culture of a people can be retrieved and renewed; that Italy, as he writes at the end of the *Art of War*, 'seems to be born to resuscitate dead things'.[5] It also neglects the fact that he repeated over and over again in all his works that the political wisdom of the ancients was far superior to the political ideas of the moderns, and that he wrote all his political works to persuade princes and leaders of republics to imitate the former and avoid the latter. 'While bowing ironically to the authority of the ancients', Harvey C. Mansfield has written, 'Machiavelli in fact uses ancient examples to reproach ancient teaching. He returns to the ancients in order to improve on them.'[6] This view entirely misrepresents the nature of Machiavelli's intellectual relationship with the ancients. He treats the ancients not as authorities to be used against other authorities, but as intellectual authorities with whom he shares the commitment and the passion for political wisdom. He does not bow ironically to them; he discusses with them—that is, he tries to understand what they did by interpreting the texts which record their actions. He treats them not with irony, but with respect; he reciprocates their kindness with gratitude, their affection with a love that compels him to give himself to them entirely and forget, thanks to them, everything else.

Machiavelli never quoted Aristotle, or Cicero, or other ancient authorities to criticize the moderns or to sustain his political advice. When his friend Vettori cites Aristotle's *Politics* to back the view that republics made up of detached territories cannot make great progress and parallel the Romans, he replies, 'I do not know what Aristotle says about confederated republics, but I certainly can say what might reasonably exist, what exists, and what has existed.'⁷ He did not believe he needed Aristotle's authority to prove the validity of his views; he relied rather on reason and historical examples. What he really used to criticize the political ideas and practices of the moderns was the authority of history as narrated by the ancient historians and interpreted by himself.

Instead of continuing to study Machiavelli as the initiator of the modern science of politics and a forerunner of modernity, we should study his works as the highest point of the tradition of Roman *scientia civilis*. He was applying and refining classical political wisdom—it is a point worth stressing—in those very pages of *The Prince* which have prompted scholars to proclaim him as the champion of modern politics who brushed aside the classical burden with a bold intellectual stroke. What Machiavelli does when he changes the conventional way of political virtue is to apply the teaching that Roman rhetoricians laid down under the rubric of deliberative rhetoric. Rules of deliberative rhetoric were intended to instruct a good citizen on how to speak when offering advice on political matters, particularly when he has to give his advice on situations in which honour and virtue have to be deferred to the security of the state. The very lines which, we have been endlessly told, mark the birth of modern politics are, in content and method, a brilliant essay of deliberative rhetoric as taught by Roman masters.

Not only did Machiavelli theorize on politics in a utterly rhetorical fashion; he also regarded political life as the exercise of the power of eloquence, and not just as the exercise of force, as he has been credited with advocating. Princes old and new, founders and redeemers, and republican leaders must know the art of war; but they need also to master the art of words, if they want to succeed. They must know how to rally, discipline, and lead an army; but they must also know how to speak eloquently to persuade, to instil hope, to calm furore, to inspire courage, and to remove fear. Rhetoric accompanies politics always and everywhere: in the battlefield before and after combat; in the prince's cabinet, in the Senate's palace, in the Grand Council's meeting hall; in diplomatic transactions.

The aspect of Machiavelli's political thought in which his intellectual debt to the Roman tradition of *scientia civilis* is particularly apparent is his theory of the republic. Yet, in spite of its magnitude, scholars of Machiavelli's republicanism have not paid sufficient attention to it. As a result, they have presented his republicanism as a commitment to, or fascination for, virtue, military valour, expansion, and predation, rather than as a commitment to the ideals of civil life, and particularly to the principle of the rule of law. I believe instead, as I argue in Chapter 4, that the genuine meaning of Machiavelli's treatment of political virtue can be grasped only if we read it as connected to his overarching commitment to the principle of the rule of law. The political virtue that he invokes and tries to revitalize is the energy, the courage, the craft that serves to institute or restore the rule of law and civil life. In his theory of political action, the rule of law and the virtue of founders and redeemers are not mutually exclusive but are integrated with one another. The virtue of great individuals is necessary when the rule of law is yet to be instituted, or needs to be restored, while the virtue of a people as a whole is necessary to preserve it, if it is already in place. Hence to interpret Machiavelli's theory of political virtue without connecting it with the rule of law ignores the sense both of his interpretation of political virtue and of his republicanism.

The commitment to the rule of law is essential also to understand the other fundamental feature of his republicanism—namely, his conception of political liberty. To be a free people means for Machiavelli not to depend on the will of others and to be able to live under laws to which citizens have freely given their consent. Accordingly, an individual is free when he is not dependent on the will of another individual, but is dependent on the laws only. Hence, to be at liberty means to be in full agreement with the Roman republican tradition, the opposite of being enslaved or in servitude. It is not just not being oppressed—that is to be forced to do something that you do not want to do. This implies that liberty

5

is incompatible not only with tyranny, in the sense of the imposition of a personal or particular interest over the city, but also with monarchy, because in a monarchy subjects obey the laws issued by the monarch and are, therefore, in a condition of dependency. Dependency causes fear, because to be in a condition of dependency means to be under the permanent possibility of being coerced and oppressed. And fear generates servile habits which are incompatible with the status and the obligations of a free citizen. Whether or not they are oppressed, the subjects of a monarch are not a free people (*populus liber*) in the sense defined by Roman jurists. True political liberty is, therefore, possible only under a republican government which properly respects the rule of law and legality. For Machiavelli, republican liberty is more than a rule of law: it encompasses the possibility to participate in sovereign deliberations, to appoint magistrates, to speak freely in deliberative bodies and councils. But it cannot exist without the essential requirements of civil life being fully respected.

However, the flavour of Machiavelli's theory of political liberty and of his republicanism cannot be appreciated without understanding his analysis of patriotism. Surprisingly, in spite of the importance of the subject, there are no studies which seriously investigate this aspect of Machiavelli's political thought, and the few incidental remarks to be found in the literature are almost all rather superficial.[8] As I discuss in Chapter 5, love of country is for Machiavelli the passion which moves citizens to pursue the common good, to resist tyranny, to ward off corruption, and to keep alive a free and civil way of living. It impels the magistrates to serve justice, gives captains and soldiers the courage to fight, and endows founders and redeemers with the strength they need to carry out their extraordinary enterprises. Patriotism in its authentic form flourishes for Machiavelli only among the citizens of free republics. Like Roman republican philosophers and historians, he interprets it as being *charitas reipublicae* and *charitas civium*— that is, a compassionate love of one's fellow-citizens and of the institutions, the laws, and the way of life of the republic which give the citizens the lucidity to see the common good and the strength to carry it out. In all his political works he appeals to love of country: the 'Exhortation to Liberate Italy' is not an extravagant addition to *The Prince*, but its necessary completion; the *Discourses* are replete with narrations of the beneficial effects of love of country; the *Art of War* opens with a praise of a model patriot; the *Florentine Histories* are written with the conviction that, 'if every example of a republic is moving, those which one reads concerning one's own are much more so and much more useful'.[9] Without patriotism, without his own distinctive interpretation of patriotism, Machiavelli's political thought becomes utterly unintelligible.

The Machiavelli that I present in this work is perhaps less interesting than the Machiavelli we admire or blame as the founder of the modern science of politics and the modern conception of political action. These images of Machiavelli, which have left a mark in the intellectual life of our century, have no doubt responded to important intellectual and political needs, fears, and hopes. But I think that another and better way of helping us is to pose new problems, to remind us of ideas that we have forgotten, rather than offering us solutions. Or, more modestly, to cast some doubt over our well-established beliefs about politics. Machiavelli's writings remind us that political action has been and can still be civil wisdom—that is, the art of founding, preserving, and reforming a civil community of individuals living together in peace under the shield of the laws. He retrieved from the classics, and handed down to us, the belief that political action has a special greatness which comes first of all from its goal. When it is practised in the right manner, it provides ordinary men and women protection against ferocity, cruelty, ambition, and oppression; it redeems from corruption; it encourages the pursuit of virtue; it provides the possibility to live one's life as one pleases within the boundaries of law.

In addition to that, political action has a special greatness which comes from the motivations and the qualities that it requires from its practitioners. The image of the political leader, and more generally of the citizen involved in political deliberations, is very different from the stereotype of the cruel, cunning, deceitful, and ambitious man that bigots and bad scholars have attributed to him. The political man is for Machiavelli a magnanimous soul who commits himself, or herself, to goals that go beyond the horizon of self-interest, or family, or social group, but encompass the entire political community, the republic at large. The passion that inspires his deliberations is, as I have already remarked, love of country, and, particularly for political leaders, a desire to attain worldly glory. While, on the one hand, he glorifies political action, on the other, he explains in the clearest possible way that the risks are very high and the rewards very uncertain. For losers, in politics more than elsewhere, there is no mercy; even the best-intended persons are soon forgotten when they fail, if they are not ridiculed. Men's judgement is volatile and often prejudiced: they often bestow love and admiration upon wicked but victorious leaders and ingratitude and contempt upon those who have whole-heartedly committed themselves to the good of their people. Nor is the historians' and narrators' judgement better: the fame of the winners fascinates them too, and the comprehension of the good historians who study and try to rehabilitate the good but defeated politicians is a meagre consolation. And there is no higher court of judgment: men—corrupt, volatile, biased as they are—are the sole judge and arbiter.

Machiavelli knew this all too well. He also knew that often good persons who are called to serve in office have to make morally dubious or repugnant choices if they want to accomplish their duty. He directly witnessed the fall of the Florentine Republic, due, in part, to the fact that the good and honest Pier Soderini, the chief magistrate of the Republic, refused to take exceptional measures against the enemies of the Republic because he did not want to incur the reputation of being an ambitious and unjust man. For Machiavelli, a good citizen should be prepared to do evil, or what is considered to be evil, to save the liberty and the life of his country. Yet, in spite of all that, in all his writings he calls for political action. And, to instil the motivation to commit oneself to politics, in all his exhortations he appeals to magnanimity—that is, the willingness to pursue grand and noble deeds, and even to waste one's life, and one's soul.

Although necessary, the qualities of the great politicians—magnanimity, love of country and desire of glory—are not sufficient to attain civil wisdom. As Machiavelli warns again and again, this sort of wisdom, which is to be attained through the study of history and the understanding of human passions, must be integrated by the mastery of eloquence. Yet scholars have considered him the intellectual father of the theory that politics is essentially a matter of military power, and the theorist of the economy of violence. But what he is in fact telling us is once again an important truth that we have forgotten—namely, that eloquence accompanies political action at all times, including times of war, and that without elo-quence civil wisdom is not a *civil* wisdom at all.

Machiavelli's most powerful intellectual challenge is perhaps that which he addresses to political theorists. He did not understand

and practise political theory as reasoning on what a just society should be like if human beings were rational and moral, or if they were to define the features of their political institutions through a dialogue in ideal conditions in which each participant leaves aside his or her passions and interests. Rather, he understood political theory as a study of the concrete behaviour of individuals and groups, and of peoples in their specific historical and cultural context, with their passions, their desires, and their memories. He focused on real polities, not on imagined or ideal ones.

None the less, all his writings, including the historical ones, have a strong normative content. When he wanted to persuade readers of the superiority of his advice on how to institute, govern, and reform republics, he used the eloquence of the narrator, rather than philosophical reasoning; he resorted to historical narrations and examples—properly coloured, amplified, and interpreted, of course. After him, and particularly nowadays, political theory has taken a different direction: more and more distant from rhetoric and history, closer and closer to philosophy and economics. Machiavelli's style has been forgotten, or transfigured, as I have remarked, into a scientific method. It is almost universally agreed that political theory's emancipation from rhetoric and history is a progress; I believe, instead, that precisely the opposite is the case, and a return to Machiavelli's style would be a salutary intellectual change. If we were to learn to frame our arguments by looking first at the reality of political life and then present our advice in an eloquent manner, free from philosophical jargon, political theory would be more interesting and more capable of exercising a positive influence on civil life, which has after all been its vocation since its beginnings.

Absurd as it may sound, however, I think the most interesting surprises for us will come from Machiavelli's philosophy of life, including his moral and aesthetic views—aspects of his thought which have been, with very few exceptions, always neglected. As is well known, he portrayed men's cruelty, ambition, meanness, and ferocity in the most vibrant way and vividly described the misery of the human condition. But this is only part of the story. He also offers us a wealth of reflections on the remedies to the miseries of the human condition. Love, politics, poetry, irony: he analysed and practised all of them, without pretending to have found the ultimate solution. He knew even too well that human fragility and weakness do not allow for the pursuit of moral perfection, which he also considered to be intolerably boring; he enjoyed the variety of individuals' inclinations, tastes, and passions and never even conceived of the idea that there is but one right way of living one's life. With its misery and its splendour, the human world was the only world that attracted him and for which he cared.[10] His conception of life encompasses different things: the grand and the ordinary, the grave and the light, rigour and transgression, commitment and irony. Many readers will find it confused, unacceptable, or even irritating. I find it a refreshing alternative to the culture of self-interest, reasonableness, and dull decency, as well as the bigotry, the moralism, and the zealotry which pervade our time.

1

Machiavelli's Philosophy of Life

The main feature of Machiavelli's thought, wrote one of his finest interpreters, is his 'spiritual narrowness'; his insensitivity 'to any spiritual movement that is not subordinate to a purely political idea': no serious religious or moral anxiety, no sincere concern for the meaning of life; only a passion for politics and for the study of political events and actions.[1] This image of Machiavelli has induced scholars to investigate his political thought as a self-sufficient and secluded province, and to leave aside his beliefs, about the cosmos, man, death, life, and history.[2]

I believe that this approach distorts Machiavelli's intellectual and moral identity and prevents us from appreciating his interpretation of the meaning and significance of political action. This is not to say that his conceptions of politics are founded upon his beliefs of the universe, and even less that they were determined or constrained by them. It means rather that we can attain a richer understanding of his views on the goals and the value of political action if we consider them within the broader spectrum of his beliefs. Also, to study Machiavelli as a purely political thinker deprives us of a moral philosophy of the highest value based upon a magnanimous conception of life pervaded by irony and self-irony, tolerant to the variety of the human world and human fragility, sympathetic to poetic abandonment to beauty and love, sensitive to the affections of ordinary life, and—a feature which I find of invaluable worth—radically, even irreverently, secular.

From the Angle of Poverty and Hardship

As for turning my face toward *Fortuna*, I should like to get this pleasure from these troubles of mine, that I have borne them so straightforwardly that I am proud of myself for it and consider myself more of a man than I believed I was. And if these new masters of ours see fit not to leave me lying on the ground, I shall be happy and believe that I shall act in such a way that they too will have reason to be proud of me. And if they should not, I shall get on as I did when I came here: I was born in poverty and at an early age learned how to scrimp rather than to thrive.[3]

Machiavelli wrote these lines to his friend Francesco Vettori in Rome, on 18 March 1513, a few days after he had been released from prison. He had been put there under the false charge of conspiracy against the new regime controlled by the Medici family which had replaced the republican government instituted in 1494. When he mentions the troubles ('affanni') which he had bravely endured, he was referring to the tortures which were inflicted upon him to obtain a confession that would have meant the death penalty. But he was also referring to another even more painful wound: his dismissal from his post as *Secretario* of the Second Chancery of the Republic and the formal ban to participate in any manner to political life. By remarking that he had bravely endured all these hardships and that he was used to face adversities, he intended to reassure his friend, whom he was hoping would have helped his political rehabilitation. But he was also disclosing important information about himself and his way of looking at life and the world. He was telling his friend that very early on in his life he had accustomed himself to look at men and life from the side of poverty, exclusion, and adversity.

Looking at the world as a defeated and poor man, from below, he had the chance to see, first of all, the power and the effects of omnipresent ingratitude. I cannot find a man, he wrote in a disconsolate letter to Vettori of 10 June 1514, 'who recalls my services or believes I might be good for anything'. Ingratitude 'lives in the breasts of princes and kings', but it also inhabits 'the heart of the populace when it is sovereign'.[4] He remarks that ingratitude makes man 'merely bear witness that he has received a benefit'. It also makes him 'forget the favours [he] receives; yet doing the giver no injury, he merely denies it', and—the most wicked of all the effects of ingratitude—it make men 'never remember or return a favour, and to the extent of their power [they] rend and bite their benefactor'.[5]

Ingratitude, Machiavelli writes, was nursed 'in the arms of Envy', the malignant passion which bites great men and prevents them from accomplishing great deeds. It cannot be placated by goodness, humility, and patience. Pier Soderini, who tried until the last minute to placate the envy of the enemies of the Republic by goodness, the favour of fortune, and 'beneficence towards all', found himself alone and scared, abandoned by all, and he failed to save the liberty of Florence. As Machiavelli remarks in the *Discourses*, the only way to overcome envy is 'the death of those who are imbued with it'; and, if their death does not occur for natural causes, the prudent ruler must 'devise some way of getting rid of the persons in question, and he should take steps to overcome the difficulty before doing anything else', as Moses did, when he 'had to kill a very great number of men who, out of envy and nothing else, were opposed to his plans'.[6]

If ingratitude and envy are the rewards for one's labours and pains for the good of one's country, the only wise thing to do would be to flee 'from courts and politics', unless, as was Niccolò's own case, another passion compels one to enter those courts where ingratitude and envy are unchallenged queens. When he wrote these lines, he believed that the years he spent serving the Republic were wasted. They had left him only poverty, sorrow, and melancholy. And yet he could not stay out of that world, because, with all its horrors and miseries, political life is the stage on which grand deeds take place.

In truth, when he served as *Secretario* from 1498 to November 1512, he enjoyed a few moments of glory. One of these was the institution of the civic militia in 1506—a personal triumph secured by a number of orations in which he persuaded his fellow-Florentines that liberty must be defended with valour and not with money, and that it is neither safe, nor honourable, to continue to rely on mercenary troops or on somebody else's sword.[7] Another was the conquest of Pisa in 1509, a diplomatic and military success for which he was highly praised.[8] He was also often praised for the precision, the insight, and the clairvoyance of his reports from the various courts he visited as orator of the Republic. But, for the most part, personal rewards were meagre, and the pains, and the risks, high.

Yet, after the fall of the Republic, he tried over and over again to re-enter the world of active politics. He was prepared, as he did so, to accept humble and even mortifying assignments: I am prepared to accept any job from 'our present Medici lords', he wrote to Vettori, 'even if they begin by making me roll a stone'.[9] He was not prepared, however, to serve a foreign prince. When he was offered the chance to become the secretary of Prince Prospero Colonna in Rome—with a very generous salary—he refused. He preferred to remain in his country villa in Sant'Andrea in Percussina to write the *Florentine Histories*, for a modest salary offered by the Medici Pope Clement VII.[10]

Machiavelli's regret for the days when he had been the *Secretario*, a regret which tormented him until his death in 1527 (21 June), must not be confused with the rancour of the ambitious and rapacious politician who no longer has the means to quench his greed. It was the anguish of a magnanimous soul forced to remain off the stage where grand events were taking place. Reduced to political inactivity, he transferred to his writings his passion for greatness and his profound disdain for the meanness, the incompetence, the cowardice, and the base ambition that pervaded the politics of his time. In *The Prince*, the first work he composed after he had lost his post, he summarized, as he put it, 'my knowledge of the conduct of great men, learned through long experience of modern affairs and continual study of ancient history'.[11] He wrote the *Discourses on the First Ten Books of Livy* (1513–17), not for 'those who are princes', but for 'those who, on account of their innumerable good qualities, deserve to be'; not for 'those who, without knowing how', actually govern, but for 'those who know how to govern'.[12] At the very outset of the *Florentine Histories*, he wrote that the actions 'of governments and states, have greatness in themselves', and they always appear 'to bring men more honour than blame', and he was referring to those who actually perform those actions and those who write on them.[13] The *Art of War* begins with praise of Cosimo Rucellai as a man 'whose spirit was more on fire for things grand and magnificent [*cose grandi e magnifiche*]' and ends with a powerful censure of the meanness and inaptitude of Italian princes:

the common belief of our Italian princes, before they felt the blows of Transalpine war, was that a prince needed only to think of a sharp reply in his study, to write a fine letter, to show quickness and cleverness in quotable sayings and replies, to know how to spin a fraud, to be adorned with gems and with gold, to sleep and eat with greater splendour than others, to be surrounded with wanton pleasures, to deal with subjects avariciously and proudly, to decay in laziness, to give position in the army by favour, to despise anybody who showed them any praiseworthy course, and to expect their words to be taken as the responses of oracles'.[14]

When he was *Secretario*, and in the last years of his life, when he was employed by Pope Clement VII in an unsuccessful attempt to counter Charles V's aggressive politics on Italy, Machiavelli tried with all his energy to provide some remedy for the inaptitude of political leaders who had caused first the fall of the Florentine Republic and then the ruin of Italy. When he wrote on politics, he tried to exhort political leaders yet to come to pursue greatness and to find for himself a path to that world of greatness from which he had been banned.

The Miseries of the Human Condition

For Machiavelli, politics has to provide a shelter against the evils that torment men's life, beginning with ambition and avarice, the causes of discord and war. Ambition and avarice penetrate every province, city, and village to deprive men of the most precious benefit of peace.[15] They are naked, seductive, all-embracing; they come followed by envy, sloth, hatred, cruelty, pride, and deceit. Wherever they arrive, they drive away concord, peace, and charity. When they enter in men's hearts, their minds become 'insatiable, arrogant, crafty, and shifting, and above all else malignant, iniquitous, violent, and savage'.[16] When possessed by ambition, men value not just whatever good their enemies have, but even the goods that they seem to have more than what they have; they suffer for the others' success, and thereby they put every effort, no matter how painful, to spoil it. They seek to affirm their superiority not by cultivating virtue, but by oppressing the others; and to oppress they wage wars.

War is the greatest evil that affects the human condition. It is, as Machiavelli writes in the poem 'Of the Blessed Spirits', a 'pitiable and cruel affliction of miserable mortals' that displeases God.[17] In war men unleash their ferocity and their cruelty, particularly on women, children, and non-combatants. When the Spaniards sacked

Prato in August 1512, he writes to a lady: 'more than four thou-
sand died; the remainder were captured and, through various
means, were obliged to pay ransom. Nor did they spare the virgins
cloistered in holy sites, which were all filled with acts of rape and
pillage.'[18] Machiavelli describes war as the outcome of ambition,
and as a cruel, inhuman, horrible sufferance, not 'as an inescapable,
grandiose and terrifying force'.[19] And civil war is even worse; even
when a people is fighting to recover its liberty, as in the case of the
Florentines who rebelled against the tyranny of the Duke of
Athens, cruelty deserves no excuse. Machiavelli's description of
the ferocity of his fellow-Florentines is meant to arouse repulsion
and to meditate over the horrors of civil strife:

Messer Guglielmo and his son were placed among thousands of their enemies, and the son was not yet eighteen years old; none the less, his age, his
form, and his innocence could not save him from the fury of the multitude.
Those whom they could not wound living, they wounded when dead, and not
satisfied with cutting them to pieces with their swords, they tore them apart
with their hands and their teeth. And so that all their senses might be
satisfied in revenge, having first heard their wails, seen their wounds, and
handled their torn flesh, they still wanted their taste to relish them; so as all
the parts outside were sated with them, they also sated the parts within.[20]

Man's life begins in weeping and often ends, because of ingratitude
and envy, in solitude, poverty, and despair. Or, because of ambition
and war, in screams, sobs, and sorrows.

For Machiavelli, man is alone and helpless in this world. Even if
God is perhaps friend to the valiant and he, or Christ, may at times
bring some relief to the wretched, man's condition in this world
remains disconsolate. Man, he writes, is more unhappy and defenceless than any other animal: 'only man is born devoid of all
protection; | he has neither hide nor spine nor feather nor fleece |
nor bristle nor scales to make him a shield | in weeping he begins
his life, | with a sound of a cry painful and choked, | so that he is
distressing to look at.'[21] These words from *The Golden Ass* are an
elaboration of Lucretius' *On the Nature of Things* which Machiavelli copied in his youth.[22] Man is not at all the master of the
universe but the victim of nature first and of Fortune afterwards.
He esteems himself highly in comparison to other species; but
without reason. In fact 'no animal can be found that has a frailer
life'. And no other animal is capable of so much cruelty; only men
slay, crucify, and plunder other men. Yet, in spite of the fragility and

the misery of his condition, man has a desire for living that is stronger than that of any other creature.[23]

For Machiavelli, men's passions do not change over history.

If the present be compared with the remote past, it is easily seen that in all cities and in all peoples there are the same desires and the same passions as there always were. So that, if one examines with diligence the past, it is easy to foresee the future of any commonwealth, and to apply those remedies which were used of old; or, if one does not find that remedies were used, to devise new ones owing to the similarity between events.[24]

This belief that men's passions, humours, and desires are the same and operate in the same manner over time rests upon a cosmology. Many believe, he writes, that the imitation of the ancients is not only difficult but also impossible, 'as if the heaven, the sun, the elements, men were changed in motion, order, and power from what they were in antiquity'.[25] This is only a passing remark, designed to discredit the belief that the imitation of the ancients is impossible by saying that this opinion would be true if it were also true that the heaven, the sun, the elements, and men were changed from what they were in antiquity. But the passage quoted above contains the core of Machiavelli's conception of the universe and of the connection between human events and celestial motions.

To make his point, he would have needed to say simply, as he did elsewhere, that it is utterly absurd to believe that men were changed from what they were in antiquity, and therefore the imitation of antiquity is perfectly possible. The reason why he brings in the heaven, the sun, and the elements is because he believes that they do influence human things heavily. Had the motion, order, and power of heaven changed since antiquity, then it would be really impossible for modern men to imitate the ancients, because the heavens would compel them to act in a totally different manner. But, since we can safely believe that no such thing as a change of the order, motion, and power of the natural world has occurred, we may also believe that the imitation of the ancients is possible.

Man and Cosmos

Contrary to the opinion of a number of scholars, Machiavelli has not at all 'declared himself for progress in terms we recognize'; nor did he share modern beliefs about men's 'perfect freedom' and capacity to gain control over themselves and the world.[26] His view of the evolution of human history is cyclical, not progressive; and he regarded human beings' freedom of action as being severely constrained by the influence that heavens and other natural or occult forces have upon them.

Machiavelli expounds his belief on the connection between heavenly motions and human things in the poem *The Golden Ass*, composed in 1517, and in other works of poetry. For him poetry was a way not only to express feelings, but also to convey beautifully his views on the human condition, on politics, and on history. He composed in verse two chronicles of Florentine political events: the *First Decennial* (1504) and the *Second Decennial* (1514). He also expressed in verse or epigrams some of his most political judgements, like the famous one on Pier Soderini: 'The night when Piero Soderini died, his spirit went to the mouth of Hell. Pluto roared: "Why to Hell? Silly spirit, go up into Limbo with all the rest of the babies."'[27] We can safely take his poems, along with his 'serious' works as a reliable guide to an understanding of his conception of the world.

For him there is a connection between celestial motions and the perennial restlessness of human things: 'the star and the heaven go wandering, | now high, now low, without any rest . . . likewise nothing on earth remains in the same condition always.'[28] He also maintained that heavenly motions and humours do in fact influence human events: 'From this [heaven's motion] result peace and war; on this depend the hatreds among those whom one wall and one moat shut up together.'[29] He also presents his general belief on the cycle of progress and decay of countries as being the will of the power which governs human things:

Virtue makes countries tranquil, and from tranquillity, leisure next emerges, and Leisure burns the town and villages. Then, after a country has for a time been subject to lawlessness, Virtue often returns to live there once again. Such a course the power which governs human things permits and requires, so that nothing beneath the sun ever will or can be firm. And it is and always has been and always will be, that evil follows after good, good after evil.[30]

In the *First Decennial*, a composition in verse in which Machiavelli condenses ten years of Florentine history from 1494 to 1504, he writes: 'I shall sing Italian hardships for those two lustres now just over, under planets hostile to her good.'[31] And in the Dedicatory

Letter to Alamanno Salviati, he says that Italy's misfortunes were caused by 'the necessity of fate, whose power could not be checked'.[32]

Fate's and heaven's plans can, in part, be detected, Machiavelli believes, by divinations, revelations, prodigies, or other heavenly signs.[33] Charles VIII's invasion of Italy in 1494 was predicted by Savonarola and, at the time, 'it was said that armed hosts had been heard and seen in the sky above Arezzo fighting one with the other'.[34] He does not question at all the value of celestial signs and of the divinations based upon them. On the contrary, he ventures as a possible explanation the idea that 'the atmosphere is full of spirits, endowed by nature with the virtue to foresee the future, who out of sympathy for men give them warning by means of such signs so that they may look to their defence'.[35]

Heaven also exercises its benign or malignant influence upon individuals. In *The Golden Ass* Circe's benevolent damsel tells the protagonist of the story that: 'From this came your first suffering; | this was altogether the cause of your toils without reward.' Heaven has not yet changed its 'opinion', nor 'will it alter it' as long as 'the fates keep towards you their hard purpose. And those humours which you have found so hostile and adverse are not yet, not yet purged; but when their roots are dry, and the heaven shows itself gracious, times happier than ever before will return.'[36]

Machiavelli's cosmos is densely populated. Heaven, Fortune, and God each has a role, though it is not always well defined. Heaven presides over orderly motions, cycles of progress, decay, death, regeneration, and corruption. Heaven (*cielo*), he writes in the *Discourses*, orders in a general way the course of all things in the world, particularly of composite bodies ('corpi misti') such as republics and religious sects. It is also in charge of periodic purges of nations and societies through pestilences, famines, and flood. As in the case of simple bodies, he writes,

when nature has accumulated too much superfluous material, it frequently acts in the same way and by means of a purge restores health to the body. Similarly in the case of that body which comprises a mixture of human races, when every province is replete with inhabitants who can neither obtain a livelihood nor move elsewhere since all other places are occupied and full up, and when the craftiness and malignity of man have gone as far as they can go, the world needs be purged in one of these three ways [pestilence, famine, and flood], so that mankind, being reduced to comparatively few and humbled by adversity, may adopt a more appropriate form of life and grow better.[37]

Whereas heaven presides over orderly and necessary motions, Fortune is the mistress of chance and accident.[38] Machiavelli carefully describes her role, status, and power in a poem in tercets.[39] She has her own kingdom and from her throne she governs the whole world and disposes of time as she pleases. Above the gates of her palace 'sit Luck and Chance, without eyes and without ears'; inside, she sits surrounded by wheels which never stop turning, day and night, 'because Heaven commands (and it is not to be resisted) that Laziness and Necessity whirl them around'.

She uses her immense power over the things of the world in a completely arbitrary way, 'without compassion, without law, without right'; she often 'keeps the good beneath her feet', and 'raises the wicked up'; deprives the just of the good that she arbitrarily 'gives to the unjust'; 'often seats the undeserving on a throne to which the deserving never attain'. She takes a special pleasure in hurting generous men, as in the case of Antonio Giacomini Tebalducci, one of the rare valiant captains on whom the Republic of Florence could count:

for his *patria* this man bore much, and long he sustained | with great justice your army's dignity. | Covetous of honour, generous with money and capable of such | virtue he is, that he merits honour much higher than I give him. | Now neglected and scorned he lies in his house, poor, old and | blind. So greatly displeasing to Fortune is he who does well.[40]

In Machiavelli's picture Fortune is not blind at all. Her eyes are ferocious and sharp; she distinguishes very well the good, whom she punishes with servitude, infamy, and sickness, and the brave and the audacious, 'who push, shove, and jostle her', whom she rewards with power, honour, and riches. However, not even the most brave and the most audacious, such as Alexander and Caesar can withstand her power or outwit her malignity: the former failed to reach 'the coveted harbour'; the latter, 'covered with wounds, in his enemy's shadow was slain'. Really to master her, men ought to be able to change their conduct according to the times and the order of things: 'anyone wise enough to adapt and understand the times and the patterns of events would always have good fortune, or would always keep himself from bad fortune; and it would come true that the wise man could control the stars and the Fates.' But, since heaven, the lord of order and constancy, does not permit individuals to change their nature, 'Fortune varies and commands men and holds them under her yoke'.[41]

When Fortune wants to accomplish great things, she chooses a man of high spirit and great virtue capable of seizing the occasion that she offers him; in like manner, when she wants to bring about a great disaster for a country or a republic, she sustains men who will help to cause that ruin, and should anyone have the power to curtail her plan, she 'either kills him off or deprives him of all the power of doing good'. Hence, Machiavelli concludes, 'men may second fortune, but cannot oppose it'; 'they may weave its warp, but cannot break it'.[42] From this belief in the power of Fortune, however, it does not follow at all that men should cease 'to sweat much over things' and let themselves be governed by fate. For one thing, Fortune is the arbiter of half of the actions of men, but 'it lets us control roughly the other half'. Men's virtue can resist her power; they can check it 'by means of dikes and dams'—that is by means of good political and military orders.[43]

Moreover, since Fortune always proceeds in unpredictable ways, we 'should never give up', we 'should never despair', however hopeless and difficult circumstances are. Placed within the intellectual context of his beliefs on Fortune's and heaven's power, Machiavelli's exhortations not to give up, to build dikes and dams ahead of time, to try to adapt one's conduct to changing circumstances and to devote oneself to political action, are vindication of a wise and magnanimous conception of life. His belief in Fortune and heaven call for resignation; his commitment to the pursuit of great things calls for political action.

A Political God

In addition to Fortune and heaven, Machiavelli also finds a place for God. In the poem *Of Ambition*, he sketches a conventional picture of God as the creator of the universe, and yet he inserts a very unorthodox reference to an occult power hidden in heaven:

Hardly had God made the stars, | the heaven, the light, the elements, and man | master over so many things of beauty | and had quelled the pride of the angels, | and from Paradise had banished Adam with his wife for their tasting of the apple, | when . . . a hidden power [*potenzia occulta*] which sustains itself in the heaven, | among the stars which heaven as it whirls encloses | to man's nature by no means friendly | to deprive us of peace and to set us at war, to take away from us | all quiet and all good, sent two Furies to dwell on the earth.[44]

A God who allows for the presence of an occult force in heaven with so much power over the things of the world, and also allows whimsical and furious Fortune to torment mortals, is surely quite different from the orthodox Christian God who governs nature and the human world through providence, as well as the heterodox Christian God of Pontano, Bellanti, and, to a degree Ficino and Pomponazzi, who governs the universe through heaven and Fortune.[45] Machiavelli's God competes with heaven and Fortune for the privilege of intervening in human affairs rather than using them both. In the *Florentine Histories*, for example, he speaks of God intervening to help Florence: 'God, who in such extremities has always had a particular care for it, made an unhoped-for accident arise that gave the king, the pope, and the Venetians something greater to think about than Tuscany.'[46] But in the same work he attributes similar acts of governance on human things to heaven—as in book II, where he describes the Duke of Athens's arrival in Florence as the consequence of heaven's malignant disposition: 'since the heavens willed that things prepare for future evil, he arrived in Florence precisely at the time when the campaign at Lucca had been lost completely';[47] or to Fortune: 'although the nobility had been destroyed, none the less fortune did not lack for ways to revive new trials through new divisions.'[48]

Moreover, God's role as creator of the universe is rather unorthodox. Although he is much more cautious than he usually is, in *Discourses* II. 5, Machiavelli seems to say that those philosophers 'who want to make out that the world is eternal' are right.[49] The reason for his caution is obvious, since the idea that the world is eternal was not only heterodox but in fact heretical. The testimony of his great-nephew, Giuliano Ricci that, in all his compositions, 'Niccolò indulged in much licence, as well as blaming great personages, lay and ecclesiastic, as in reducing all things to natural or fortuitous causes', has to be taken very seriously, particularly because, in other circumstances, Giuliano Ricci laboured very hard to protect the name of his great-uncle from the charge of atheism.

Machiavelli's God is the last hope of a derelict, like Italy, which, 'remaining almost lifeless', 'beseeches God to send someone to rescue it from the cruel and arrogant domination of the foreigners'.[50] At times God intervenes to attenuate heaven's malignity, as in the case of Niccolò himself. 'It is a miracle that I am alive,' he writes to his nephew Giovanni Vernacci; 'because my post was taken from me and I was about to lose my life, which God and my innocence have preserved for me', and, with the help of God's grace, I shall live as best as I can 'until the heavens show themselves to be more kind'.[51] More often, though, God helps those who help themselves: 'but there should be no one with so small a brain | that he will believe, if his house is falling, | that God will save it without any other prop.'[52] And, of all men, he likes the strong and the brave: men, the Lucchese captain Castruccio Castracani used to say, 'ought to try everything, not to be afraid of anything', as 'God is a lover of strong men, because we see that he always punishes the powerless by means of the powerful'.[53]

Like Castruccio's, Machiavelli's God has little resemblance to the Christian God who sent his own son to die to redeem humanity. He is the God of captains, princes, lawgivers; or, perhaps, more precisely, a rhetorical God, to be used to persuade princes to commit themselves to grand enterprises of innovation, reform, and redemption. Machiavelli resorts to God particularly in exhortations; he promises God's help and God's reward to assure that the enterprise he is urging to undertake is feasible, and shall bring glory. Although references are almost absent in the *The Prince*, he mentions God five times in the 'Exhortation to Liberate Italy' that concludes *The Prince*.[54] The 'exceptional and remarkable men', men such as Moses, Cyrus, and Theseus who redeemed their countries, he writes, were none the less human, and their causes 'were not more righteous', nor 'easier', than the liberation of Italy; and, more importantly, he remarks that 'God was not more a friend to them than to you'.[55] Italy is well disposed 'and the difficulties to be confronted cannot be very great when the circumstances are propitious'; moreover, God shows his friendship through clear signs: 'the sea has opened; a cloud has shown you the way; water has flowed from the rock; manna has rained down here.' But God, Machiavelli concludes, 'does not want to do everything, in order not to deprive us of our freedom and the glory that belongs to us'.[56] A similar rhetoric is employed also in the *Discourse on Remodelling the Government of Florence*, which he wrote in 1520. To persuade Cardinal Giulio de' Medici to restore a republican constitution in Florence, he assures him that no other deed would be 'most pleasing to God'.[57]

For rhetorical purposes, Machiavelli adapts the classical idea of God the friend to founders and saviours of republics whose origin is to be found in Cicero's *Scipio's Dream* edited by Macrobius around

AD 430.[58] The presence of this theme, which had been kept alive with little variation by Petrarch and by Quattrocento humanists like Matteo Palmieri, is visible in Machiavelli's texts. In the *Discourses* he writes that the founders of republics, like Romulus, lived their lives secure and after death became glorious; in the *Discourse on Remodelling the Government of Florence* he refers to the great reformers of republics as 'Gods' ('Iddii'). However, his political God is more 'understanding' than the God of Cicero and the humanists. For them, God is ready to help and reward founders, rulers, and redeemers of republics who have practised the political virtues: justice, fortitude, prudence, and temperance. For Machiavelli, God is willing to excuse also princes who perpetrated 'well-committed' cruelties, if that was necessary to establish their power, or to redeem kingdoms or republics.[59]

Machiavelli's way of speaking of God's propensity to excuse princes who perpetrate cruelties or injustices was remarkably in tune with princes' views on the matter, at least with the views of the most shrewd of them, like the Duke Valentino. During a conversation, Machiavelli writes to the Ten of Liberty, (the Committee of the Florentine Republic in charge of foreign affairs), the Duke told him that he counted on being 'excused before God and men', had he tried to secure by any means his own position with regard to Florence.[60] And in another letter, reporting again a conversation, he writes that the Duke had told him that, had he been forced by necessity to levy a war against the people of Siena, he would have 'excused himself before God, men, and the Sienese themselves'.[61] By assuring princes that they can count on God's help and reward, even if they have often to abandon the path of virtue, he was offering a powerful exhortation which was well in harmony with princes' beliefs and expectations. Or, at least, he was speaking a familiar language.

Irony, Love, and the Variety of the World

However magnanimous and resolute men are to pursue great things, still their fate is disconsolate, marked as it is by the certainty of death. Machiavelli speaks of death as a dreadful event. He does not see it as the end of sufferance and the beginning of eternal life. Christian salvation and hope is absent from his writings and he speaks with contempt of Christian glorification of 'humble and contemplative men'.[62] In the last years of his life he composed an *Exhortation to Penitence*, which his biographer Roberto Ridolfi believes to be a document of a serious spiritual crisis.[63] In this text he writes that God, out of his immense compassion, has offered men the chance to redeem themselves through penitence. He urges them to practise the celestial virtue of *charitas* and warns that those who lack it shall find no help, no consolation in human affliction, no salvation.

Ridolfi suggests as the date of composition of the 'Exhortation to Penitence' April 1527, upon Machiavelli's return from the camp of the papal army around Milan. At the time Niccolò was 'a man getting on for sixty', 'marked with the labours of the mind and the spirit', a 'tired and unhappy man', who 'has stopped smiling' and defending himself against the ingratitude, the stupidity, the ambition and the malignity of his fellow men.[64] A man who is no longer capable of laughing at the world may well have written that 'Exhortation to Penitence' and found consolation in the possibility of gaining celestial happiness through penitence.

However, the 'Exhortation to Penitence' is an oration composed for a friar addressing his 'honoured fathers and greater brothers'. Even if we accept the idea that Machiavelli had in his later years a spiritual crisis, he certainly never joined a religious order. He did in fact spend some time in a monastery, more specifically in the monastery of the Minor Friars, in Carpi, in the spring of 1521; but he occupied his time plotting, with the complicity of Governor Francesco Guiccciardini, hilarious tricks and jokes at the expense of the friars. Part of his mission was to find a 'prudent, honest, and genuine' monk to preach in Florence at Lent. Instead he was looking for a friar 'madder than Ponzo, wilier than Fra Girolamo, and more hypocritical than Frate Alberto', as he believed that the true way to go to Paradise was to learn the way to Hell in order to steer clear of it. The hope of eternal beatitude in Paradise does not console him; but neither does the thought of eternal damnation scare him. He laughs irreverently about Hell.[65] In *La Mandragola*, a comedy which he composed in 1518, he makes Callimaco say to himself that 'the worst that can happen is that you'll die and go to Hell. But how many others have died! And in Hell how many worthy men there are! Are you ashamed to go there?'[66]

Niccolò was not the kind of man to search for relief to the misery of the human condition in religious faith. Becoming devout would have been for Machiavelli to break completely with himself, and a great surprise for those who knew him well. Your honour would be blemished, Guicciardini wrote to him on 17 May 1521, 'if at this age you started to think about your soul, because, since you have always lived in a contrary belief, it would be attributed rather to senility than to goodness'.[67] Machiavelli did not disappoint his friend, nor did he compromise his reputation. If repentance and penitence were not his way to find shelter or relief from the miseries of life and the horror of death, what then were his defences?

One was irony. To laugh at one's own and others' weaknesses alleviates 'the pains that every man bears'. Life 'is short', and 'many ills and strange events crush almost all mortals': it makes no sense to live only with labour and toil. When life is miserable, when we are powerless against men's stupidity and meanness, it is time to look at the world and ourselves with irony. It is time for a Machiavellian smile—a smile which is not a sign of scorn or indifference, but a mask which covers sufferance, but only on the surface.

In this spirit he wrote *La Mandragola* for the sole purpose of finding some solace and making the audience laugh: if this story does not suit a man who wants to appear wise and grave, he writes, 'make this excuse for him, that he is striving with these trifling thoughts to make his wretched life more pleasant, for otherwise he doesn't know where to turn his face, since he has been cut off from showing other powers with other deeds, there being no pay for his labours'.[68] No captains, no lawgivers, no princes; the heroes this time are 'a doleful lover, a judge by no means shrewd, a wicked friar, a parasite beloved by Malice'. The story is not designed to instil the desire to imitate a grand example of virtue, but simply to arouse laughter: 'if you do not laugh,' he says, I am ready 'to pay for your wine'.[69]

If comedies are to give pleasure, Machiavelli explains in the Prologue to *Clizia*, another comedy which he wrote in 1525, 'they must incite the audience to laughter'. To obtain this goal, the composer must 'put on the stage persons who are either stupid, or sarcastic, or in love'.[70] Everyday life offers a wealth of subjects for comedy: the misadventures of a homosexual friend in Florence, which Machiavelli describes to Vettori in a graceful and colourful manner, or his own inglorious adventure with an old prostitute in Verona.[71]

With the help of irony Machiavelli went through the hardships of life. He laughed, joked, and told stories even on his deathbed. It was, once again, an irony coming from an inner sadness, from

powerlessness against men's ferocity and stupidity, from hopeless-
ness. On 6 May 1527 Catholic Spaniards and Lutheran pikemen
under the command of Charles of Bourbon overwhelmed the poor
defences of Rome and ferociously sacked it. It was the conclusion
of the tragedy of Italian weakness long since predicted by
Machiavelli. A few days later, on 16 May, the citizens of Florence
took advantage of the defeat of the Medici pope and proclaimed the
Republic. The following day the Medici left Florence. The new
republican government, however, did not return Machiavelli to
his post as *Secretario*, in part because his fellow-Florentines dis-
liked the fact that in the last few years he had associated himself
with the Medici, but above all because they were not prepared to
forgive him 'for his greatness which made him different from
others in his ways, bold in his words, frank in his vices'.[72]

In the brief space of a month, his dearest aspirations, for which
he had fought all his life—the liberation of Italy from barbarian
domination and his return to a post of responsibility in a free
republican government in Florence—were brutally crushed. What
else was there to do but to laugh and continue telling funny
stories?

One of them, which became famous as 'Machiavelli's dream', is
worth reporting. To the few good friends who remained with him
in his last days, he told how 'he had seen a sparse crowd of poor
people, ragged and emaciated; and when he asked who they were,
he received the answer that they were the blessed souls of Paradise,
of whom we read in Scripture: *Beati pauperes quoniam ipsorum est
regnum caelorum*. When they had disappeared, he saw a large
crowd of people of noble appearance in royal and courtly robes,
who were gravely discussing affairs of state, and among them he
recognized Plato, Plutarch, Tacitus, and other famous men of antiquity. Having asked who these newcomers were, he was told that
they were condemned to Hell, because it is written: *Sapientia
huius saeculi inimica est Dei*. When they too had vanished, he
was asked which lot he would like to be with. He replied that he
would rather go to Hell with noble minds to discuss politics than to
be in Paradise with that first beggarly contingent.[73]

Even if it is probably not true that Machiavelli died 'unrecon-
ciled and jeering', the story of his dream fits him perfectly well:
he went through life laughing and telling stories; so he faced
death.[74] It is not a laughter which provides release from unhappiness
and fear, but it at least gives solace, for a while, and saves from

penitence, repentance, and religion. But irony helps only for a while. Laughter is only a temporary and superficial relief: 'I laugh, but my laughter does not pass inside.'[75] It helps to forget pain, but not to overcome it. It expresses sadness, not joy: 'Therefore, if at times I laugh or sing, | I do so because I have no other way than this | To give vent to my bitter tears.'[76] But what else did he believe was available in life to escape from grief and unhappiness?

One possibility is loving a woman. When it comes, love can turn a miserable life into the most sweet dream, and the only thing to be done in this case, Machiavelli has no doubt on the matter, is to abandon oneself. Women can perform the miracle of changing one's whole sense of life because of their beauty, grace, and nobility of soul. Love, Machiavelli reports to Vettori, captured me with nets 'of gold woven by Venus, so soft and gentle that though an insensitive heart could have severed them, none the less, I declined to do so. For a while I reveled within them, until their tender threads hardened and locked into untieable knots.'[77]

Love turns the body and the mind upside down. 'I try to give myself courage,' says Callimaco to himself in *La Mandragola*, but 'I feel as though my whole body from the soles of my feet to my head has gone wrong: my legs tremble, my vitals are shaken, my heart is torn out of my breast, my arms lose their strength, my tongue falls silent, my eyes are dazzled, my brain whirls'.[78] Just as it can turn an unhappy life into a sweet dream, it can give endless pain: 'the soldier dies in a ditch and the lover dies in despair.'[79] The miracles of love do not last. Women turn cold. Riccia, a Florentine courtesan who for a long time was his lover, 'allows me to kiss her, but in a fugitive manner', Machiavelli laments.[80] And when a man turns old, and vigour no longer corresponds to the intensity of desire, women turn their attention to the young men: 'so much beauty', he writes in a disconsolate sonnet for his lover Barbera, 'loves younger men'.[81]

Another lamentable aspect of human condition; but it is not women's fault. On the contrary, Machiavelli finds women much more generous and charitable than men. In the darkest moments of his life, when he was jobless and penniless, he found in Riccia 'so much faith and so much compassion'.[82] He reported this judgement to Vettori, who, as a result of Machiavelli's word, revised his misogynist belief that 'women are wont to love Fortune and not men', and that, when fortune abandons men, they leave them altogether.[83]

Unlike Vettori, who was very cautious in these matters,

Machiavelli believes that one should abandon oneself to the experience of love, as Horace recommends, because 'whatever pleasure you seize today may not be there for you tomorrow'.[84] And when he was not in love, he liked to read and dream about it: 'I have a book under my arm: Dante, Petrarch, or one of the minor poets, like Tibullus, Ovid, or some such. I read about their amorous passions and their loves, remember my own, and these reflections make me happy for a while.'[85]

On love matters, he has one fundamental rule, which he takes from Boccaccio: 'I believe now, I have always believed, and I shall continue to believe that what Boccaccio says is true: it is better to act and to regret, than not to act and regret it.'[86] For Hanna Pitkin this remark 'could serve as an emblem of Machiavelli's political teaching, for autonomy is intertwined with manhood. Dependence is characteristic of women, children, and animals; for men it is despicable and fatally dangerous.'[87] She overlooks the fact that what Machiavelli is urging his friend Vettori to do is precisely to abandon himself to love—that is, to give up autonomy and become fully dependent, indeed to become a slave. Dependence and abandonment to the love of women are for Machiavelli one of the best conditions of men's life. As his own life amply illustrates, he was always more than happy to trade autonomy for love.

Machiavelli describes loving a women as an experience of enchantment, sweetness, and abandonment. 'I know of nothing', Vettori wrote to him on 16 January 1515, 'that gives more delight to think about and to do than fucking. Every man may philosophize all he wants, but this is the utter truth, which many people understand this way but few will say.'[88] Machiavelli responds with this sonnet on the power of love which ends with these words: 'With such great force he let one fly, | That I feel its painful wound still; thus I | Confess and recognize his power.' He then writes that even if he knew the way to free himself of the chains of love, he should not use it, because he finds these fetters 'now sweet, now light, now heavy—and they make such a tangle that I believe I cannot live happily without that kind of life'.[89]

He knows that love will bring him much pain, but the perception of woman's beauty is too overwhelming and seducing: 'I nevertheless feel so great a sweetness in it, both because of the delight that rare and gentle countenance brings me and because I have laid aside all memory of my sorrow, that for anything in the world, would I desire my freedom—even if I could have it.'[90] A remarkable dialogue between two men in their mid-forties: one celebrates fucking (or the thought of it); the other chants woman's beauty and the sweetness of abandoning oneself to love. Yet the latter has been considered the symbol of *machismo*. But if *machismo* means, as Hanna Pitkin writes, 'the anxious and defensive effort of men to prove their manliness', and if the central element of manliness is autonomy,[91] then the exchange with Vettori shows that Machiavelli's conception and manner of life have nothing to share with *machismo*.

The experience of forgetfulness that love permits is remarkably similar to the one which he describes in the famous letter to Vettori of 10 December 1513:

When the evening comes, I return home and enter my study; on the threshold I take off my workday clothes, covered with mud and dirt, and put on the garments of court and palace. Fitted out appropriately, I step inside the venerable courts of the ancients, where, solicitously received by them, I nourish myself of that food that *alone* is mine and for which I was born; where I am unashamed to converse with them and to question them about the motives for their actions, and they, out of their human kindness, answer me. And for four hours at a time I feel no boredom, I forget all my troubles, I do not dread poverty, and I am not terrified by death. I absorb myself into them completely.

This man, who has been said to have been totally insensitive to the dimension of the infinite and the transcendent, had in fact at least two ways of experiencing both: love of woman and love of ancient masters of politics.

Machiavelli speaks of the ancients with reverence; of women as friends and equals. He calls Riccia woman-friend (*amica*), and portrays their relationship as one between equals, and at times even as one in which Niccolò is, once again, in a position of subordination. Riccia speaks frankly to him, just like a man-friend would. When she is tired of having the unemployed Niccolò in her house, she calls him 'house-pest' (*impaccia-casa*), just like Machiavelli's old friend Donato del Corno, who calls him 'shop-pest' (*impaccia-bottega*). Like Donato, she does not recognize Machiavelli's eminence at all: 'Wise men, oh these wise men, I don't know what they have upstairs; it seems to me they turn everything topsy-turvy.'[92]

Machiavelli describes the relationship with women in terms of equality and friendship also in *The Golden Ass*, which contains, as has been noticed, several autobiographical allusions.[93] After some time, says the hero of the story, she (Circe's damsel) and I talked together of many things, as one friend speaks to another.

'Another', in the Italian, is rendered in the masculine (*l'altro*); they discussed many things and conversed in the manner in which a man chats with a man-friend—that is, as equals. And the many things of which the hero of the story speaks with his woman-friend as he would do with a man-friend include political matters.

Hanna Pitkin remarks that, in *The Golden Ass*, Circe's damsel plays a very active, even a dominant role and has a developed personality. She encourages, teaches, feeds, and seduces him.

She and the hero talk together 'of many things, as one friend speaks with another', a degree of mutuality between the sexes that is not even approached anywhere else in Machiavelli's writings. Yet even this woman holds the hero captive in her room and he, 'surrendering' himself into her 'power', swoons 'all prostrate on her sweet bosom'. Her presence also keeps him from 'reflection', and particularly from reflection on politics'.[94]

This interpretation omits the fact that the hero's political reflections (ch. 5, ll. 28–126) are prompted by the woman's considerations on the variations of earthly things (ch. 3, ll. 75–132) and on the best way to face them. She introduces political reflections and he meditates upon her words. It also omits the fact that, as soon as the damsel returns, the male hero immediately loses interest in political reflections, and he is very happy about that: 'and though I was intent on that thought which all day had | pulled me to itself and from my breast had driven every other care | when I heard my lady, of a truth I thought that every other thing | was vain except her whose servant I had been made' (ch. 6, ll. 10–14). Trading one's autonomy, becoming a servant out of love, is for Machiavelli a most desirable condition.

In the only letter he addressed to a woman that we possess, Machiavelli analyses political events in a manner which is not in the least different from the letters he composed for his male correspondents. He reports the dramatic events that led to the fall of the Florentine Republic with his usual precision; no tones of condescendence, or patronage. He says that he does not intend to indulge in the description of the horrors of the sack of Prato in order 'to spare Your Ladyship cause for worry in your spirit';[95] but he never goes into horrific details, even when he writes to males.

He knows well that history is full of examples of women who did much better than men in political affairs. In his second mission in his capacity of *Secretario*, in July 1499, he had the opportunity to meet Caterina Sforza Riario, widow of Girolamo Riario, and his reports to the Signori of Florence all show that Caterina deeply impressed him for her political skills.[96] And the impression was a lasting one; both in the *Discourses* and in the *Florentine Histories*, some fifteen or twenty years later, he recounts with transparent admiration how she bravely defeated the conspirators who killed her husband on Christmas Day 1476.[97] He admits, with pleasure, that many women would do much better than men in politics— like Lucrezia, the wife of Nicia in *La Mandragola*: 'she is beautiful, virtuous, courteous, and fit to rule a kingdom,' says the impartial observer Ligurio.[98]

Other affections—love of one's wife, of children, of friends—give tenderness, relief, and joy to life. He was fond of his wife, Maria Corsini 'Marietta' or 'mona Marietta', and his children Primerana, Bernardo, Lodovico, Guido, Piero, Bartolomea (Baccina), and Totto. When he was home, Niccolò was surely great company for all. 'Remember to come back home. Nothing else,' Marietta wrote to him when he was in Rome, in 1503–.[99] He also longed to be with her, particularly when he knew that they might be in danger: 'greet Mona Marietta for me and tell her that I have been expecting—and still do—to leave here any day; I have never longed so much to return to Florence as I do now, but there is nothing else I can do,' he wrote in one of his last letters, on 2 April 1527.[100] He was, for all his 'brigade', as he calls his family, a source of reassurance and fun. Since you have promised that you will be with us, his son Guido wrote to him, 'we are not worrying about the lansquenets', and mona Marietta 'is no longer worried'.[101] When, because of his poverty, he felt he had become a burden for his family, he considered leaving home:

But I cannot possibly go on like this for long, because I am rotting away and I can see that if God does not show a more favorable face to me, one day I shall be forced to leave home and to place myself as tutor or secretary to a governor, if I cannot do otherwise, or to stick myself in some deserted spot to teach reading to children and leave my family here to count me dead; they will do much better without me because I am causing them expense, since I am used to spending and cannot do without spending.[102]

He tried, as much as he could, to be close to all of them with his affection and advice. He was hoping for a better future for his sons and daughters: 'If God grants you and me life, I believe that I may make you a man of good standing, if you are willing to do your share.' And the part that his son Guido should play is 'study, do well and learn', because what gives true honour, he reminds his son, is virtue.[103]

He not only recognized that there are many ways of living one's life, but he also saw beauty and value in the variety of the world. One of his favourite occupations in Sant'Andrea in Percussina was 'to learn various matters' and 'to observe mankind: the variety of its, the diversities of its fancies'.[104] One of his closest friends, Filippo Casavecchia, was a well-known homosexual; his best woman-friend was a courtesan. He believed that in the world there should be room for all, for those who like men and those who prefer the company of women. When Filippo Casavecchia and Giuliano Brancacci were guests of Vettori in Rome, Filippo posed the Ambassador a difficult moral dilemma. 'You will not take it ill', Filippo said to him, 'I have been, from childhood . . . '. He meant to say that he did not at all like the fact that the Ambassador was receiving women, and more precisely courtesans coming from the nearby papal court, 'more to stay and chat with them than for any other reason', as Vettori puts it in a letter to Machiavelli of 24 December 1513. Consulted to offer his advice on such a delicate matter, Machiavelli responds with total confidence: the house must be open to both boys and courtesans. I should come to Rome, he writes, and appear in the house saying: 'Ambassador, you are going to be ill; I do not think you're allowing yourself any diversion; there aren't any boys here, there aren't any girls here; what kind of a fucking house is this anyway.'[105]

He backs his profound moral advice with an even more profound piece of moral reasoning on how one should live one's life in a world inhabited, as is the case, only by crazy people:

Magnificent Ambassador, there are nothing but crazy people here; only a few are familiar with this world and are aware that whoever seeks to act according to others will accomplish nothing because no two men who think alike can be found. These people are unaware that whoever I considered wise by day will not be considered crazy by night and that whoever is deemed a decent, able man will occasion honor, not blame, whatever he does to refresh his spirit and live happily; instead of being called a sodomite or a lecher, people will say he is well-rounded, easy-going, and a boon companion. They are also unaware that he gives of himself and takes nothing from others and that he acts as the must does when it boils; it imparts its own pungency to dishes that reek of mold without taking on the mold from the dishes.[106]

Yet, Niccolò has very high standards concerning morals. He believes that civil life requires a certain propriety and decorum in words, gestures, and dressing. His disgust for licence, excessive elegance, and arrrogance is transparent from his description of the way of life of Florentine youth at the time of his childhood:

Hence arose those evils in the city that are customarily generated most often in peace, because the young men, more unrestrained than usual, were spending beyond bounds on dress, banquets, and other similar abandonments; and, being at leisure, they consumed time and substance in games and women; they studied to appear splendid in their dress, and to be clever and smart in their speech, and he who was more deft at biting the others was wiser and more esteemed.[107]

Each person has to follow his or her way, so long as one does not hurt others. In a world inhabited by crazy people, this is for Machiavelli the best philosophy of life. Crazy creatures need not be punished or suppressed; they should just be left alone, even if most people think otherwise. He offers advice of this sort to his son Guido, who had probably consulted him on what to do with a little mule who turned crazy. Though it is crazy, Machiavelli responds,

it must be treated just the reverse of the way crazy people are, for they are tied up, and I want you to let it loose. Give it to Vangelo and tell him to take it to Montepugliano and take off his bridle and halter and let him go wherever it likes to regain its own way of life and work off its craziness. The village is big and the beast is small; it can do no one any harm. [108]

A little animal who has become crazy should be left free; it will do no harm, and left free will perhaps recover its sanity. A good lesson on the connection between liberty and sanity, a lesson of compassion and respect for unfortunate, and defenceless creatures; a moral philosophy of the highest kind.

The proponent of this conception of the world has been presented as a man possessed by the demon of power, with his mind and heart all fixed on politics alone. In more recent years, it has also been claimed that Machiavelli advocates a one-dimensional way of life: 'Intellectually and physically, man must become fierce, resolute, and in a sense, one-dimensional, if he is not to be overwhelmed by his weakness in the world.'[109] In fact he advocated with the greatest conviction, and sustained with eloquent arguments, that life is and has to be made of different passions, concerns, attachments, and desires:

Anyone who might see our letters, honorable *compare*, and see their variety, would be greatly astonished, because at first it would seem that we were serious men completely directed toward weighty matters and that no thought could cascade through our heads that did not have within it probity and magnitude. But later, upon turning the page, it would seem to the reader that we—still the very same selves—were petty, fickle, lascivious, and were directed toward chimerical matters. If to some this behavior seems contemptible, to me it seems laudable because we are imitating nature, which is changeable; whoever imitate nature cannot be censured.[110]

For him love of women, of family, and of friends, as well as the pleasures and the pains of ordinary life, are important. In the letter to Vettori of 10 December 1513, he describes a typical day in Sant'Andrea in Percussina as divided in two parts: in the morning he attends to his properties and various business; he then takes some time to read poetry, and fancy about love, and to chat 'with those who pass, and ask news of their villages, learn various things'. He lunches with his family and returns to the tavern where he 'sinks into vulgarity' for the rest of the day, playing cards with the host, the butcher, a miller, and two furnace tenders and quarrelling with countless insults and shouts that are heard 'as far as San Casciano'. In the evening, properly reclothed with 'regal and courtly garments', he enters 'in the ancient courts of ancient men' to discuss with them grand matters of politics.

Politics is his deep vocation; it is the nourishment of his spirit 'that food that alone is mine and for which I was born'. It makes him forget the anxieties of everyday life and fear of poverty and death, the greatest of all fears. And yet, all he did before dusk was also important: caring for his properties, being with his family, playing cards at the tavern, listening to men's fancies, dreaming of love when he was not in love, are not just consolations for not being able to pursue politics. When he was the *Secretario* he did exactly the same things, and many others of a similar sort. And, more importantly, he believed that in life there is room for the serious and the trivial, the ordinary and the grand, the contingent and the infinite.

Magnanimity and the Pursuit of Glory

Although ordinary life has a worth and a sweetness of its own, although it may offer episodes of transcendence and infinity through the experience of love and moments of lightness through irony, something else is needed. One must integrate it with the experience of the grand, and the road to it is political action or the writing of politics. For Machiavelli, magnanimous men have to enter the universe of political action to search for the eternity which glory alone ensures.

As Cicero had defined it, glory is the praise given to right actions and the reputation for great merits in the service of the republic which is approved not merely by the testimony of the multitude but by the witness of all the best men.[111] This piece of Roman political philosophy was eloquently restated by Florentine humanists. To attain glory, so the conventional argument runs, one must enter public life, even if the principle of confining oneself to the pursuit of honour and tranquillity in private life is surely a praiseworthy one. Fame, wrote, for instance, Leon Battista Alberti in *Of the Family*,

is born not in the midst of private peace but in public action. Glory springs up in public squares; reputation is nourished by the voice and judgement of many persons of honor, and in the midst of the people. Fame flees from every solitary and private spot to dwell gladly in the arena, where crowds are gathered and celebrity is found; there the name is bright and luminous of one who with hard sweat and assiduous toil for noble ends has projected himself up out of silence and darkness, ignorance and vice.[112]

Like that of Cicero and of the humanists, the glory that Machiavelli presents as a reward is worldly glory which does not need to be 'recognized and authenticated in heaven'.[113] In a page of the *Discourses*, where he compares the ethos of pagan religion with that of Christianity with regard to love of liberty, he remarks that, while the former 'beatified only men full of worldly glory (*mondana gloria*), the latter has seen 'humility, abjection and contempt of the world (*dispregio delle cose umane*)'. One of the main differences between the two sorts of education consists precisely in the fact that Christianity teaches us not to attach much value to the honour of *this* world (*l'onore del mondo*), and instead instils in men the desire to go to paradise; ancient paganism, on the contrary, esteemed worldly honour very highly and motivated men to pursue it as the greatest good.[114]

Once again, Machiavelli wants to restore the ancient view over modern beliefs and to see again men committed to *worldly* glory rather than to salvation of their soul. Every human being, he writes, should be afraid to imitate bad emperors and endeavour to follow the example of good princes who lived 'glorious and respected by all' in a triumphant world.[115] And a prince who truly seeks worldly glory (*la gloria del mondo*) should desire to live in a corrupt city, not to complete its corruption, as Caesar did, but to reform it, as Romulus did. Heavens (*i cieli*) cannot offer men a better opportunity to attain glory than this, Machiavelli writes, and he means the glory certified by future generations in *this* world.[116]

Although worldly glory is subject to the inconstancy and the arbitrariness of men's judgement, it can be eternal, if it is true glory. Those who institute and preserve a republic or a kingdom, he writes, obtain 'immortal honour'; and death makes redeemers of republics glorious forever in this world, as opposed to those who have corrupted a republic, who obtain, as a just reward for their ignorance or wickedness, eternal infamy (*sempiterna infamia*).[117] In *The Prince*, he assures the new ruler that, if he diligently follows his advice, he shall obtain the 'double glory [*duplicata gloria*]' of founding a new state and of adorning it with good laws, good armies, good friends, and good examples.[118] And if the same new prince accomplishes the grand deed of liberating Italy from the barbarians, he will certainly attain a glory comparable to that of Moses, Cyrus, and Theseus.[119] When he addresses princes, he insists on the fact that good princes live more securely and are more glorious than bad ones; but he also remarks that God loves reformers of republics, and that immortal glory shall be the reward for their deeds. And when he addresses members of the Medici family, he specifies that, if they follow his counsel, they will obtain a glory greater than that of their ancestors: 'Of all the many blessings God has given to your house and to Your Holiness in person, this is the greatest: that of giving you power and material for making yourself immortal, and for surpassing by far in this way your father's and your grandfather's glory.'[120]

However heaven or God may contribute to it, glory is a worldly reward; it is one way of living eternally in this world by remaining alive in the memory of humanity; the other is eternal disgrace, a destiny which ought to be as frightening as the other is appealing. Like virtues and vices, the path of glory and that of infamy are very close to one another. It is very easy to miss the former for the latter, and it is also easy to enter paths that, though they may look similar to that of glory, do in fact lead in the opposite direction.

The first and most categorical piece of advice that Machiavelli has to offer on this matter is never to become a tyrant. Tyranny makes princes and kings lose 'glory, security, tranquillity', and 'peace of mind', and brings instead 'infamy, scorn, abhorrence, danger and disquiet'.[121] Since they destroy republics and kingdoms and are enemies of virtue, tyrants are the most infamous and detestable of all men. And yet, in spite of the dangers and the infamy, many men have become tyrants, and many more would have, had they not been stopped. They err either voluntarily or by mere ignorance; in both cases, however, the cause of their error is deceit, and what they are precisely deceived by is 'a false good and a false glory',[122] like the Florentines, who long 'not for true glory, but for the contemptible honors on which hatreds, enmities, differences, and sects depend'.[123]

To this sort of false glory, which has caused humanity innumerable sufferances, belongs Caesar's glory. In spite of the lauds of historians and writers, no one should 'be deceived by Caesar's renown (gloria)', Machiavelli admonishes.[124] By Machiavelli's standards, military prowess and the ability to preserve one's power are not sufficient to attain glory. The infamous Agatocles was an excellent captain of great virtù in confronting and surviving dangers and he displayed an 'indomitable spirit' in enduring and overcoming adversities. By killing his fellow-citizens, betraying his friends, being treacherous, merciless, and irreligious, he gained and maintained power, but 'not glory'; and, Machiavelli specifies, he does not deserve to be ranked 'among the finest men'.[125]

To attain glory, it is not sufficient to be a valiant captain; one has to be valiant and good, like the Roman generals before the last Punic War who 'gained glory as brave and good', whereas the captains like Caesar and Pompeus acquired only 'fame as brave men'.[126] In spite of their outstanding qualities, they missed the path of glory because ambition perverted their judgement and instigated them to break laws, plunder provinces, usurp and tyrannize over their country, and gain wealth for themselves.[127] As he remarks in the *Discourses*, love of true glory is a restraint which drives men to be good.[128]

Machiavelli fully endorses the classical view that there is a clear distinction between fame (*fama*) and glory (*gloria*).[129] Fame is the reward for military or political deeds which are in one way or another grand, noteworthy, and extraordinary, and thereby give a lasting or even an eternal reputation and renown. Had the tyrant of Perugia Giovanpagolo Baglioni had the courage to kill his archenemy Pope Julius II when he imprudently arrived in Perugia accompanied only by the cardinals and a few soldiers, he would have gained 'an immortal fame [*memoria eterna*]' but would not have attained glory. He would have gained a lasting reputation because he would have been the first 'to show prelates how little men are respected who live and rule as they do, and would have done a thing the greatness of which would have obliterated any infamy and any danger that might arise from it'. But the wickedness of that action and the fact that he was an evil man, parricidal and incestuous, prevented him from entering the true path to glory.[130]

In some cases, however, men's judgement on fame and glory is less severe than Machiavelli's. Common people are impressed by 'appearances and results'.[131] They equate fame with glory, as in the case of King Ferdinand of Aragon, who has become 'in fame and glory [*per fama e gloria*]' the 'first king of the Christendom'.[132] He was raised to such a status in a very short time because, Machiavelli explains, he performed great enterprises and extraordinary deeds. In an earlier chapter, Machiavelli remarks that, had Ferdinand of Aragon been trustworthy, he 'would have lost either reputation or power several times over'.[133] However, when he speaks in his own voice, Machiavelli attributes King Ferdinand with reputation, but not with glory. His wording is consistent with the belief that he expresses in *Discourses*: 'I will say but this, I do not mean that a fraud which involves breaking your word or the contracts you have made is glorious; for, although on occasion it may win a state or a kingdom . . . it will never bring you glory.'[134] It is also perfectly consistent with the classical meaning of reputation. Reputation is the recognition of astonishing qualities that escape our understanding and therefore compel us to think about them over and over again (*re-putare*). Any person capable of doing great things obtains reputation, but glory requires a clearer splendour of both the ends and the means.

Unlike his friend Guicciardini, who believed that modern men do not long for glory, Machiavelli maintains that glory, along with riches, is one of the ends 'which everyone aims at'. The work to be done was then for him to rekindle the love of glory and direct it towards its proper goals. To this effect he puts before his contemporaries' eyes the grand deeds of princes, captains, and lawgivers who founded or reformed republics and kingdoms. He also puts before their eyes the example of the Roman people, which had been for 400 years 'lover of glory and of the common good of its country',[135] as well as the example of eminent compatriots, like

Lorenzo il Magnifico, who, upon his return from a dangerous diplomatic mission in which he had put his own life at risk for his fatherland, was received as a 'very great man'.[136]

At the same time, he expresses all his contempt for princes who are insensitive to the allure of glory, like the 'lesser princes' of Italy, who were 'unmoved by any glory' and sought only 'to live either more richly or more securely'.[137] His belief in the possibility of reviving love of glory inspires most of his reflections on politics. He saw love of glory as the only motive that might enable peoples to accomplish the grand deeds that liberty at times demands, like resisting tyranny and mobilizing against arrogant men who want to impose their domination. He also considered love of glory as the only motive that could drive leaders to accomplish the grand deeds that they alone can accomplish—that is, founding republics or kingdoms, liberating countries, redeeming a corrupt city.

The Tree of Politics

Pace the view which holds that Machiavelli had his eyes fixed on politics alone, he did in fact reflect on political action from different angles, in relation to a number of beliefs on the world, on life, on man, on history. Against heaven's overwhelming power over countries and men, political action is for him an emancipatory force, while, against Fortune's malignity, politics is an effort to construct a moral order where the good people are rewarded, honoured, and remembered and the wicked punished, blamed, and forgotten. Looked at from God's angle, politics is a fulfilment of his desire; its goal is in fact to build a city where the common good of justice is properly preserved,[138] and God, Machiavelli writes, 'loves justice and mercy'.[139] With regard to the inevitable tendency of republics and countries to decline and corrupt, political action takes the form of an effort designed to rediscover and bring back to life original energies and principles; the right way to renew political bodies, Machiavelli writes, 'is to bring them back to their foundational principles. For at the start religious institutions, republics, and kingdoms have in all cases some good in them, to which their early reputation and progress is due.'[140]

When he considers political action with regard to men's cruelty and ambition, he recommends it as a necessary protective endeavour; with regard to the variety of the world, he sees politics as the commitment to build a city in which each individual can live his or her life in the way he or she likes, following fantasy, inclinations, and craziness. From the perspective of everyday life, politics appears to him as the main road to escape monotony and dullness and attain the sphere of the grand and the momentous. Lastly, when he reflects on politics having in mind his beliefs on man's fragility and mortality, he perceives it as the only path open towards eternity, as the only way to defeat death.

To express all these meanings of politics, Machiavelli uses the metaphor of 'planting trees beneath the shade of which mankind lives prosperously and happily'.[141] Like a tree, the good republic that politics is supposed to create and preserve offers protection and solace to all, regardless of what they do under its shade. It must have deep roots in the past from which it takes the moral lymph which keeps it healthy and defends it from corruption and decay. If the planting has been made wisely, it can resist for long hostile weather and the malignity of natural adversities; finally, like trees, each republic has a beauty of its own.

To do the work properly, many qualities are needed; it takes experience, knowledge of the terrain, care, patience, and, if necessary, the courage to cut and trim, to give the plant the necessary treatment to resist corruption and disease. It takes a special art which Machiavelli never takes pain to define. Only in a very few instances does he use the term 'art of the state'. The expression, which is almost a neologism, is usually rendered by modern scholars as 'statecraft'. But that wording does not convey the richness of its meaning; it is worth analysing it more closely.

2

The Art of the State

Machiavelli considered himself to be an expert on a special art which we call statecraft, and he called 'arte dello stato'. 'If I could talk to you,' he wrote to Vettori on 9 April 1513, 'I could not help but fill your head with castles in the air, because Fortune has seen to it that, since I do not know how to talk about either the silk or the wool trade, or profits or losses, I have to talk about the state.'[1] A few months later, in the famous letter of 10 December 1513, he puts forth his long and assiduous apprenticeship in the art; if the Medici read *The Prince*, he writes, it 'would be evident that during the fifteen years I have been studying the art of the state I have neither slept nor fooled around, and anybody ought to be happy to utilize someone who has had so much experience at the expense of others.'[2] And Vettori, like all who knew Machiavelli well, acknowledged with pleasure his mastery: even if you have been out of the workshop for two years, Vettori wrote to him in December 1514, 'I know you have such intelligence that although two years have gone by since you left the shop, I do not think you have forgotten the craft'.[3]

Spending years in the study of the art of the state; to be able to discuss only the art of the state; to be in or out of the workshop in which the art of the state is practised, and taught to apprentices: what did Machiavelli mean when he claims to have applied himself to the study of the art of the state? What precisely was the subject of the art? And what kind of expertise or skill did the mastery of the art precisely entail? Was it the same as being a master of civil science or politics, or was it something different, something more or something less? These questions need to be raised, not only to understand the shades of meaning implicit in Machiavelli's self-presentation as an expert of the *arte dello stato*, but also to identify the intellectual project which oriented the writing of *The Prince*.[4]

Politics as Civil Wisdom

The first observation to be made in this respect is that Machiavelli does not describe himself as an expert on politics or civil science, nor on 'government and public administration', nor on 'the theory of the best governments', nor on 'the theory and practice of civil affairs', to mention some of the expressions used by his contemporaries.[5] He prefers instead to present himself as an expert on the art of the state, a choice all the more strange because, in Machiavelli's Florence, politics, or civil science, was praised as the most noble of all intellectual endeavours, while the word 'state' had, as we shall see, a dubious connotation. In early sixteenth-century Florence, public rhetoric, philosophy, and historiography were in fact still pervaded by the Aristotelian and Ciceronian interpretation of politics as the art of instituting, preserving, and reforming a *respublica*—that is, a community of free and equal citizens living together for the common good under the rule of law—and by the ideal of the political or civil man, understood as an upright citizen who serves the common good with justice, prudence, fortitude, and temperance.

This interpretation of politics and of the political man had deep and old roots in Florentine public discourse. According to the chronicler Giovanni Villani, the founder of Florentine political rhetoric was Brunetto Latini, who, in the early thirteenth century, taught the Florentines to speak well and to steer and rule their republic 'according to politics'.[6] In *Li livres dou Tresor*, (*The Books of Treasure*), composed around 1260, he presents the science of politics (*politique*) as the highest among the human sciences and the most noble activity of man, because its aim is to teach how to rule the inhabitants of a kingdom and a city (*ville*), and a people and a commune, in times of both peace and war according to reason and justice ('selonc raison et selonc justice').[7] The science of politics, continues Latini paraphrasing Aristotle, orders the arts and the knowledge that are to be cultivated in the city, and through language it preserves civil order. An essential component of politics are then the sciences that teach us how to speak: grammar, dialectic, rhetoric. Following Cicero, Latini stresses that language is the prerequisite of the city and civil life, because without language there can be no justice, no friendship, no humane community.[8] The proper place where men can express themselves through speech and conversation is the political community, which must be seen as the natural place for men living a truly humane life.[9] Aptly, then, Cicero said that rhetoric is the most important, and the noblest, component of the science of ruling a city.[10]

Latini's emphasis on rhetoric as a fundamental element of the art of government—a theme that I shall discuss at length in the next chapter—should not, however, obscure another equally important aspect of the conception of politics that he introduced in thirteenth-century Florence. When he says that politics is the discipline that teaches how to rule according to reason and justice, he means that politics consists in governing impartially, giving each citizen his due and ensuring that rational assessment of individual and social claims is not perturbed by partiality and private interests. The reason he is referring to in his definition of politics is civil reason, or civil wisdom—that is, the reason that presides over the framing and the implementation of civil laws; 'justice' stands here for civil justice, the principles of justice that ought to regulate the relationships among citizens. By saying that politics means to rule according to reason and justice, Latini was keeping alive an even older tradition of communal self-government based upon the idea of reason as civil justice. In a model speech composed by Guido Faba in the early thirteenth century, for instance, the new Podestà solemnly declares that his main goal is to live according to the laws of the commune and ensure justice to every person.[11]

At the same time, Latini was restating another equally important piece of pre-humanist political language—that is, the view that civil society, and above all free republics, are kept together by the principles of civil wisdom, which consists in the correct administration of justice and respect for laws.[12] What Latini taught was then a conception of politics based upon the principle of legal reason—that is, the sort of reason which presides over making and implementing civil laws and therefore preserves the civil community. He taught the Florentine, in other words, to regard politics as the civil science *par excellence*, to be cultivated with the support of rhetoric and the knowledge of civil law.

Like the idea that politics is based on rhetoric, the interpretation of politics as civil science (*civilis scientia*), or civil philosophy (*civilis philosophia*), or civil reason (*civilis ratio*) also belongs to Roman political philosophy. When he speaks of civil science, or civil reason, or civil philosophy, Cicero, to mention the most obvious example, does not mean just the knowledge or the competence in civil law, but the more general art of ruling the republic. As he says in *De finibus*: 'the topic of what I think may fitly be entitled Civil Science was called in Greek *politikos*.'[13]

The affinity between politics and civil law was refined and strengthened by fourteenth-century jurists. They maintained that the subject matter of civil law is the political or civil man—that is, the man living in a civil community. As one of the most eminent jurists of the time—Baldus of Ubaldis (1327–1400)—wrote, to say that the subject matter of civil law is the political man means that the goal of civil law is to make men political—that is, capable of living the sort of life appropriate to the *polis*. Because it compels individuals to behave with restraint and moderation, to respect other citizens' liberty, and to discharge their civic duties, civil law forges the citizens who keep the *civitas* alive.[14]

The identification of politics and law and therefore of politics and *recta ratio* became one of the basic tenets of the civic humanists' ideology. Politics and the laws, wrote Salutati in his dialogue *De nobilitate legum et medecinae* (*Of the Nobility of Law and Medicine*), are actually the same thing ('idem esse politicam atque leges').[15] He speaks of 'political reason' (*politica ratio*) as a synonym of the Ciceronian 'civil reason' (*ratio civilis*).[16] Even if it is a human creation, the Law, he writes, is the rational norm of human life. True laws come in fact from nature, and therefore their origin is ultimately divine. A true law must in fact respect the highest norm of equity, which is the precept of eternal reason.[17] The task of political reason, Salutati remarks, is that of introducing measure, proportion, and justice into the human world—a task accomplished through the laws, which are the arrangement and the rule of political reason.[18]

Both politics and laws aim at the preservation of civil society. Politics' goal is the good citizen; so is the legislator's.[19] His concern is the good and the order of the city and the whole of humanity. As Aristotle aptly said, the political good (*bonum politicum*) is greater and nobler than the individual one. Politics, therefore, is responsible for the health of the soul, and for men's happiness. True happiness is political happiness (*politica felicitas*), the life of virtue in the human city. Only politics, through laws, makes political or civil felicity available to men by creating the condition for a virtuous life.

The logical corollary of this interpretation was the idea that politics deserves the highest status among human sciences and arts. This view, which had been amply discussed by scholastic political philosophers, became another conventional theme of Florentine public rhetoric. After Salutati's forceful defence of the superiority of jurisprudence and politics over medicine, Leonardo Bruni, his successor as Chancellor of the Florentine Republic, restated the same point in the 'Proem' to his translation of Aristotle's *Politics*. The *respublica*, as he translates the Greek *politia*, is a self-governing community where the common good prevails over particular interests, and only in such a community can individuals enjoy happiness and a truly human life. Because a civil society where men can attain self-sufficiency and the perfection of their moral life is the most precious common good, Bruni remarks, the art that teaches what a *civitas* is, and how it is to be preserved, deserves the highest rank among human disciplines.[20]

Celebrations of the excellence of politics also continued to be part of Florentine intellectual life in the second half of the Quattrocento. In the 'Proem' to his translation of Aristotle's *Politics* composed in 1472, Donato Acciaiuoli remarks that Aristotle's intention in writing the *Politics* was to argue that, even if civil discipline relies upon probable arguments, rather than infallible demonstrations, it is none the less the most excellent of practical sciences because through politics men can moderate and rule the republic and therefore enjoy a most happy life on earth.[21] In 1478 Donato Acciaiuoli issued a new Latin translation of Aristotle's *Nichomachean Ethics*, and in his commentary he remarks that the goal of civil science is the highest good of man ('summum bonum hominis'), and that the highest good of the individual is one and the same as the good of the civil community, even though the good of the civil community (*civitas*) is more divine and beautiful than the good of the individual; for this reason, civil science (*scientia civilis*) is the most noble of all practical sciences.[22]

From the Aristotelian literature and the works of jurists, the ideal of political life spread into Florentine public rhetoric. In an oration delivered in 1493, for instance, Alamanno Rinuccini remarks that both ancient history and modern experience prove that justice and good laws are the necessary foundations for the liberty of the city and for the preservation of the political and civil life. As long as cities and empires are governed in justice, they increase in glory and reputation. People are content with justice and, if justice is provided to all, the city enjoys concord and peace. Cicero, remarked Rinuccini, was then perfectly right in ranking justice as the queen of virtues.[23]

The Limits of Civil Wisdom

Machiavelli was perfectly acquainted with the conventional language of politics. Donato Acciaiuoli's summary of Aristotle's *Nichomachean Ethics* was among the books borrowed by Niccolò's father, Bernardo Machiavelli, and even if he did not attend Rinuccini's orations and did not read Acciaiuoli's works, he surely had many other opportunities to hear that political or civil life is based upon justice and law, that politics is therefore the most noble of human activities, and that political science is the highest of all practical sciences.[24]

To this one must add that Machiavelli was acquainted with the language of public law and civil jurisprudence, and the traces of his acquaintance are visible in all his works. At the very outset of the *Discorsi*, for instance, he writes that 'civil law is nothing but a collection of decisions, made by jurists of old, which the jurists of today have tabulated in orderly fashion for our instruction'.[25] In the *Ritracto delle cose di Francia* (*Portrait of the Affairs of France*), composed in 1510, he describes the authority of the barons over the subjects as 'mera', that is absolute, in accordance with the classic legal concept of *merum imperium*.[26] His interpretation of the concept of political life and his assessment of the value of political action and political philosophy are perfectly consonant with the tradition that I have outlined. For him the *vivere politico* or the *vivere civile* is the civil community based upon the rule of law and the common good.

He also fully endorses another fundamental tenet of the conventional language of politics—namely, the view that laws make men good:

All writers on civil life [*vivere civile*] have pointed out that . . . in constituting and legislating for a republic one must presuppose that all men are wicked . . . and that men never do good unless necessity drives them to it . . . Hence it is said that hunger and poverty make men industrious and that laws make them good.[27]

For this reason he considers civil life based upon the rule of just laws the highest good on earth on which human felicity depends and regards philosophers such as Aristotle and Plato, who wrote with competence on the *vivere civile*, as the greatest of all men.[28]

Like classical republican writers, Machiavelli sees civil and political life as based upon the principles of equality before the law (*aequum ius*) and the equal access to office on the basis of virtue (*aequa libertas*).[29] Because a true civil or political community has to be based on these two principles of justice, the first obligations of rulers is to respect the rule of laws, as did those emperors 'who acted, like good princes, in accordance with the laws'.[30] Obedience to the laws is the best means to secure one's power:

princes should learn, therefore, that they begin to lose their state the moment they begin to break the laws and to disregard the ancient traditions and customs under which men have long lived . . . For it is much easier to acquire the affection of good men than of the bad, and to obey laws rather than to override them.[31]

And the second obligation is to be absolutely fair in the administration of punishments without allowing for discriminations or privileges, and to reward citizens on the basis of virtue alone, as the Romans used to do as long as their republic remained incorrupt.[32]

However, ruling and legislating according to justice and reason presuppose the existence of the state as a dominion—that is, a political structure having the power to exercise jurisdiction over a people in a territory.[33] It is to this sense of the word 'state' that Machiavelli is referring when he claims to have spent fifteen years studying the art of the state. As his diplomatic correspondence, and his writings of the time, amply document, the problems he had been dealing with while he was the *Secretario* were problems of dominion, and, more precisely, the problems of the preservation and the expansion of the dominion of Florence and the problems that other sovereigns had to face in instituting new dominions or defending old ones. He applied himself to the study of what comes before legislating and governing, when states are confronted with enemies determined to cause their death. When the states are threatened as dominions, princes and rulers have to face situations of necessity, when the choice is not between policies that are more or less advantageous or more or less just, but between the life or

death of the state. When it is the very life of the state which is at
stake, matters turn particularly harsh. These are the times when
justice and reason have to be postponed and politics, in the classical sense, is powerless.

All that was well known, in Machiavelli's Florence. The word
'state', in fact, evoked not only the unpleasant features of the
power of a man over the city, but also the equally disturbing business of the conflict between the interest of the state, on the one
hand, and Christian ethics and civil and international law, on the
other. Machiavelli was, of course, perfectly aware of the dubious
connotations of the state. When he reports in the *Florentine Histories* Cosimo's famous line that 'states were not held with prayer
books [*paternostri*] in hand', for instance, he makes it very clear to
the readers that Cosimo meant *his own* state, the state of the
Medici, not the sovereign political community of Florence. He
also highlights the contrast between the interest of the state (*stato*)
and the interest of the city by reporting another of Cosimo's mot-
tos—namely, that it is 'better a city ruined than lost'. What Cosimo
was concerned with was the preservation of his *stato*. He exiled, or
sentenced to death, or confiscated the properties of Florentine
citizens, not because they were enemies of the republic, but
because they were enemies of *his* state, just as he rewarded others
because they were *his* friends and partisans.[34]

The conflict between state and justice was also debated by Florentine citizens, as we can see from the records of the *Consulte* and
Pratiche, the advisory bodies of the Florentine Republic attended by
members of the Florentine élite.[35] In the *Pratica* summoned to
debate the treason of Paolo Vitelli—at which Machiavelli was
almost certainly present—the issue to be decided was whether
Vitelli ought or ought not to be treated 'according to reason'—
that is, according to justice and the law.[36] As one of the speakers
remarks, since it would be dangerous for the republic to leave Vitelli
alive, in his case one 'should not proceed according to the precepts
of reason [*secondo e termini di ragione*]'. And to justify the violation of the principle of civil wisdom that prescribes obeying the rule
of justice, the speaker appeals to the usual practice of states: matters of state, he says, are not to be handled according to reason.[37]

By the beginnings of the second decade of the century, the
conflict between moral and legal reason, on the one hand, and
the interest of the state, on the other, began to be described not as
a divergence between reason and the practice of the state, but as a

conflict between moral and legal reason and another 'reason'—namely, the 'reason of the state'. The concept of 'reason of state' appears for the first time in Francesco Guicciardini's *Dialogo del reggimento di Firenze* (*Dialogue on the Government of Florence*), composed between 1521 and 1524. Citing the example of the Genoese who did not release the prisoners they had captured at the battle of Meloria in 1284, thereby inflicting an irreparable blow on their Pisan enemies, Bernardo del Nero argues that what the Genoese did was a cruelty of which moral conscience could never approve. However, since all states—with the sole exception of republics within their own territory—are grounded on nothing but sheer violence, to preserve them it is necessary to resort to violence again and again. Therefore, Bernardo del Nero concludes, 'when I talked of murdering or keeping the Pisans imprisoned, I didn't perhaps talk as a Christian: I talked according to the reason and practice of states [*secondo la ragione e l'uso degli stati*]'.[38] He then says, and it is an important remark, that

anyone who doesn't acknowledge this has no excuse before God because—as the friars like to say—it shows 'crass ignorance'. Anyone who does recognize it cannot say it is reasonable to listen to one's conscience in one case and to disregard it in the other. I wanted to say this not to pronounce a verdict on these difficulties, which are immense, since anyone who wants to live totally according to God's will can ill afford not to remove himself totally from the affairs of this world, and it is difficult to live in the world without offending God. I did so in order to talk realistically about things as they are in fact, since chance has drawn us into this discusssion. We can cope with this argument among ourselves, but we shouldn't, however, use it with others, nor where there were more people.[39]

Machiavelli's Critique of Classical Politics

The last thing that Machiavelli would have liked to be told was that he was ignorant on how matters of state ought to be handled. When he says that he has distilled in *The Prince* what he has learnt on the art of the state, he implies that his little book contains *all* that it is necessary to know how to preserve a state, including indications on what a prince should do when the interest of the state compels him to violate the norms of moral reason. Since a ruler who intends always to be good among many who are not good will necessarily be ruined, he remarks, it is necessary for a ruler to learn to be able to be 'not good' and to use or not to use this capacity according to necessity.[40] And in Chapter 18 he states in even clearer terms that for a prince it is often (*spesso*) necessary to act against the principles of Christian morality, if he wants to preserve his state: 'and it must be understood that a ruler, and especially a new ruler, cannot always act in ways that are considered good because, in order to maintain his state, he is often forced to act against good faith, against charity, against humanness, against religion.'[41]

What was truly bold about it was not so much what he said, but the fact that he wrote it in a text intended for public circulation. Cosimo was reported to have *said* that states cannot be held with prayer books ('paternostri') in the hand; the Florentine citizens who remarked that there are questions pertaining to the security of the state that are not to be handled according to justice and reason were speaking in restricted gatherings; Guicciardini developed the concept of a reason of the state which supersedes Christian morality in a text never intended for publication, and even in the text itself he makes the protagonist of the dialogue say that discourses on a reason of the state are not to be made in public. Machiavelli's choice was an act of intellectual courage instigated by his longing for great accomplishments and, perhaps, also by the compelling need to see his expertise on the art of the state acclaimed. For people already accepted within the élite, a letter or a memorandum was sufficient to be credited as a reliable adviser. But Machiavelli had been the *Secretario* and was 'a man of very low and humble condition'.[42] He had to do something of much higher intellectual quality, even at the cost of breaking well-established conventions.

In his explanations as to why a new prince 'cannot always act in ways that are considered good', his language remains quite close to the conventions that the Florentine élite and princes used in discussing matters of state and diplomatic transactions.[43] Like them, he argues that the practice of states amply proves that it is sometimes necessary to leave aside the precepts of moral reason, and points to the great accomplishments of princes who have held uprightness in little respect:

everyone knows how praiseworthy it is for a ruler to keep his promises, and live uprightly and not by trickery. Nevertheless, experience shows that in our time the rulers who have done great things are those who have set little store by keeping their word, being skilful rather in cunningly deceiving men; they have got the better of those who have relied on being trustworthy.[44]

He continued to speak of a conflict between the precepts of moral reason that teach us 'how men should live' ('come si doverrebbe vivere'), and how men live, rather than of a contrast between moral reason and a reason of the state.[45] He did not go so far as to say that derogations of moral norms can be excused by a 'reason of the state'. He gave the art of the state a public dignity, but did not provide it with a new theoretical foundation, nor did he in fact construct a new language. The true intellectual masterstroke was his friend Guicciardini's invention or rediscovery of the concept of reason of the state. Before the invention of the concept of reason of the state, all political practices repugnant to the principles of moral and civil reason—waging an unjust war and fighting it unjustly, denying citizens their legal rights, distributing offices to one's friends, perpetrating cruelties, not keeping promises— were excused, as we have seen, by appealing to the practice of the state. After the construction of the concept of a reason of the state, they can be excused, even justified, by appealing to this new reason—namely, the reason of the state. With his background in jurisprudence, Guicciardini knew well that an excuse or a justification for actions which violate moral and legal reason based upon a reason, or a law, are more powerful than excuses or justifications based upon reference to current practices or customary behaviour. Even if he was acquainted with the language of jurisprudence, Machiavelli did not feel the need, or did not see the possibility and the importance, of coupling reason and state, or to oppose the classical moral and civil reason with a reason of the state.

This does not, however, at all diminish the intended subversive meaning of *The Prince*. As Quentin Skinner has shown, the arguments that Machiavelli put forth in it were a radical critique of the views on princely government discussed in fifteenth-century advice for princes.[46] Against the conventional Ciceronian precept that to attain glory and preserve his state the prince must be virtuous, he states, in the clearest possible way, that, if a prince wants always to behave according to moral virtues, he will surely lose his state and attain no glory at all.

Most of the passages of *The Prince* which have gained Machiavelli a sinister reputation are explicit attacks on the main principles of Ciceronian political theory. 'Wrong', Cicero had remarked in *Of Duties* 1.13.41, may be done 'by force or by fraud'; both are bestial: 'fraud seems to belong to the cunning fox, force to the lion. Both ways are wholly unworthy of man, but fraud is the more contemptible.' To this Machiavelli replies:

You should know, then, that there are two ways of contending: one by using laws, the other, force. The first is appropriate for men, the second for animals; but because the former is often ineffective, one must have recourse to the latter. Therefore, a ruler must know well how to imitate beasts as well as employing properly human means. This policy was taught to rulers allegorically by ancient writers: they tell how Achilles and many other ancient rulers were entrusted to Chiron the centaur, to be raised carefully by him. Having a mentor who was half-beast and half-man signifies that a ruler needs to use both natures, and that one without the other is not effective. Since a ruler, then, must know how to act like a beast, he should imitate both the fox and the lion, for the lion is liable to be trapped, whereas the fox cannot ward off wolves. One needs, then, to be a fox to recognize traps, and a lion to frighten away wolves.[47]

Commenting upon the foundations of political authority, Cicero had stressed that 'of all motives, none is better adapted to secure influence and hold it fast than love; nothing is more foreign to that end than fear'. From this principle he had derived a straightforward piece of advice: 'let us, then, embrace this policy, which appeals to every heart and is the strongest support not only of security but also of influence and power—namely, to banish fear and cleave to love. And thus we shall most easily secure success both in private and in public life.'[48] On this issue, too, Machiavelli's position is a clear rejection of Cicero's views. Men are, he writes, 'ungrateful, fickle, feigners and dissemblers, avoiders of danger, eager for gain. While you are of benefit to them, they are all devoted to you: they would shed their blood for you; they offer their possessions, their lives, and their sons, as I said before, when the need to do so is far off. But when you are hard pressed, they turn away.' The right advice to offer princes is, therefore, that it is better to be feared than to be loved, if one cannot be both, because 'men are less hesitant about offending or harming a ruler who makes himself loved than one who inspires fear'.[49]

Last, Cicero had proclaimed that 'no cruelty can be expedient; for cruelty is most abhorrent to human nature, whose lead we ought to follow'. To which Machiavelli responds in Chapter 8 of *The Prince*, that there are cruelties that 'may be called well committed (if one may use the word "well" of that which is evil) when they are all committed at once, because they are necessary to establish power, and are not afterwards persisted in, but changed for measures as beneficial as possible to one's subjects'. Therefore, as he writes in Chapter 18, 'every ruler should want to be thought merciful, not cruel; nevertheless, one should take care not to be merciful in an inappropriate way. Cesare Borgia was considered cruel, yet his harsh measures restored order to the Romagna, unifying it and rendering it peaceful and loyal.'

Radical as it is, however, Machiavelli's critique of the Ciceronian tradition and of the conception of politics as civil wisdom is intended to restrict the range of its validity rather than to dismiss it altogether. More precisely, he claims that the Ciceronian precepts are to be followed except in situations of necessity when princes and rulers are dealing with enemies who are prepared and capable to use any means to destroy their states. The use of fraud, for instance, is 'detestable'; yet 'in the conduct of a war is praiseworthy and glorious'. A fraud which involves breaking your word or the contracts you have made, he clarifies, is not glorious at all: 'for, although on occasion it may win for you a state or a kingdom . . . it will never bring you glory.' What turns a fraud into a praiseworthy and glorious deed is the fact that a prince or a ruler uses it 'with an enemy who has not kept faith with you, i.e. of a fraud which is involved in the conduct of a war'.[50]

The same considerations apply to cruelties, injustices, simulation, deceit; in brief, to all the derogations to the commitment to virtue that Machiavelli discusses in *The Prince*. His wording on this delicate matter is extremely precise. He writes, in fact, that a man, who wants 'always [*in tutte le parte*] to act honourably' will inevitably fall, because he is surrounded by many unscrupulous men; therefore, 'it is necessary for a prince, if he wants to maintain his power, to learn to be able not to be good and to use it [the capacity to be not good] or not to use it according to necessity'. A few lines later he restates the same point in even clearer terms:

I know that everyone will acknowledge that it would be most praiseworthy for a ruler to have all the above-mentioned qualities that are held to be good.

But because it is not possible to have all of them and to comply with them at all times, because the reality of human life [*le condizioni umane*] does not permit it, it is necessary to know how to avoid becoming notorious for those vices that would destroy one's power and seek to avoid those vices that are not politically dangerous.

To put Machiavelli's argument in a nutshell, as long as a prince or a ruler is able to ['potendo'], he must not 'deviate from right conduct'; but he must 'be capable of entering upon the path of wrongdoing, if forced by necessity', or better to render his wording, 'necessitated' ['necessitato'].[51]

It is perhaps because of these emendations to the language of politics based on the principle that politics is only government according to moral reason and justice that he describes *The Prince* as being not an essay on politics, or civil science, or public government, but a work on the art of the state. As I remarked at the beginning of this chapter, in Machiavelli's time politics was identified with the activity of legislation, government, and the administration of justice, inspired by the ideal of a civil community based upon the rule of law. In *The Prince* he explains the virtue, made of force and cunning, which is quite different from civil wisdom and yet is necessary for founding and preserving states.

In this sense, *The Prince* is an integration of the language of politics. The long-term goal of his advice in *The Prince* is the establishment of a new principality adorned and strengthened with 'good laws, strong arms, reliable allies, and exemplary conduct' in which the subjects will feel encouraged to attend to their ordinary occupations both in trade and agriculture without fearing that their gains and their properties will be taken away from them.[52]

The best evidence on this regard can be found precisely in that infamous Chapter 7 of *The Prince* which does contain the disconcerting advice to imitate the methods used by the Duke Valentino to institute his dominion over the peoples of Romagna. As soon as the Duke had conquered the Romagna, Machiavelli writes,

he found that it had been controlled by violent lords, who were more disposed to dispoil their subjects than to rule them properly, thus being a source of disorder rather than of order; consequently, that region was full of thefts, quarrels and outrages of every kind. He considered it necessary to introduce efficient government, because he wanted the region to be peaceful and its inhabitants obedient to his monarchical authority. He therefore sent there messer Remirro de Orco, a cruel and energetic man, giving him full powers.

After Remirro had succeeded in 'restoring order and peace', with his cruelty and his unrestrained powers, the Duke, Machiavelli reports, 'set up a civil tribunal, under a distinguished president, in the centre of the region, to which each city sent a lawyer'. As soon as a dominion is consolidated, cruelties and absolute powers have to be replaced by ordinary civil justice and reason, as the tradition of civil wisdom prescribes; but before the rule of law is in place, politics in the conventional sense of the art of ruling according to reason and justice needs the help of the ambivalent but powerful art of the state.

The Critique of the Medicean Art of the State

Firmly to establish his reputation as an expert on the art of the state, however, Machiavelli could not confine himself to the discussion of general issues, particularly in a work composed with the intention of presenting it to the Medici. He had also to address the specific problems of the consolidation of the Medici's regime in Florence, and the whole interpretation of the art of the state that had been guiding the Medici political conduct since the times of Cosimo. For the Medici and their advisers, the word *stato* meant the power of a *signore* or a family over the institutions of the city, as exemplified by expressions like the '*stato de' Medici*', which Machiavelli himself uses.[53]

To be competent on the art of the state in this sense meant, therefore, to know what needs to be done in different circumstances to found and preserve a regime. In his times the undisputed example of this kind of expertise was Cosimo de' Medici, whose 'understanding of the states of princes and civil governments' was second to none, as Machiavelli acknowledges. Because of his skill, he succeeded in building and preserving the Medici's regime over Florence ('tenere lo stato') for thirty-one years, in such a variety of fortune and in so varied a city.[54]

The key of Cosimo's success was his outstanding prudence and the skill of building, through a policy of favours and patronage, a large network of partisans and friends which ensured the Medici substantial control over the republic's institutions. At the same time, Cosimo, and also Lorenzo after him, were attentive to govern 'with civility'—that is, in a civilized manner and behind the scene, without introducing constitutional changes nor claiming for themselves princely titles.

Cosimo's legacy was well represented in the advice offered by experts on the art of the state on the best ways to secure the Medici regime which was restored upon the ashes of Soderini's republic in

September 1512. However, they also recognized that the republican experience had significantly affected the spirit of the Florentines and changed the political geography of the city in a way that
posed serious threats to the regime. In a memorandum addressed to
Cardinal Giulio de' Medici, to instruct him on what should be done
for the security of the Medici regime and of all those who had
obligations to it ('per la salute di questo Stato e di chi si è ubligato
seco'), Paolo Vettori remarks that, in the previous ten years, under
the republic, the city had lived very well and therefore the memory
of those happy times would always threaten the new regime. In
comparison with the times of Cosimo and Lorenzo, the new regime
has more enemies and less means to satisfy them; hence, to be able
to last, the new Medici regime must rely on force rather than on
the traditional policy of patronage.[55]

The same issue is also discussed in a text composed by Francesco
Guicciardini in October 1512, in the aftermath of the restoration,
to discuss, as he puts it, what the Medici should do 'to keep the
state and the government of the city of Florence'.[56] The regime
instituted by Cosimo in 1434, he remarks, did not replace a popular
government but the power of the factions led by Rinaldo degli
Albizzi and Palla Strozzi; moreover, the Medici did not immediately impose themselves as the absolute masters of the city, but
built their power up gradually over the years. The new regime, on
the contrary, has replaced 'a very popular and democratic government ('uno stato affatto populare e larghissimo'), in which the
citizens enjoyed the greatest liberty and equality, and power has
been suddenly concentrated in the hands of one man alone. For this
reason, the Medici are now seen as those who have deprived the
people of Florence of their state, with the obvious consequence
that a great number of citizens are hostile to the new regime.[57]

Another widespread belief in the analyses of the Medicean state
was that, because of the way in which it had been imposed over
the republic, the new regime could do very little to gain the
people's support and had therefore to seek to reinforce the loyalty
of the nobles. There was, in other words, a large consensus that
the Medici, as Paolo Vettori put it, 'will not be able to regain the
city'.[58] In the same vein, Guicciardini notices that the people ('lo
universale della città') are not at all happy with the new regime,
because they think that under the republic they had some role in
the state and do not accept the fact that they have now to be
dependent on one or a few men. As with the nobles, they can be

divided into two groups: those who are compelled to bet everything on the Medici because no other regime can possibly satisfy their most onerous requests, and those who had important posts in the former government because of their goodness and their prudence in civil affairs. Whereas the requests of the former are difficult to satisfy because those men are keen to violate the laws and have a predatory nature, those of the latter are easy to meet and it is therefore reasonable to believe that they will become friends of the new regime.[59]

While the accounts of the state and the problems of the regime were convergent, the suggested solutions were quite dissimilar. Vettori urged the Medici not to try to placate their enemies and to be sure instead to intimidate them. To this effect, he advised them to leave aside the old policy of patronage and count on military force. The policy of patronage was instead forcefully recommended by a member of the Medici family, Giuliano de' Medici, in a memorandum composed between May and August 1513. In this text Giuliano de' Medici urges Lorenzo to devote the greatest care to be sure to put friends of the family in the most important institutions of the city, and to choose for these posts people who are both loyal ('fedeli') and bold ('animosi').

If we now turn to *The Prince*, it is easy to see that Machiavelli addresses all the key issues concerning the security of a regime like that of the Medici, and on each of them he offers clear advice, beginning with the hotly debated theme of the difficulty to secure the new Medici regime because of the still vivid memory of the Republic of 1494–1512 and the presence of a significant number of supporters of the bygone republic. With his typical briskness, he assures that, unlike what other advisers believed, the truth of the matter is that 'men are much more interested in present things than in those that are past, and if they find that their affairs are flourishing, they are content and do not seek changes'.[60]

With equally straightforward words, he rebuffs the idea that the new regime has to worry about those who were content with the old republic and sustained it. Again, he claims that precisely the opposite is the case: the true danger for the new regime comes not from those who were content with the republic, but from those who were dissatisfied with it. They were dissatisfied with the republic because of their immoderate ambition, and for this reason it will also be very difficult for the new regime to turn them into loyal friends.[61] Even if they have helped him to attain power, a new prince must always regard the nobles as a serious threat to the state, because they have the means and the audacity openly to attack him, if they are dissatisfied. A prudent prince, he writes in the chapter on 'Civil Principality', must therefore distinguish among the nobles those who are prepared to associate their fortune with that of the prince and those who are not:

You should honour and esteem those . . . who are not rapacious. As for those who do not commit themselves to you, two different kinds of reason for their conduct must be distinguished. If they act in this way because of pusillanimity or natural lack of spirit, you should make use of them, especially those who are shrewd, because in good times they will bring you honour, and in troubled times you will have nothing to fear from them. But if they do not commit themselves to you calculatingly and because of ambition, it is a sign that they are thinking more of their own interests than of yours. And a ruler must watch these nobles very carefully, and fear them as much as if they were declared enemies, because if he finds himself in trouble they will always do their best to bring him down.[62]

The Medici, who always presented their regime as a civil one, would hardly have failed to read these lines of *The Prince* as strong advice not to ground their power on the nobles' support, as their counsellors were urging them to do. Against the trite proverb 'he who builds upon the people builds upon mud' ('chi fonda sul populo fonda sul fango') endorsed as we have seen by influential Florentine experts on matters of state, Machiavelli remarks that to secure a civil principality 'it is necessary for a ruler to have the people well disposed towards him'.[63] A prince, he explains, 'can never protect himself from a hostile people, because there are too many of them; but he can protect himself from the nobles, because there are few of them'.[64] Moreover, 'a ruler is always obliged to co-exist with the same people, whereas he is not obliged to have the same nobles, since he is well able to make and unmake them at any time, advancing them or reducing their power, as he wishes'.[65]

Much as they were subversive, these pieces of advice were less scandalous than his comments on the time-honoured Medicean practice of ruling behind the scene through loyal friends suitably appointed to the important posts of the republic. Civil principalities, Machiavelli warns, do collapse when the prince needs to take absolute authority; and, since such a need may well arise, it is utterly unwise to believe that a principality in which the prince rules indirectly could last for long. Princes who 'rule through public officials', Machiavelli explains, are highly unstable because they depend completely on the goodwill of those citizens who act as their officials. And they can very easily remove him from power either by moving against him or simply by refusing to obey him. Moreover, in troubled times the ruler does not have enough time to assume absolute authority, because the citizens or subjects, accustomed as they are to obeying the officials, will not be disposed to obey him in such a crisis. And in difficult times, he will always lack men on whom he can depend.[66]

It is difficult to imagine a more eloquent way of saying that the old traditional practice of ruling behind the scenes had to be abandoned, and new policies needed to be put into practice, if a truly solid state had to be built.

Along with the tradition of 'civil government', Machiavelli also directly attacks the other foundation of the Medicean art of the state—namely, the policy of patronage and favours: 'because friendships that are acquired with money, and not through greatness and nobility of character, are paid for but not secured, and prove unreliable just when they are needed.'[67] Favours and honours, he explains, generate a loyalty based on gratitude. But, since men easily break the bonds of gratitude when they see that it is in their interest to do so, friendships acquired through private favours do not offer at all a solid basis for the state.[68] Much more effective than gratitude is fear, sustained by the threat of punishment. If one really regards interest and fear as the most powerful motives for men's conduct, as the Florentine theorists of the state were claiming, one must conclude that for a prince it is not at all safe to rely on the gratitude of the partisans he has benefited, and that he should rather look for ways of making himself constantly feared.

As we have seen, the advisers of the Medici who were urging them to continue the old policy of favours and patronage were not claiming that the prince should expect from the people who had benefited from him a loyalty based upon gratitude. They were in fact stressing that the loyalty of partisans originates from self-interest, indeed from necessity: partisans are willing to do everything to sustain the regime because they know that they owe all their honours and their wealth to it, and fear the consequences of a change of government. They have no other choice but to sustain the regime with all their energy.

Machiavelli responds to this argument with the observation that the partisans of the regime, particularly the nobles, can never be securely bound to the regime because 'they are more far-seeing and cunning, they are able to act in time to save themselves, and seek to ingratiate themselves with the one whom they expect to prevail'.[69] Against the view of other students of the state, he can, therefore, conclude with the utmost confidence that the policy of favours does not have at all the power to compel partisans to be loyal and sustain the regime in moments of danger; it cannot tie them to the prince through the bonds of interests and fear.

Once he has dismantled the core tenets of Florentine wisdom on matters of state, Machiavelli puts forth his own reinterpretation of what the true art of securing a principality should consist of. It cannot be the astute skill of controlling public institutions through one's own friends, nor that of dissimulating power under the habiliments of civility. It must first of all be the ability to create and discipline the militia:

A ruler, then, should have no other objective and no other concern, nor occupy himself with anything else [né prendere cosa alcuna per sua arte] except war and its methods and practices, for this pertains only to those who rule [perché quella è sola arte che si espetta a chi comanda]. And it is of such efficacy [virtù] that it not only maintains hereditary rulers in power but very often enables men of private status to become rulers. On the other hand, it is evident that if rulers concern themselves more with the refinements of life than with military matters, they lose power [lo stato loro]. The main reason why they lose it is their neglect of the art of war; and being proficient in this art is what enables one to gain power.[70]

By saying that the prince should apply himself to the art of war and work to institute an army composed of his own subjects, Machiavelli was not only rejecting the view that the best way to secure a state was to disarm the subjects, but was in fact claiming that the most secure way to transform the subjects into loyal partisans was precisely to enrol them in the militia:

New rulers, then, never disarm their subjects; indeed, if they find them unarmed, they always provide them with weapons. For when you arm them, these weapons become your own: those whom you distrusted become loyal, those who were loyal remain so, and subjects are converted into firm adherents. Since it is not possible to provide all your subjects with arms, when you benefit those whom you arm, you will also be able to secure yourself better against the others. Since the former are treated favourably, they will be more attached to you. The latter will excuse your conduct, because they will realize the need to treat favourably those who carry out more dangerous duties.[71]

If the most important aim of a prince is to preserve himself and the state, as the masters of the art of the state maintained, then the old way of building and preserving a regime theorized and practised in Florence since the times of Cosimo had to be abandoned to embrace a new conception of the art of the state based on the principle that no state is a true dominion unless it is sustained by an army composed of citizens or subjects. This piece of wisdom which Machiavelli was offering in *The Prince* was exactly, as he wrote to Vettori, the result of the many years he had spent in studying the art of the state. As early as 1503, in the oration composed to persuade the deliberative bodies of the Republic to pass a law which would authorize new taxes to levy new troops, he had written that

all cities which have been governed either by an absolute prince, or by the aristocracy, or by the people . . . have defended themselves through military force and prudence. Military force and prudence are therefore the backbone of all forms of dominion which have existed or shall exist in history.[72]

Three years later, writing again on the same subject, he stresses with even greater eloquence that *any* dominion needs justice and armies.[73] Because of the special competence he had gained serving the Republic, he was capable of saying with great authority that for any new prince the best way to secure his state was to build a reliable army, not a regime based on favours.

Moreover, he considered a state based on patronage particularly inadequate to permit a new prince to accomplish great things, as Machiavelli wanted a true prince to be willing and able to do.[74] He intended his art of the state to suit a prince capable of liberating Italy from the barbarians, not just a *signore* ruling Florence by conferring benefits on this or that individual, giving marriage portions to the daughters of his partisans, protecting friends from the magistrates, and the like. He was dreaming of a new Cyrus, not just another Cosimo. He offered his mastery of the art of the state necessary to attain such a grand endeavour.

The Methods of the Art of the State

While these remarks hopefully clarify the goals of the art of the state as Machiavelli understood it, we still need to elucidate its limits and methods. As is well known, the view which still commands wide consensus among scholars is that Machiavelli considered the aim of the student of the art of the state to be that of discovering the truth about political action by looking for a 'direct contact with things' beyond appearances, deception, and self-deception.[75] As a number of scholars have stressed, Machiavelli investigated political matters in a scientific way; indeed he founded the modern science of politics. As a title of praise, his name has been associated with that of his compatriot Galileo: 'What Galileo gave in his *Dialogues*, and what Machiavelli gave in his *Prince*', wrote Ernst Cassirer, were really 'new sciences'. Just as Galileo's dynamics became the foundation of our modern science of nature, so Machiavelli paved a new way to political science.[76] Through his method based upon empirical observations and rigorous mathematical calculations, Galileo identified the laws that govern the natural world; through empirical observations and rigorous generalizations, Machiavelli identified the laws of politics.

Scholars who stress the scientific nature of Machiavelli's approach remark that he believed that the human world, like the natural world, displays regular or recurrent features which form the basis of general laws of politics. The text most frequently cited on this regard is a passage from the *Discorsi*, where Machiavelli writes:

Prudent men are wont to say—and this is not rashly or without good ground—that he who would foresee what has to be, should reflect on what has been, for everything that happens in the world at any time has genuine resemblance to what happened in ancient times. This is due to the fact that the agents who bring such things about are men, and that men have, and always have had, the same passions.[77]

This belief in the sameness of human passions over history was a common one in early sixteenth-century Florence, but it certainly did not encourage a scientific study of politics aiming at the discovery of general laws. Rather, it was the premise for an interpretive work aiming at understanding the specific features of political life and events, attempting predictions, offering practical advice, and writing historical narratives based upon the identification of the political actors' intentions. Francesco Guicciardini, for instance, wrote in a letter to Machiavelli that 'the very same things return', and all events have already occurred in past times. What changes are 'only the faces of the men and the extrinsic colors' of things.[78] This assumption, however, did not lead him to search general laws of political behaviour; on the contrary, it led him to conceive of the study of politics, which consists in 'recognizing' things and 'seeing them again' with the help of historical knowledge. Understanding political events is therefore recognition in the literal sense: we understand when we see things for the second time.

However, precisely because the faces of men and the external appearances change, and so do 'the names and the forms of things', the recognition is arduous; it is not at all an easy task to identify in histories the events that can illuminate the ones that we are witnessing or are about to witness. To read and to understand the complex geography and alchemy of human passions and intentions in narrations of past events and to apply this knowledge to present political affairs, it takes, as Guicciardini wrote in the *Ricordi* a 'sharp and discerning eye'.[79] It takes good eyes capable of identifying specific signs and traits rather than general or common features; it is, as he puts it, a job for prudent men,[80] not for philosophers or scientists inclined to investigate the eternal and immutable underneath the ever-changing flux of things.

Also Machiavelli believes that men have, and always have had, the same passions; but he also knows very well that each individual has his own passions and temperament and acts accordingly. 'I believe', he writes to Piero Soderini, 'that, just as Nature has created men with different faces, so she has created them with different intellects and imagination. As a result, each man behaves according to his own intellect and imagination.'[81] To be able to understand and predict their behaviour, one must therefore be capable of identifying the particular disposition and imagination of individual actors—an arduous task which requires a sophisticated work of interpretation and historical analysis.

The student of politics must be 'there' or at least close to the event or to peoples performing political acts, and must diligently collect and review facts and information. But uncertainty as to what is really going on remains, and the clouds that surround political action never go away, in part because of the ability of political actors to deceive themselves and others, in part because the student of the art of the state himself is not an impartial observer at all but looks at things through his own hopes, fears, and beliefs. The interpretive work is valuable and fascinating, but hardly conclusive; the best one can hope for is to come up with stories and advice which will be questioned by other students coming up with different stories and by other advisers offering different counsels. Judgements about men's actions, and particularly princes' actions, can never be final, because, as Machiavelli remarks, there is no judge to whom one can appeal for a conclusive verdict ('non è iudizio da reclamare').[82]

Machiavelli learnt very soon in the course of his activity as *Secretario* that to understand political events means to be able to interpret the intentions of men from their acts and their words; but he also learnt that even the most accurate and insightful analyses do not go beyond conjectures. On 2 December 1502 he writes to the Ten of War: 'I have tried all I could to be able to understand [*intendere*] whether the French are going to move to the Kingdom of Naples with or without the Duke Valentino, but I have not been able to reach any certain conclusion [né mai ne ho possuto trarre alcuna cosa certa].' From many signs, he continues, 'I see this *Signore* [the Duke Valentino] resolved to leave in three or four days, but of all that time shall be the judge'.[83]

A year later, writing this time from Rome, he conveys once again to the *Signori* how difficult it is to interpret the intentions of the Duke, even if he is almost an eyewitness to all his man- œuvres: 'one does not know how to interpret [*interpretare*] what he intends to do, but many conjecture that it will be an unhappy outcome.'[84] However attentive he is in observing gestures and acts, and even the smallest details, our student of the art of the state cannot even come close to anything like the truth of the matter. He does not venture to present conjectures as certain assessment and recognizes the limits of his own capacity to understand the significance of the events which are unfolding under his eyes. On the sudden departure of French troops from the Duke Valentino's headquarters in Cesena, in late December 1502, for instance, he writes that 'every man is making his own castles in the air'; but, he confesses, 'from authentic sources nothing can be extracted that seems reasonable to anyone else', even if he has not spared himself all the efforts which were necessary 'to get to the truth of the matter'.[85]

The 'truth of the matter' has often to be uncovered by decoding theatrical performances that princes stage in order to impress, scare, or stupefy their subjects as well as their enemies. The obvious example is the murder of Remirro de Orco by the Duke Cesare Borgia. In *The Prince* (Ch. 7) Machiavelli reports the episode as a harsh but necessary measure to allay the subjects' hatred. He emphasizes the efficacy of the power of the staging:

because he [the Duke] recognized that the severe measures that had been taken had resulted in his becoming hated by some people, in order to dispel this ill-feeling and win everyone over to him, he wanted to show that if any cruel deeds had been committed they were attributable to the harshness of his government, not to himself. And availing himself of an appropriate opportunity, one morning the Duke had Remirro placed in two pieces in the square at Cesena, with a block of wood and a blood-stained sword at his side. This terrible spectacle left the people both satisfied and amazed [*satisfatti e stupiti*].

While, in *The Prince*, Machiavelli registers the power of the performance over the subjects, some thirteen years before, when he saw the scene on 26 December 1502, in Cesena, he had suggested a more subtle interpretation of the meaning of that staging. The body of the man who had turned the scattered parts of Romagna into a united and ordered political body was turned into two pieces and placed in the square in Cesena. A dubious way of rewarding his merits; surely a powerful affirmation of the prince's total and arbitrary control over bodies, political and individual.[86]

Even when the prince does not act behind the scene, or a mask, as in the case of the Duke, the interpretive work remains difficult because of the secrecy with which political actors cover their intentions. In the fifteen years that he spent in the apprenticeship of the art of the state he had far too many opportunities to appreciate this distinctive quality of princes. As I have written to you many times, he reports from Cesena on 22 December 1502,

this Lord is very secretive, and I do not believe that what he is going to do is known to anybody but himself. And his chief secretaries have many times asserted to me that he does not tell them anything except when he orders it . . . Hence I beg Your Lordships will excuse me and not impute it to my negligence if I do not satisfy Your Lordships with information, because most of the time I do not satisfy even myself.[87]

Some years later he registers the same secretness in the Emperor Maximilian and expresses again his sense of frustration at the impossibility of attaining full intelligence of the situation and therefore of offering solid materials on which certain prediction could be built.[88]

The student of the art of the state may attempt various tricks to 'infiltrate' the defences that princes put forth to cover their intentions, but he is unlikely to succeed, no matter how able he is, as it occurred to Machiavelli himself in the course of a long conversation with the Duke on 7 October 1502: 'notwithstanding that I was inveigling him to get from him some particulars, he always kept his distance and made wide turns.'[89] However great the difficulty of the task and the frustration it generates, Machiavelli accepts the limitations in the understanding of political events. Other disciplines may hope to attain truth; the art he practices does not. The awareness of the limits of one's art is precisely what distinguishes serious practitioners from amateurs, beginners, and zealots.

In addition to princes' secrecy, what makes understanding political events arduous is princes' equally notable ability to deceive those who attempt to grasp their intentions. Once again the Duke was a master in colouring his hostile intentions with words full of friendship and noble purposes.[90] He had an excellent mentor in his father, Pope Alexander VI, who 'was concerned only with deceiving men, and he always found them gullible. No man ever affirmed anything more forcefully or with stronger oaths but kept his word less. Never the less, his deceptions were always effective, because he well understood the naivety of men.'[91] And so did King Ferdinand the Catholic: 'one present-day ruler, whom it is well to leave unnamed, is always preaching peace and trust, although he is really very hostile to both; and if he had practised them he would have lost either reputation or power several times over.'[92]

Unlike the majority of men who 'judge more by their eyes than their hands', the good student of the art of the state has ways of guarding himself from princes' deceptive skills. He must, first of all, not be credulous at all, and not let himself be deceived by appearances or by anybody's authority.[93] He must 'judge by the hands'. As Giovanni Bardazzi has finely observed, the metaphor of 'judging by the hands' as opposed to 'judging by the eyes' is a reminiscence of Luigi Pulci's *Morgante* and of Poggio Bracciolini's *Facezie*, which tell the story of a thrush who, seeing tears in the eyes of a man who is killing his cage mates, believes that the man will have compassion on the remaining birds until an older bird tells him to look, not at the man's eyes, but at his hands. As Poggio comments, to judge well one must look at what people do, not at what they say.[94] Machiavelli surely endorses the old bird's wisdom, but also knows that even man's actions are not clear at all. They must be interpreted. To do that one must touch who the prince is. But what precisely does it mean to be able to touch who the prince is? What is there to be 'touched'?

The metaphor of touching who somebody is indicates a kind of knowledge which requires closeness. It means to be able to under-

stand the passions and humours which orient particular princes'
and rulers' conduct, to identify the passions that dominate their
mind. One is dominated by the desire of glory, another by hatred;
another by the desire of revenge; another by lust for money;
another still by fear of losing his territory or power. Because they
are moved by passions, at times they make mistakes; they pursue
policies that have disastrous consequences for them, just like any
other men.

To assume that they will do what is best for their states is a
typical view of the amateur of the art of the state. As Vettori wrote
to Machiavelli on 12 July 1513, things often 'do not proceed according to reason'; therefore it is a vain exercise to investigate political
matters and speculate solutions designed to put order in the world
of international relations ('rassettare questo mondo').[95] None the
less, for Machiavelli, the student of the art of the state must
attempt to assess the state of things and try to predict what the
people are likely to do, given the fact that they are—each in a
different way, and each in a different way at different times—
dominated, or at least affected, by particular passions.

When Vettori asks him his opinion on the politics of European
powers and Italian states, Machiavelli bases his comments on a
consideration of the 'quality' or 'nature' of kings and peoples; and
by 'quality' or 'nature', he means their passions and their
temperament:

As for the state of affairs in the world, I derive this conclusion from them.
The sort of princes who govern us possess, whether by nature or by chance,
the following qualitites: we have a wise pope, and therefore a serious and
scrupulous one; an unstable and capricious emperor; a haughty, timorous
king of France; a niggardly and avaricious king of Spain; a rich, inpetuous,
and glory-hungry king of England; the brutish, victorious, and insolent Swiss;
and us Italians—poverty stricken, aspiring, and cowardly.[96]

In the case of kingdoms and principalities, the passions of kings
and princes are the decisive factor.[97] In the case of republics, peoples' temperament needs to be considered, for it does indeed affect
political deliberations. The Swiss, Machiavelli warns, were at first
content to defend themselves; then it was enough for them to take
stipends from others, to keep their young men ready for war, and to
get honour; as a result of their military achievements, they have
now acquired 'an aspiring spirit and a will for soldiering on their
own'. From his analysis of the change in the temperament of the

Swiss, Machiavelli concludes that they will not give up the control over Northern Italy that they have gained through wars, and that they will, on the contrary, labour to increase it.[98]

Though they are based on the interpretations of tangible or at least visible elements such as passions and humours, Machiavelli is perfectly aware that his predictions, like anybody else's, contain much guesswork, as his friend Vettori says.[99] When he discusses whether the alliance between France and England of August 1514 is likely to last or not, he remarks that Henry VIII of England could break the treaty either out of fear or out of envy, and speculates that neither passion will be strong enough to move the king to change his alliances. He interprets the king's intentions on the basis of a general assumption about the way in which passions operate and on the basis of his knowledge of who the king is.

In other cases he relies on the prince's past conduct. The example is Machiavelli's assessment of the behaviour of Ferdinand the Catholic. Whereas Vettori considers the conduct of the king of Spain utterly inexplicable, Machiavelli finds it perfectly consistent, given the fact that his policy has always been that of rousing 'great expectations about himself, all the time keeping men's minds occupied in considering what is going to be the end of new decisions and new undertakings'. The goal of the king's strategy, which has proved to be very effective in holding on to new states and distrusted subjects, is not

so much this, that, or the other victory, as to win prestige among his multifarious activities. Therefore, he always started things off ardently, later giving them that end which chance places before him or which necessity teaches him; up until now no one has been able to complain about either his luck or his courage.[100]

To recognize that princes' conduct is affected by passions does not mean that they behave foolishly or irrationally. The king of France and the king of Spain whom Machiavelli has portrayed as inclined to be angry and timid, and stingy and avaricious, respectively, shall make an agreement between themselves because, he says, 'reason requires' it.[101] In an earlier letter he had written that 'I have always believed and still believe that it would please Spain—and still does—to see the King of France out of Italy, provided that he was able to hound him out of Italy with his own army and his own prestige' because it is 'reasonable'. Elsewhere, he describes the pope as reasonably 'eager for glory'.[102]

However reasonable they are, each of them is reasonable given the kind of person he is—that is, given the sort of passions which affect his choices. This implies that general theories of political behaviour are little more than a futile exercise. Effective evaluations and predictions are to be made by 'touching' the prince or the king whose actions we want to understand or predict.

Interpretive knowledge obtained by touching is always tentative and conjectural, no matter how close the student of the art of the state is, no matter how accurate his information is. Still, this is the only sound knowledge that a wise student of the art can try to gain. Uncertain as it is, it is highly valuable, as it permits the student to picture a narrative within which each actor's intentions and conduct will make sense and which therefore provides a basis for political choices.

> Your Lordships [he wrote from Rome on 21 November 1503] wish to understand how matters are proceeding here and what judgement [iuditio] and conjecture one should make of them. It seems to me that all along I've been writing to you in such a way that, if Your Lordships take my letters in hand, I believe you would see a history [storia] of everything happening here.[103]

Before the facts, the student of the art of the state attempts predictions based on his interpretations; after the facts, the work of interpretation resumes to provide this time a plausible account of what has happened; until another narrative is proposed.

Interpretations and predictions on matters of state are tentative, not only because of the intricacy of the object of their investigations, but also because the students themselves have their own beliefs and their own passions, as Machiavelli openly admits:

> I suspect that your not wanting it [a particular proposal for peace in Europe] and my wanting it have the same basis—a natural feeling or temperament that causes you to say 'no' and me to say 'yes'. You justify your 'no' by pointing out that, were the king to regain Lombardy, there would be more difficulty in achieving peace; to justify my 'yes', I have pointed out that this is not true—furthermore, peace gotten by my method will be more secure and more stable.[104]

His correspondent Vettori has a different view. He stresses that his own, and his friend Niccolò's analyses are not affected at all by passions.[105] But Vettori's very words prove that Machiavelli was right to claim that their disagreement was based on different fears and different hopes. Vettori in fact admits that his foremost concern is the good of Florence, and that after the sack of Brescia by the French troops on February 1512 he feared very much that Florence might suffer a similar fate. Machiavelli, on the other hand, is above all concerned with the Swiss. They are a republic, they are well armed, they have tasted the sweetness of domination; all that, given Machiavelli's assumptions concerning republics' behaviour, makes him believe that they will pursue expansionist politics, even if they will not parallel the Romans:

I certainly do not think that they will create an empire like the Romans, but I do think they can become masters of Italy thanks to their proximity and thanks to our disarray and bad situation. And because these things appall me, I should like to remedy them; if France is not adequate, I see no other remedy—and now I am ready to start weeping with you over our collapse and our sevitude that, if it does not come today or tomorrow, will come in our lifetime.[106]

The dispute can hardly be settled on empirical grounds. Time shall be the judge, afterwards. Before time's verdict, all one can have is little more than a rhetorical contest in which each contender puts forth his partisan views, and colours them with general criteria. Even time's verdict concerning princes' and kings' actions is far from being conclusive; there is still ample room for dispute and conflicting interpretations on why they did what they did, what they were hoping to attain, or, as Machiavelli wrote in the letter of 10 December 1513, 'the motives for their actions ('della ragione delle loro azioni'). Out of their kindness, Machiavelli continues in the same letter, the great men of antiquity 'answer me'; he means that their works and the histories which record their actions disclose to him their meaning because he knows how to question them.[107] That skill, which he uses to interpret the intentions of ancient men and modern men alike, is the core of the art of the state. It is because he is confident he possesses the skills of the interpreter that he can also claim, a few lines later, that he has been a serious apprentice of the art.

Be they predictive or historical, assessments on political matters can at times be made by referring to general principles. To settle the debate on whether the peace between the king of Spain and the king of France of April 1513 shall last, for instance, Machiavelli puts forth a general criterion which ought to be used to evaluate all peace treatises: one 'must among other matters figure out what parties are disgruntled with it and what the ramifications of their discontent may be'.[108] In other cases, he bases his interpretations on the assessment of the psychological status of a prince at a given time which he has been able to grasp by 'being there' and judging by his hands. In his dispatch of 2 December 1502, for example, he reports to the *Signori* that the Duke 'begins to get used to not having his whims satisfied, and he realizes that fortune is not always on his side'; and from this interpretation he infers that he will be more disposed to accept Florence's proposals.[109]

A few months before, on 26 June 1502, Francesco Soderini and Machiavelli had warned the Signori of Florence that the Duke was a very bold man who feared nothing and was sustained by a perpetual good fortune.[110] Machiavelli has 'touched by the hands' the changes in the Duke's passions; what was true in June is no longer true in December. As a consequence, what was the right conduct in June was wrong in December. If science is, as it was considered to be in Machiavelli's time, the true knowledge of things which cannot be otherwise, his work has nothing to share with that of the scientist.[111]

Appeals to general principles, references to past examples, remarks on particular individuals' inclinations are all perfectly compatible. They can all be used in the same argument; they are all part of the effort of making one's positions persuasive. To describe Machiavelli's way of addressing matters of state in terms of pursuit of truth as opposed to imagination only in part renders what he was in fact doing, and, more importantly, it distorts what he believed was the right way to discharge his task as a student of the art of the state.

To find out what the truth of the matter is—that is, to interpret princes' and rulers' intentions and to understand the reasons of their actions—is only one aspect of the assignment of the student of the art of the state. Another equally important part of it is to make one's views sound true, to present them in the best light, and to sustain them with eloquent examples, powerful metaphors, and appropriate similitudes. When he offers in *The Prince* his own comprehensive study on the art of the state, he infuses in it not just his knowledge of the truth of the matter, which he has acquired by 'touching with the hands' and by interpreting ancient and modern histories, but also his mastery of rhetoric, as we shall see.

3

The Power of Words

Machiavelli composed all his political works, and above all *The Prince*, in the manner of the rhetorician following the rules illustrated by the Roman masters of rhetoric, particularly Cicero, Quintilian, and the anonymous author of the *Rhetorica ad Herennium*. (*To Gaius Herennius: On The Theory of Public Speaking*) He did not write to explain a scientific or a moral truth, but to persuade and to impel to act. Yet, students of Machiavelli's political thought have been quite unaware of this important feature of his language, or, when they have noticed it, have not studied it with sufficient care. As a result, we still do not know the kind of texts we are reading. We have failed to understand not only how Machiavelli composed his works, but also what he meant to say, particularly what he meant to say on the much-contested issues of political ethics. We have yet fully to appreciate both Machiavelli's distinctive way of practising political theory, and his conception of political action—two aspects of his intellectual legacy that could greatly help us to improve our political theory.

The rhetorical nature of Machiavelli's works is so obvious that scholars' silence on it is perhaps one of the most spectacular examples of misinterpretation of texts of the past. But even more astonishing are the comments of the scholars who have noticed the embarrassing presence of a typical rhetorical piece like the 'Exhortation to Liberate Italy' at the end of *The Prince*—that is, at the end of the text which has been celebrated as the foundation of the modern scientific study of politics. To this effect, some have concluded that Machiavelli the scientist does not go very well with

Machiavelli the partisan, just as Machiavelli the republican citizen is not easily compatible with the author of *The Prince*; others that the two Machiavellis do in fact go rather well together: the rhetorician reinforces the scientist and vice versa. The prevailing view, however, is that the true Machiavelli is the scientist: the pages that he did write in a non-scientific manner are to be treated as the result of moments of intellectual weakness: he composed them while he was possessed, as an Italian student put it, 'by a sort of rhetorical raptus that went beyond his scientific mind'.[1]

In more recent years a similar conclusion has been reached by scholars who have studied Machiavelli's text from the point of view of literary criticism. The 'Exhortation', writes Nancy Struever, is

disjoined, unsuccessful, because Machiavelli can not substitute a nationalist myth of redemption for a Christian one, since he has undermined not simply the motivation, but the narrative structure of the redemptive mode of politics. He has abandoned a linear structure of events for one of repetitious sequence[2]

In a much-quoted essay we read that the 'Exhortation to Liberate Italy' 'radically alters the rhetorical mode from deliberation to apocalypse'; it indicates that in the last third of the book 'scientific pretentions are quietly withdrawn as the semblance of conclusive law fades from the text'.[3]

The truth of the matter is precisely the opposite—namely, as I shall illustrate, that the 'Exhortation' far from being a disjointed, unsuccessful alteration of the mode of the text, is a splendid, necessary, and perfectly connected conclusion of a text like *The Prince*, if we understand what sort of text *The Prince* is.

To be sure, a number of scholars have correctly identified and made fine investigations of the rhetorical dimension of *The Prince* and, though to a lesser extent, Machiavelli's other works. Eugene Garver, for instance, has remarked that, 'throughout the history of its influence, people have found Machiavelli's *Prince* to be many things, but a work of rhetoric has rarely been one of them'.[4] A valuable suggestion can also be found in an essay by John Tinkler, who rightly remarks that 'the rhetorical directions for deliberative oratory provide a number of important insights into Machiavelli's political emphases', and in the works of Victoria Kahn, who stresses that, 'in contrast to many of the standard scholarly works . . . Machiavelli does not supplant rhetoric with a more realistic view of politics but rather makes politics more deeply rhetorical than it had been in the earlier humanist tradition'; a Machiavellian politics, she concludes, 'is rhetorical through and through'.[5] Lastly, Quentin Skinner has paved the way for a historically accurate interpretation of the very core of *The Prince* by pointing to the fact that 'Machiavelli's book is one in which the technique of rhetorical redescription is not only put to sensational use, but is used specifically as a means of depreciating and undermining the so-called 'princely' virtues of clemency and liberality'.[6]

Along the lines that these works have indicated, what needs further investigation is the precise rhetorical structure and content of Machiavelli's *Prince* and of his other major political works, particularly the *Discourses on Livy* and the *Florentine Histories*. As I have already stresssed, by bringing to the surface the rhetorical structure and content of Machiavelli's works, we ought to be able to cast a fresh light on the most controversial and debated aspects of Machiavelli's political thought as well as gain a new understanding of his conception of the role of eloquence in political life. The goal of this chapter is precisely to investigate Machiavelli's practice and theory of the power of words.

The Tradition of Political Rhetoric and the Rhetorical Structure of The Prince

Machiavelli grew up in a city pervaded by the cult of eloquence.[7] As we read in the statutes of the Studio Fiorentino, eloquence is the 'highest ornament of political life'; indeed the necessary component of the education of a civil man, as Angelo Poliziano put it in the opening lecture of his course on rhetoric at the Studio Fiorentino in 1480. Nothing is more beautiful, Poliziano explains, than to distinguish oneself in the very art that makes men superior to other animals; nothing is more marvellous than to be able to penetrate the mind and the soul of a multitude, to captivate the people's attention, to drive their will and dominate their passions. Eloquence permits us to embellish and celebrate virtuous men and their actions, and to darken the wicked; to persuade one's dearest fellow-citizens to pursue what is useful for the common good and avoid what is damaging and malignant. Eloquence is like the breastplate and the sword with which we defend ourselves and the common good against our enemies and the enemies of the republic. Thanks to eloquent men, Poliziano remarks, states have obtained the greatest advantages, and for this reason oratory has in all times been rewarded and held in the highest honour.[8]

Like other Florentines of his social status, Machiavelli received a training in rhetoric. He had available in his house the *To Gaius Herennius* attributed to Cicero, along with Cicero's *Of the Orator*.[9] Under the rubric of the deliberative genre (*genus deliberativum*), these works offered the instructions on how to compose an oration on state affairs (*cose di stato*), as Machiavelli was later to say. Though many rules of rhetoric apply to the deliberative as well as to the forensic and the epidectic genre, the rules of the deliberative genre were in fact especially crafted for the orator engaged in counselling or consulting on affairs of state.[10]

These texts explained that a citizen giving advice on state matters has to be able not just to persuade an audience or a readership—that is, to win their support—but also to persuade or impel the addressees of his speech or text actually to put his advice into practice. To be able to persuade a ruler or a council, the orator must master the different parts of the *ars rhetorica*, particularly, for written texts, the Invention (*Inventio*), the Arrangement (*Dispositio*), and the Expression (*Elocutio*).[11] In addition to that, he must be sure that the oration is properly divided into the *exordium*, the narrative (*narratio*), the partition (*partitio*), the confirmation (*confirmatio*), the refutation (*refutatio*) and the final peroration (*peroratio*).

The oration must begin with an appropriate *exordium* that serves the purpose of bringing 'the mind of the auditor into a proper condition to receive the rest of the speech', a task that can be attained by making the auditor or the reader 'well disposed, attentive, and receptive' ('*benivolum, attentum, docilem*').[12] He can win the goodwill of the auditors by referring to his own acts and services ('*de nostris factis et officiis*') without arrogance, and by weakening 'the effects of charges that have been preferred, or of some suspicion of less honourable dealings' which has been cast on him, by insisting 'on the misfortunes which have befallen' him or the difficulties which still beset him; and, finally, by using prayers and entreaties with a humble and submissive spirit'.[13] As for making the audience attentive, the good orator should announce at the very outset that he is about to discuss matters that are 'important, novel, or incredible, or that they concern all humanity, or those in the audience, or some illustrious men, or the immortal gods, or the general interest of the state'.[14] Finally, to be sure to make the audience receptive, an eloquent adviser should promise at the very outset that he will prove the case briefly, and in 'plain language'.[15]

If we now turn our attention to *The Prince*, we can see that our alleged scientist of politics did in fact compose his treatise following the rules of Roman rhetoric. As we know, he composed that piece of work to establish his competence on matters of state, and he intended to do that by demonstrating his capacity to offer good advice on political affairs. The way to do that was to compose a good oration according to the rules of the deliberative genre.

What was at stake was not so much the chance to obtain a new post in the Medicean regime. For that, a flattering letter or a short memorandum would have been more suitable, and Machiavelli knew it. What was at stake was his reputation in the art of the state. He wanted this reputation as a wise man on matters of state to be recognized by good and wise men, as the competence of the great men of ancient times had been recognized by wise and good men of all times. He wanted to be in their company, and the way to be accepted in such a distinguished circle was to persuade that his advice on all the fundamental issues of statecraft was wiser than the advice usually offered either by the writers of advice for princes' books or by the more pragmatic counsellors and friends of the Medici.

What was needed was an oration; he wrote it in an impeccable form for readers who were perfectly capable of recognizing the good rhetorical quality of a text, and to identify the author's mastery of rules of rhetoric.[16] The recognition of his competence on the art of the state was a matter of content as much as it was a matter of form and style. For us, the only way to understand what he meant to say is to understand both what he in fact said, and how he said it.

Machiavelli's diligent application of the rules of deliberative rhetoric in *The Prince* is manifest from the very first page—namely, the well-known, but often misunderstood, *Dedicatory Letter to His Magnificence Lorenzo de' Medici*.[17] Machiavelli uses the Dedicatory Letter to Lorenzo de' Medici as an *exordium* designed to fulfil the important requirement of rendering the reader well disposed and attentive. In Machiavelli's case the task was particularly delicate, as he had to remove the ill-disposition of the Medici towards him which was due not only to the fact that he was the former *Secretario*, and had been suspected of having been involved in the Boscoli's conspiracy (February 1513), but also to the fact that he was a man of low social status. Among the various rhetorical strategies outlined by Roman theorists, he chooses to try to gain the reader's benevolence by putting forward the good qualities of his own person, the services he has rendered, his knowledge on matters of state, the hardships he has endured, and the ill-fortune that malignantly strikes him. He writes, in fact, that he is offering the product of the knowledge of the 'conduct of great men' he has attained through a 'long experience of modern affairs and continual study of ancient history', and what he has learnt 'in so many years', and with 'much difficulty and danger'.[18]

To remove the diffidence due to his status, Machiavelli presents his political and diplomatic experience as a *Secretario* of the Republic as a guarantee of his competence. He claims that the fact that he is one of the people actually puts him in the best position to treat matters of state:

I hope it will not be considered presumptuous for a man of very low and humble condition to dare to discuss princely government, and to lay down rules about it. For those who draw maps place themselves on low ground, in order to understand the character of the mountains and other high points, and climb higher in order to understand properly the characters of the plains. Likewise, one needs to be a ruler properly to understand the character of the people, and to be a man of the people to understand properly the character of rulers.[19]

To complete the work, again in strict adherence to the classics' directions, he then moves to laud the person of the dedicatee: 'my deep wish will be revealed—namely, that you should achieve that greatness which your propitious circumstances and your fine qualities promise.' Finally, he attracts the reader's attention to the bad fortune that oppresses him: 'you will see how much I am unjustly oppressed by great and cruel misfortune.'[20]

The rhetorical texture of *The Prince* becomes transparent as we proceed in the analyses of the other parts of the work: In their treatises his Roman mentors had in fact stressed that, after the *exordium*, having hopefully gained the benevolence and the attention of the prince or the council he is addressing, the expert on state matters should turn to the other parts of the oration—namely, the narrative, the partition, the confirmation, the refutation, and the final peroration. While the narrations have to aim at verisimilitude,[21] the function of the partition is to render the whole speech 'clear and perspicuous'. In the partition the orator must therefore 'briefly set forth' the subjects which he intends to discuss'.[22] Finally, after having confirmed his points and refuted the adversaries' theses, the adviser on state affairs should sum up by saying that he has in fact proved what he had promised to prove at the outset,[23] and then end the speech with a peroration in which he should use both the topic of *indignatio*, in which he excites indignation, and the *conquestio*, in which he arouses pity. [24] Of the various ways to arouse indignation, Cicero recommends, it is particularly effective to mention a 'foul, cruel, nefarious and tyrannical' deed,[25] whereas pity can be aroused by insisting on the 'helplessness and weakness' of the victim of violence, injustice, and cruelty.[26]

As to be expected, in *The Prince*, after the *exordium*, we find the partition, where Machiavelli announces the subject matter of the work in a brief and methodical way, as Cicero had recommended: 'I shall not discuss republics, because I have already treated them at length. I shall consider only principalities . . . examining how principalities can be governed and maintained.'[27] As he proceeds towards the end of the work, after he has laid down his advice, he diligently completes a summary of the main point of his oration and reminds the reader that he has fulfilled what he had promised—namely, to instruct how a principality, and particularly a new principality, can be maintained and secured: 'If the above-mentioned measures are put into practice skillfully, they will make a new ruler seem very well established, and will quickly make his power more secure and stable than if he had always been a ruler.'[28]

Having diligently composed the summary, he then concludes his treatise with the famous 'Exhortation to Liberate Italy'. Far from being incompatible with the alleged 'scientific' style of the whole text and insecurely attached to it, the Exhortatio is perfectly consistent with the rhetorical structure of *The Prince*. Without it, Machiavelli's essay would have been missing and incomplete, as it would have lacked the final peroration that has to conclude a good deliberative oration. It would have lacked the device which is most necessary in order to arouse the readers' emotions and move them to do what he was urging them to accomplish.

Following the rules of the *ars rhetorica*, Machiavelli constructs the 'Exhortatio' on the topics of *indignatio* and *conquaestio*. He

tries to arouse indignation by stressing the cruelties and the insolences that the barbarians have inflicted upon Italy ('crudeltà et
insolenzie barbare'), and endeavours to arouse compassion by
pointing to Italy's weakness and helplessness: 'more enslaved
than the Hebrews, more oppressed than the Persians, more scattered than the Athenians, without an acknowledged leader, and
without order or stability, beaten, despoiled, lacerated, overrun,
in short utterly devastated.'[29] Seen from the right perspective—
that is, from Machiavelli's perspective—the 'Exhortation' is simply
perfect.[30]

In addition to directions concerning the formal arrangement of
the oration in the deliberative genre, canonic texts of Roman masters of rhetoric also contain a number of suggestions on matters of
style. Both Cicero and Quintilian agreed that in deliberative oratory 'the whole speech should be simple and grave ('simplex et
gravis'), because the matter being discussed has a splendour and
magnificence of its own.[31] Finally, Roman authorities recommended that a very effective way to persuade and move a person
or a council to adopt a particular policy is to offer examples taken
from history. Exemplification, as the author of the *For Gaiius
Herennius* wrote, 'renders a thought more brilliant when used for
no other purpose than beauty; clearer, when throwing more light
upon what was somewhat obscure; more plausible, when giving
the thought a greater verisimilitude; more vivid, when expressing
everything so lucidly that the matter can, I may almost say, be
touched by the hand.'[32] And of various types of examples, those
taken from recent and ancient history are particularly effective to
arouse emotions and therefore move the audience to accept the
view that the orator is putting forth.

Machiavelli diligently follows both the advice on the plain style
and the advice on examples. As he promptly declares in the Dedicatory Letter, he does not embellish his work 'by filling it with
rounded periods, with high-sounding words or fine phrases, or with
any other beguiling artifices of apparent beauty which most writers
employ to describe and embellish their subject matter'. He does so,
he explains in a perfect Ciceronian way, because 'my wish is that, if
it is to be honoured at all, only its originality and the importance of
the subject should make it acceptable.'[33] This does not mean that
The Prince is composed in the manner of a scientific text; it means,
on the contrary, that it is a text composed according to rhetorical
technique appropriate to the subject matter.

Machiavelli also amply resorts to the use of examples. As he openly states at the outset of his essay: 'nobody should be surprised if, in discussing completely new principalities, both as regards the rulers and the type of government, I shall cite very great examples', because a prudent man ('uno uomo prudente') must always follow the footsteps of great men, and, even if 'he does not succeed in matching their ability, at least he will get within a sniffing distance of it'.[34] His examples are always designed to embellish, and to make clear, visible, and tangible, and therefore persuasive, political advice. He cites, for instance, the case of Hannibal, who succeeded in keeping his army disciplined and obedient, even if it was very large and composed of men from different countries, by his 'inhumane cruelty', to clarify and exemplify political advice that 'when a prince is with his army, and commands a large force, he must not worry about being considered harsh [*crudele*]', and to add force to his more general advice that, if it is not possibile to be both loved and feared, 'it is much safer to be feared than loved'.[35]

Machiavelli supports the advice that 'it is much safer to be feared than loved' by the remark that

for this may be said of men generally: they are ungrateful, fickle, feigners and dissemblers, avoiders of dangers, eager for gain. While you benefit them they are all devoted to you: they would shed their blood for you; they offer their possessions, their lives, and their sons, as I said before, when the need to do so is far off. But when you are hard pressed, they turn away.

It would be mistaken to consider Machiavelli's examples as particular cases of general laws of human behaviour established inductively through the review of a significant number of facts.[36] They are ornaments, in the technical sense, rhetorical devices that serve the orator to attain his goal—that is, to persuade. They pursue the truth. The example of Hannibal illustrates the truth of the advice that it is much safer to be feared than to be loved.[37] Still, to equate them as particular cases of empirical laws misrepresents their function in Machiavelli's text, as they are there primarily to make political advice more vivid, to make its validity appear as clear as if the reader or the listener could literally see or touch it, and to instil a desire to imitate the heroes of the stories being told.

As an adviser on matters of state, Machiavelli is committed to a particular type of truth, which he calls 'la verità effettuale della cosa', usually but wrongly translated as 'what really happens', or

'the real truth of the matter', as opposed to 'theories or specula-
tions' or 'what people have imagined'.[38] The adjective 'effettuale'
which Machiavelli adds to the noun 'verità' [*truth*] means effective,
productive. To pursue the effective truth of the matter means to
pursue the truth which permits one to attain the desired result—
that is, as Machiavelli says in the same sentence, what is useful
[*utile*] for the prince. He is committed, in other words, to the truth
of the orator, not the truth of scientist. *Pace* the innumerable
commentators who have praised *The Prince* as a scientific text,
Machiavelli aims to discover not plain and uncoloured truths
about political action, but adapted or accommodated truths
obtained by minimizing anything that might make the argument
less persuasive and maximizing all the considerations that make
the advice plausible.

As he remarks at the very outset of *The Prince*, Machiavelli
believes he possesses what Cicero and the other rhetoricians had
commended as one of the main qualities of the orator—namely,
wisdom, in the sense of a wide and profound knowledge of matter
and the ability to produce logically rigorous arguments.[39] He also
claims to know the truth of the matter. But he also knows that it is
not a truth that can be proved or demonstrated beyond doubt, and
that the whole point can be argued on both sides. The best that the
orator can do is to empower the truth with appropriate examples,
metaphors, amplifications, and narratives, as Machiavelli in fact
does in his oration. He must try to combine reason with eloquence,
ratio with *oratio*. His truths will never attain the status of a scientific or philosophical truth; they will remain partial, probable,
adorned, accommodated, and coloured truths, identified because
they offer useful advice.

As is well known, Machiavelli tends to cast his advice in a
universal or general form. The list could be very long, but a few
examples shall suffice: 'men should either be caressed or crushed;
because they can avenge slight injuries, but not those that are very
severe';[40] 'from this may be derived a generalization, which is
almost always valid: anyone who enables another to become
powerful, brings about his own ruin. For that power is increased
by him either through guile or through force, and both these are
reasons for the man who has become powerful to be on his guard';[41]
'I conclude, then, that any principality that does not have its own
army cannot be secure; rather, it must rely completely on luck or
the favour of others, because it lacks the strength to defend itself in

difficult times';[42] finally, the well-known words from Chapter 17: 'it is much safer to be feared than loved.'

Machiavelli's habit of framing his advice in general terms should not be equated with a scientific style of producing inductive general laws of politics. To discuss political matters in general rather than specific terms was yet another rule of classical deliberative rhetoric. As Quintilian put it, questions debated in deliberative orations are generally definite questions (*'quaestio finita'*) that contain reference to persons, time, place, and the like, and are questions of action rather than questions of mere knowledge. However, 'in every special question the general question is implicit, since the *genus* is logically prior to the *species'*, and it is highly advisable to treat matters of state by abstracting from particular persons and occasions, because, as he remarks, quoting from Cicero, 'we can speak more fully on general than on special themes, and because what is proved of the whole must also be proved of the part'.[43]

Moreover, it must be taken into account that Machiavelli himself repeatedly warns his readers that no rule of political behaviour—however general its form—is as certain as a scientific law. If they were, political wisdom and political success would be the norm, not the exception. Political deliberations are always highly uncertain and tentative, because the subject matter does not allow for certainty:

no government should ever believe that it is always possible to follow safe policies. Rather, it should be realised that all courses of action involve risks: for it is in the nature of things that when one tries to avoid one danger another is always encountered. But prudence consists in knowing how to assess the dangers, and to choose the least bad course of action as being the right one to follow.[44]

Political precepts, even when presented in the most general terms as plain truths, do not offer secure guidance at all. The rule 'it is much better to be feared than loved', for instance, is subject to many exceptions. As Machiavelli notices in *Discourses*, III. 20:

This authentic incident affords us an excellent example of how a humane and kindly act sometimes makes a much greater impression than an act of ferocity or violence; and how districts and cities into which neither arms nor the accoutrements of war, nor any other kind of human force would have been able to obtain entry, it has been possible to enter by displaying common humanity and kindness, contingence or generosity.

Contrary examples aside, what makes the general rule 'it is much better to be feared than loved' highly tentative is that its effectiveness ultimately depends on the virtue of the prince or captain who puts it into practice—that is, on a completely contingent element. Princes and captains make serious mistakes, Machiavelli remarks, either when they make themselves loved too much, or when they make themselves feared too much: 'for he who desires too much to be loved becomes despicable, however little he departs from the true way; the other, who desires too much to be feared, becomes hateful, however little he exceeds the mode.'[45] What makes the rule a 'verità effettuale', an effective truth as opposed to a truth that leads to disastrous results, is the virtue of the political leader—that is, his capacity to put the rule into practice according to the specific circumstances within which he is operating, as well as his personal reputation. It is the virtue of the commander which mitigates ('mitigare') the excessive desire to be feared or the excessive desire to be loved, and 'properly seasons' ('condisca bene') every mode of life. Machiavelli's general rules of political conduct are therefore not only subject to many counter-examples and exceptions, but also require a substantial work of temperament, adaptation, and the addition of qualities which only the virtue of the political leader can provide.

Along with the formal and stylistic requirement of eloquence on political matters, Roman rhetoricians amply discuss the issue of the goal or the goals that the orator has to have in mind when he offers his advice. Although their views on this topic are more nuanced than in other cases, both Cicero and Quintilian do in fact stress that counsellors on matters of state have to offer advice that is advantageous (*utilis*) and honourable (*honestus*). Speeches before deliberative bodies, Cicero explains in *Of Invention*, are about 'what is honourable ('quid honestus') and 'what is advantageous' ('quid utile'). Unlike Aristotle, who accepts advantage as the end of deliberative speeches, Cicero remarks that the end is 'both honour and advantage'.[46] He then specifies that the actions that are to be called honourable are all those that fulfil the requirements of virtue, which he defines as 'the habit of mind in harmony with reason and the order of nature', and he divides it into four parts: wisdom, justice, courage, and temperance.[47] Advantage, on the other hand, primarily concerns the body, and in the case of the body of politics, advantage or interest primarily consists in those things which protect its safety and its liberty—namely, fields, harbours, money, the fleet, sailors, soldiers, and allies, and in those things that pertain to the greatness of the state, such as money, friendships, and alliances.[48] Advantage in matters of state, concludes Cicero, then has two parts, security (*'incolumitas'*) and power ('potentia').[49]

The *For Gaius Herennius* offers a slightly different account of the aim of the orator offering advice in political deliberations ('in civili consultatione'). Instead of advantage and honour, the author indicates only advantage, and remarks that 'the complete economy of his entire speech may be directed to it'. He divides advantage ('utilitas') into security ('tuta') and honour ('honestas')[50] and subdivides security in might and craft ('vim et dolum') and honour in the right and the praiseworthy ('rectum et laudabile').[51] Under the heading of might are to be discussed issues pertaining to armies, fleet, arms, engines of war, and re-creating of manpower; craft is exercised by means of 'money, promises, dissimulations, accelerated speed, and deception'.[52] Honour consists in virtue and duty, and its subdivisions are, as for Cicero, wisdom ('prudentia'), justice ('iustitia'), fortitude ('fortitudo'), and temperance ('temperantia').[53] The praiseworthy (*laudabile*) is 'what produces an honourable remembrance, at the time of the event and afterwards'.[54]

As with Quintilian, he claims that, if one has to assign one single aim to deliberative oratory, he would say that 'this kind of oratory is primarily concerned with what is honourable ('quod honestum'). However, he clarifies, the good orator has often to address an 'ignorant audience' composed of uneducated men who do not admit that what is honourable is also advantageous. For this reason, they must distinguish 'what is honourable and what is expedient' and adapt their speech to ordinary understanding.[55] The goals of deliberative rhetoric, Quintilian concludes, are then both honour and expediency.

The view which commends the consensus of the scholars is that in *The Prince* Machiavelli straightforwardly indicates and pursues advantage as the only aim that a political adviser must pursue. Serious political debate, John Tinkler has written in a seminal essay,

which is directed at advising future action, must be practical, and must therefore take *utilitas* [advantage] as its ultimate aim. Certainly, this was the aim laid down in both the *Rhetorica ad Herennium* and the *De Inventione*, the two most important classical rhetorical treatises in both the Middle Ages and the Renaissance. It is this ultimate concern of deliberative rhetoric with *utilitas* that sheds light on Machiavelli's concern with political success.[56]

Machiavelli, therefore, not only questions 'the Ciceronian ideal of harmony between the *honestum* and the *utile* (the good and the useful),[57] but also endorses the subversive suggestion that 'the question of what is *utile* in such matters of statecraft may have no connection with what is *onesto* at all', as Quentin Skinner put it.[58]

I think that it is certainly true that Machiavelli intends his political counsels to be directed to what is useful for the prince. However, following the guideline of the *For Gaius Herennius*, he understands the useful ('utilitas') to be composed of two elements—that is, security ('tuta') and honor ('honestas')—and he intends his advice to ensure the prince the attainment of both security and honour. In fact, he clearly states that his goal is to write 'what will be useful [*utile*] to anyone who understands'. But when he recapitulates the sense of all the counsels he has offered throughout *The Prince*, he says that 'If the above-mentioned measures are put into practice skilfully, they will make a new ruler seem very well established, and will make his power more secure [*sicuro*] and stable than if he had always been a ruler.' And in Chapter 18, concluding the discussion on the conflict between honesty and advantage, he stresses that, if the prince 'contrives to conquer, and to preserve the state, the means will always be judged to be honourable and be praised by everyone'; and even more honourable will be judged the aim of the new prince's actions: 'nothing brings so much honour to a new ruler as new laws and new practices that he has devised.' Which is to say that, if the prince should follow Machiavelli's advice, he will attain both security and honour—that is, the two components of advantage as described by the author of the *For Gaius Herennius*.

Machiavelli's allegiance to the teaching of the *For Gaius Herennius* emerges from the analysis of the *dispositio* of the arguments. As we have seen, under the heading of security, the adviser on matters of state has to be able to offer suggestions on issues that pertain more specifically to might—that is, armies, manpower, and the like—and to craft—that is, money, promises, and dissimulation—while under the heading of honour he shall speak of what is right—that is, of virtues, and of what is laudable. In the first part of *The Prince* he in fact discusses matters pertaining to the security of principalities; in the second he offers his advice concerning the qualities that make a prince laudable or blameworthy, and virtue—which are the two subheadings of honour.

He addresses in more detail the issue of security by discussing the territory, the number of men the prince can count on, the strength of his enemies, and the quality of his army. On these issues, he puts forth his views concerning the specific kind of difficulties that new princes have to face as they consolidate their powers and argues that a new prince is insecure because 'men are very ready to change their ruler when they believe that they can better their condition', and because 'anyone who becomes a new ruler is always forced to injure his new subjects, through both his troops and countless other injuries that are involved in conquering a state'.[59] On the crucial issue of the territorial extension of the state, he stresses that it makes a remarkable difference whether the new territories are of the same country, with the same language, or not. If the latter is the case, Machiavelli suggests that the best thing that a new prince can do is 'to go and live there', or to 'establish colonies in a few places'. At the same time, the prince should become 'the protector of the neighbouring minor powers and contrive to weaken those who are powerful within the country itself'.

Machiavelli brings the discussion on the might of the state to an end in Chapter 10, where he addresses the issue 'How the strength [vires] of all principalities should be measured' and explains that the difference between a prince who 'has sufficient territory and power to defend himself' and one who 'will always need some help from others' consists in the fact that the former can put together an army that is good enough to fight a battle against any power that attacks him (either because he has many soldiers of his own or because he has sufficient money).[60] As he stresses with typical briskness in Chapter 10, if security is the goal, the might that a state must possess is that which permits him to defend his state without anybody's help—that is, to have good armies composed of his own subjects.

Having accomplished the first duty of the adviser, he then considers the issues that properly pertain to craft ('dolus')—that is, taxation, promises, dissimulation, deception. If a prince wants to keep up a reputation for being generous, he offers this advice on taxation: that he will consume all his resources in sumptuous display; and if he wants to continue to be thought generous, he will eventually be compelled to become rapacious, to tax the people very heavily, and raise money by all possible means. Thus, he will begin to be hated by his subjects and, because he is impoverished, he will be held in little regard.[61]

A prudent prince should therefore be parsimonious, because in this way his revenues will always be sufficient to defend his state 'without imposing special taxes on the people'. As for promises, dissimulation, and deception, he condenses his views in Chapter 18 and offers here one of his most subversive pieces of advice: 'a prudent ruler cannot keep his word, nor should he, when such fidelity would damage him, and when the reasons that made him promise are no longer relevant.' And he adds, a few lines later, that to put the above advice into practice, the prince must be 'a great feigner and dissembler'.

Finally, he links his considerations on generosity and meanness, on cruelty and mercifulness, and on promises to the discussion of 'The things for which men, and especially rulers, are praised [*laudati*] or blamed [*biasimati*] and of virtue—that is, the two subdivisions of the general theme of honour ('honestas'). His concluding comment on this issue, it is a point worth noticing, is that, if a prince 'contrives to conquer and preserve the state, the means will be judged to be honourable and be praised by everyone'.

The fact that the counsellor on matters of state has to bear in mind both security and honour does not mean that the attainment of the former requires the sacrifice of the latter. Roman authorities on the art of rhetoric amply discuss the delicate issue of possible conflicts between honour and expediency, or between what is praiseworthy and what is advantageous, and suggest ways of settling it. One solution is to rank the different alternatives, as Cicero accurately does in *Of Invention*: the greatest necessity is that of doing what is honourable, next comes the necessity of security, last the necessity, of much lesser weight, of convenience.[62] This ordering can, however, be altered and, if security is really at stake, the orator can put security before honour, particularly if honour, momentarily lost, can later be recovered by courage and diligence.[63] An argument based on honesty and fairness is always a strong one, but it can be countered if we prove that the position we are advocating is 'necessary', and, in deliberative rhetoric, necessity refers to the security of the state.[64] Even when he offers advice that puts security before honesty, however, the orator can still claim to be committed to uphold honour, because 'without security we can never attain to honour'.[65] In a later work, *De partitione oratoriae*, Cicero recognizes that interest is often in contrast with moral virtue ('persaepe evenit ut utilitas cum honestate certet') and leaves the choice concerning the priority of the two goals to considerations of opportunity: if the orator is speaking before an audience composed of uninstructed and uncultivated people who consider interest more important than moral virtue, he should put forward considerations of profits and rewards, of pleasures and of modes of avoiding contumely and disgrace. If the audience, or the addressee of the counsel, believes that virtue is more important than interest, the orator should sustain his point by reference to glory and honour.[66]

Another rhetorical device that the adviser can use if he wants to recommend that security has to have priority over virtue is to be found in the *For Gaius Herennius*. Certainly, the author remarks, 'no one will propose the abandonment of virtue', but the orator can say, for instance, that in the case being discussed the virtue does not consist in what it is ordinarily believed to consist of. More specifically, the adviser can describe in a different way the course of action that he is advocating. He should show that what his opponent or other advisers name justice is in fact cowardice and sloth or perverse liberality; what they call wisdom should be termed impertinent, babbling, and offensive cleverness; what they call temperance is in reality inaction and lax indifference; what they define as courage is nothing but 'reckless temerity'.[67]

In addition to that, the orator who prefers considerations of security to virtue can resort to the following topics: 'nothing is more useful than safety, no one can make use of his virtues if he has not based his plans upon safety; not even the gods help those who thoughtlessly commit themselves to danger', and, a topic of particular importance, 'nothing ought to be deemed honourable which does not produce safety'.[68]

Yet another way of solving conflicts between honesty and interest is the one discussed by Quintilian in book III of the *Institutio*. If we have to advise to put interest before honesty, we should do it without 'openly admitting' that the course of action we are recommending is 'dishonourable' ('inhonestum').[69] This can be done by changing the names of the actions that we are advocating.[70] If, for instance, we advise Julius Caesar to become emperor, we shall say that the republic is doomed to dissolution unless it is ruled by a monarch. The reason for doing that is that, on the one hand, 'there is no man so evil as to wish to seem so', and, on the other hand, 'the aim of the man who is deliberating about committing a criminal act is to make the act appear as little wicked as possible'.[71] If the orator offers this kind of advice for the safety of the state, Quintilian remarks at the end of his work, he does not cease at all to be a 'good man, skilled in speaking' ('oratorem esse vir bonum dicendi peritum').[72]

Machiavelli discussess the contrast between honour and advantage in four central chapters of *The Prince*: 'The things for which men, and especially princes are praised or blamed' (Ch. 15); 'Generosity and meanness' (Ch. 16); 'Cruelty and mercifulness; and whether it is better to be loved or feared' (Ch. 17); 'How rulers should keep their promises' (Ch. 18). Although this section of *The Prince* has been subject to endless exegetic scrutiny, we have not yet been able to see that what Machiavelli was in fact doing was to discuss the classical theme of *honestas* versus *utilitas* from the perspective laid down by Roman rhetoricians. As a result we have failed to understand the sense of what he was trying to say and we have attributed to him a political ethic which has only a very pale resemblance to his views.

The fact that Machiavelli was following the teaching of the Roman rhetoricians does not rule out the fact that in those chapters he was at the same time submitting to a severe critique the conventional view repeated by the humanist writers on political affairs that honour (*honestas*) must always have priority over advantage (*utilitas*), or, as Cicero put it in *Of Duties*, that 'nothing is really expedient that is not at the same time morally right, and nothing morally right is not at the same time expedient'.[73] However, as we have seen, Cicero himself, and the other Roman rhetoricians, had not only recognized the possibility of a conflict between honour and security, but had actually suggested ways of solving it by putting security before honour. While Machiavelli explicitly rejects the euphoric Ciceronian view that honour must always have precedence over interest, he follows the Roman rhetoricians in claiming that there are circumstances when security must come before honour. Moreover, and the point needs to be emphasized, he frames his advice on the need for princes and rulers to derogate to the principle of the priority of *honestas* over *utilitas* according to the directions laid down by Roman rhetoricians. He resorts in fact to both the topic of necessity and the device of redescribing what has to be counted as virtue in political affairs.

Machiavelli grants that the humanists' advice that the prince should never abandon the path of virtue is perfectly fair, but remarks that there are indeed circumstances in which it is necessary to abandon the path of virtue. 'It is necessary', he writes, for a prince to learn to be 'not good'—that is, to violate the principles of *honestas* that qualify the good man ('bonus vir'), if necessary ('secondo la necessità').[74] And in Chapter 18 he remarks that a prince, and especially a new prince, 'cannot always act in ways that are considered good because, in order to maintain his power, he is often forced [*necessitato*] to act treacherously, ruthlessly, or inhumanly, and disregard the precepts of religion'; therefore, he must not deviate from right conduct ('*bene*') if possible, but be capable of entering upon the path of wrongdoing when this becomes necessary ('*necessitato*').[75]

Another rhetorical strategy, this too derived from the classics, that Machiavelli employs in cases in which security is in conflict with honour is to put security first and to say that, though honour is momentarily lost in the pursuit of security, it may be recovered afterwards by being good. This is precisely the rhetorical device that Machiavelli commends in a well-known text of the *Discourses*:

For when one deliberates [*si delibera*] on the safety of one's country [*della salute della patria*], no consideration should be paid to either justice or injustice, kindness or cruelty, or its being praiseworthy or ignominious. On the contrary, every other consideration being postponed [*posposto ogni altro rispetto*], that advice should be whole-heartedly adopted which will save the life and preserve the freedom of one's country.[76]

In *The Prince* he resorts to a similar argument in Chapter 18; after having explained at length that a prince must be capable of putting security before moral considerations when necessity requires it, he remarks that, if he 'contrives to preserve his state' even by deviating from the path of honour, his actions will be 'judged to be honourable and be praised by everyone'.[77] By putting security first, he can, therefore, soon recover his honour, particularly if he 'contrives that his actions should display grandeur, courage, seriousness and strength', and endeavour 'to achieve through all his actions the reputation of being a great man of outstanding intelligence', as Machiavelli urges in the subsequent chapters.[78] If we add to that the other part of Machiavelli's advice—namely, that the prince should avoid being rapacious and show himself 'a lover of talent', honour 'those who excel in any art', 'encourage the citizens to follow quietly their ordinary occupation, both in trade and agriculture and every other kind', and display 'affability and munificence'[79]—we have a full sense of Machiavelli's advice: honour momentarily lost by being not good for security's sake can be properly recovered by preserving the state, and by displaying greatness, justice, generosity, and strength—that is, by re-entering the path of virtue, which is precisely the line of conduct that, according to Cicero, a good man should follow when counselling on state matters.

To be able to argue in a persuasive manner that nothing can be deemed honourable if it does jeopardize the security of the principality or of the republic, Machiavelli also resorts to the other device laid down by Roman rhetoricians—namely, to redescribe as vices the actions that other theorists on state matters qualify as virtues but are in fact leading to the loss of the state, and redefine as virtues those actions that are considered to be vices but do in fact lead to the preservation of the state. As Roman rhetoricians had explained, virtue and vices are neighbours.[80] What counts as a virtue can therefore be redescribed as vice and what counts as a vice can be redescribed as a virtue, if the necessity to achieve the goal of the security of the state so requires. Machiavelli writes in fact that a prince should not be troubled at all

about becoming notorious for those vices [*vizii*] without which it is difficult to preserve one's power, because, if one considers everything carefully, doing some things that *seem* virtuous ('parrà virtù') may result in one's ruin, whereas doing other things that *seem* vicious ('parrà vizio') may strengthen one's position and cause one to flourish (emphasis added).[81]

Actions which are usually blamed as wicked not only can, but indeed should, be redescribed as good and recommended, if one wishes to be a serious adviser on political matters. In the discussion of cruelty in Chapter 8 he in fact introduces the distinction between 'well-committed' and 'badly committed cruelties': to the former kind belong cruelties 'all committed at once because they are necessary for establishing one's power'; to the second the cruelties 'that at first are few in number, but increase with time rather than diminishing'. As Machiavelli himself openly admits, what he is after here is to redescribe evil as good, and he promptly excuses himself: 'if one may use the word "well" of that which is evil.'[82] A few lines above he had used the same rhetorical device, this time in a contrary fashion—namely, to claim that some kind of actions cannot be *called* virtuous, even if they assure the preservation of the prince's power. Of the infamous Agathocles he says: 'yet it cannot be *called* virtue to kill one's fellow-citizens, to betray one's friends, to be treacherous, merciless and irreligious; power may be gained by acting in such ways, but not glory' (emphasis added).[83]

If these remarks are correct, a number of well-established interpretations of *The Prince* are to be reconsidered, beginning with the influential idea that Machiavelli is the theorist of power politics—that is, the idea that political action is primarily, if not exclusively, concerned with military might. [84] He surely recognizes that military might is a fundamental component of successful political action, but this is only one aspect of Machiavelli's advising. He also amply highlights the essential role of the power of words—that is, eloquence. Although the best soil for political rhetoric is the free republic, the prince too needs a rhetoric of his own, and above all the ability to use the topics of simulation and dissimulation. The author of the *For Gaius Herennius* had listed dissimulation ('dissimulatio') and deception ('mentitio') as two means to exercise craft ('dolus'), which, alongside might ('vis'), is one of the two components of security, as I have remarked earlier.[85] Quintilian defines simulation and dissimulation as two 'almost identical proceedings' ('vicina et prope') that consist in the pretention of having a certain opinion of one's own and in feigning that one does not understand the meaning of someone's words. Dissimulation, he specifies, is the most effective means 'of stealing into the minds of men'.[86] If we now turn to *The Prince*, Chapter 18, we read that the prince must be a great 'feigner and dissembler' ('simulatore e dissimulatore') and be able to offer plausible reasons to 'colour' his failure to keep his promises—a task which has to be accomplished by words. To be able to seem to be merciful, trustworthy, humane, upright, and devout, a prince must 'be very careful that everything he *says* is replete with the five above mentioned qualities; to those who *hear* he should seem to be exceptionally merciful, trustworthy, upright humane and devout' (emphasis added).[87]

Alongside the interpretation of Machiavelli as founder of the doctrine of power politics is the idea of Machiavelli as the founder of the doctrine of the autonomy of politics from ethics—that is, as Croce put it, 'the necessity and autonomy of politics, of politics which is beyond good and evil, which has its laws against which it is useless to rebel, which cannot be exorcised and driven from this world with holy water'.[88] This description misrepresents the intended meaning of his work. What Machiavelli was in fact doing in the central chapters of *The Prince* was to restate and refine a view on conflicts between security and virtue which did not affirm or vindicate the autonomy of politics from ethics, but was in fact considered to be the view which a *good* man should offer on political matters. When he stresses that, when the safety of the state is at stake, moral considerations are to be postponed, or when he redescribes virtues and vices, he was doing what a *vir bonus dicendi peritus* as defined by Roman masters of eloquence was supposed to do.

We may agree or disagree with the validity of his, and his Roman mentors' conception of the duties of a good man offering political advice, but Machiavelli was perfectly serious whan he claimed, as he does in the *Discourses*, that his teaching was the teaching of a good man ('uno uomo buono').[89] Although it has been rarely noticed, he places at the very core of his discussion on cruelty and mercifulness the words that Virgil in the *Aeneid* puts in the mouth of Dido: 'Harsh necessity and the newness of my kingdom force me to do such things, and to guard all frontiers.' Virgil was the guide of Dante, and the symbol of virtue.

If we really intend to accept Machiavelli's intellectual challenge, we must frame our discussions on political ethics differently. Even the best discussions on the 'dirty-hands' issue assume in fact that Machiavelli's paradox consists in the view that 'the good man who aims to found or reform a republic must do terrible things to reach his goal',[90] and that this paradox depends upon Machiavelli's own commitment to the existence of moral standards and upon the stability of those standards. But Machiavelli's arguments about the necessity to learn how not to be good are based not so much upon the existence and the stability of moral standards, but on the consideration that 'whenever men are discussed, [*quando se ne parla*] and especially princes (because they occupy more exalted positions), they are praised or blamed [*o biasimo o laude*]', as he puts it in *The Prince*, Chapter 15.

Machiavelli's most famous or infamous pages of *The Prince*, in other words, are not so much an ethical investigation about moral standards and the problem of their violation or their acceptance, but a set of advice on the typically rhetorical issue of praise and blame. To learn to be 'not good' means to learn not to fear to be blamed for having qualities which are not considered to be good—that is, to be 'sufficiently prudent to know how to avoid becoming notorious for those vices that would destroy one's power and seek to avoid those vices that are not politically dangerous; but if one cannot bring oneself to do this, they can be indulged in with fewer misgivings'.[91]

He is offering his advice, as I have already remarked, on how to attain security and praise, not on how to do or not to do what is right and good. He is not speaking as a philosopher who believes in the existence of a moral truth, but as a rhetorician whose aim is more modestly to indicate the best means to attain praise and avoid blame. As he forcefully puts it, 'with regard to all human actions, and especially those of rulers', there is no court of appeal, there is no moral truth, but only men's volatile changing, malleable praise and blame.[92]

This does not mean that one cannot argue for political values such as liberty, justice, peace, security, and greatness. Nor does it imply that one cannot whole-heartedly commit oneself to pursue these ideals and work to persuade others to share one's commitment. Machiavelli did precisely all that, for all his life. He knew, however, that the ideals he was struggling and arguing for could be sustained in different ways, or redefined, or utterly repudiated. His commitment was a commitment without truth, which makes it even more generous and intelligent.

Also the much-quoted considerations on Romulus in the *Discourses*, I. 9, are on praise and blame, not on means and ends. It is not a philosophical discussion about moral truth which assumes the existence of stable moral standards and of a clear way of demarcating right and wrong, but a rhetorical discussion on opinions about what is praiseworthy and what is blameworthy which assumes that there are no stable moral standards; and that good and evil are not far apart but close, and therefore demarcations are always tentative.[93]

The difference with the similar discussion which occupies Machiavelli in Chapters 15–18 of *The Prince* is that, in the case of the actions discussed in *The Prince*, the alternative is between praise and blame; in the case of Romulus, the alternative is between excuse and blame. Praise in this case is out of the question, probably because of the enormity of the crime. In a similar case, that of the Spartan king Cleomenes, which he comments upon in the same chapter, Machiavelli speaks of a 'just and praiseworthy' plan. Cleomenes 'had all the ephors killed and anyone else who might be able to stand against him' because he realized that he could not restore the vigour of the laws of Lycurgus 'unless he became the sole authority there, and since it seemed to him impossible, owing to man's amibition to help the many against the will of the few'.[94]

The discussion on Romulus is, like that in *The Prince*, a rhetorical argument on a typical issue of the deliberative genre. Machiavelli is, in fact, taking issue with the view, which comes directly from Cicero's *Of Duties*, that it was a bad example that a founder of a civil way of life, as was Romulus, should have first killed his brother, and then consented to the death of Titus Tatius the Sabine, chosen by him as a partner in the kingdom. Against this judgement he remarks that never will 'a wise man *reprove* anyone for any extraordinary action that he uses to order a kingdom or constitute a republic' (emphasis added). He then specifies that, while 'the deed accuses him, the effect excuses him; and when the effect is good, as was that of Romulus, it will always excuse the deed', and as a justification for this statement he puts forth an observation which is again, like the previous one, connected to praise and blame: 'for he who is violent to spoil, not he who is violent to mend, should be *reproved*' (emphasis added). The real subject of the whole discussion is once again what deserves praise and what deserves blame, not how can an effect excuse a means or 'how can it be wrong to do what is right'.[95]

The redefinition of what deserves praise and what commands blame is the basis for the political advice of the chapter—namely, that a prudent orderer of a republic, 'whose intention it is to govern not in his own interest but for the common good . . . should contrive to be alone in his authority'. And the connection between the two themes, which is entirely lost if we do not take into account that the discussion is about praise and blame, is eloquently restated in the comment which concludes the chapter: 'All things considered, therefore, I conclude that it is necessary to be the sole authority, if one wants to order a republic; and for the death of Remus and Titus Tatius, Romulus deserves excuse [scusa] and not blame [biasimo].'

The rhetorical structure of *The Prince* also helps properly to explain the much-debated theme of necessity. As I have stressed, one of the basic rules of Roman deliberative rhetoric was that considerations of necessity take priority over both advantage and honour. Machiavelli's best-known remarks are all framed in terms of necessity. But this does not mean that necessity in politics is just a rhetorical, in the sense of crooked, excuse. Even if appeals to necessity or to extraordinary circumstances have been endlessly used over history to cover injustices and abuses, it remains true that states do find themselves in situations of emergency or necessity, particularly in the formative phases of their history. Unlike individuals, who are normally protected by the state, states cannot count on a superior authority which protects them against external and internal enemies. Choices that individuals very rarely have to make are more likely to occur for representatives of states. A serious adviser on state matters, as Machiavelli was, cannot ignore them.

The Rhetorical Power of History

Like *The Prince*, the *Discourses on Livy* and the *Florentine Histories* were also written to move the readers to pursue the useful, honourable, or necessary course of action that Machiavelli was illustrating for them; with the difference that this time he was offering his advice on how to found, preserve, and reform republics. Still, he was not content with just persuading them; he wanted, in his words, to motivate and encourage them to act in the right manner. To carry out his undertaking, he resorted to yet another valuable lesson of Roman rhetoricians—namely, the idea that history is not only a source of political wisdom which helps to understand what should be done, but also incites men to do what should be done.

History, Cicero writes, 'bears witness to the passing of the ages, sheds light upon reality, gives life to recollection and guidance to human existence, and brings tidings of ancient days'.[96] Quintilian expands the same point in the *Institutio*: 'history seems to repeat itself and the experience of the past is a valuable support to reason.' For this reason, he remarks, the study of history is particularly suited to deliberative oratory, and the speeches delivered to the people and the opinions expressed in the Senate provide precious examples of advice and dissuasion.[97]

History has also a great power to arouse love of virtue through the narration of grand examples of antiquity, and for this reason it is much more valuable than philosophy:

it is still more important that we should know and ponder continually all the noblest sayings and deeds that have been handed down to us from ancient times. And assuredly we shall nowhere find a larger or more remarkable store of these than in the records of our own country. Who will teach courage, justice, loyalty, self-control, simplicity, and contempt of grief and pain better than men like Fabricius, Curius, Regulus, Decius, Mucius, and countless others. For, if the Greeks bear away the palm for moral precepts, Rome can produce more striking examples of moral performance, which is a far greater thing.[98]

This advice of classical rhetoricians was taken up by Florentine historians. In his preface to the *Istoria Fiorentina* Leonardo Bruni writes that to compose the history of the Florentine people is a most useful pursuit ('utilissima') both for private and public purposes, because history allows us to know the deeds and the deliberations ('partiti presi') of ancient peoples in different epochs, and should therefore make us prudent ('fare prudenti') and teach us what we should do and what we should avoid.[99] In addition to that, by placing before our eyes the examples of excellent men, it arouses our soul to pursue virtue.[100]

The same themes are reiterated by Iacopo Bracciolini, in the Proem to the Italian translation of his father Poggio Bracciolini's *Florentine History*. History, he remarks, permits us to know the lives of men and of peoples, the different views that ancient peoples discussed in their councils, their deliberations, the different customs of republics, the various games of fortune, and the events of war; therefore it helps us to deliberate what is useful for us and for our country.[101]

Machiavelli fully endorses the main tenets of this intellectual tradition. Like Roman rhetoricians and Florentine historians, he believes that history is the basis of political wisdom and a powerful source of commitment and engagement, if properly written and commented upon. He composes the *Discourses* to restore the value of history as the basis of political enquiry and political education against the prevailing mode of reading history to take pleasure in hearing of human vicissitudes. He comments upon Livy to give the pages of the Roman historians a new life, to extract from them the political wisdom necessary to find new 'modes and new orders', and to stimulate in his fellows the desire to imitate the grand deeds of the ancient Romans. He intends to restore the rhetorical power of history to arouse the moral energies necessary to redeem his own epoch from corruption.

More specifically, in the *Discourses*, Machiavelli sets himself two main goals: to read history to gain a better knowledge of the political wisdom of the ancients, and to use it as the basis for political advice. He pursues a twofold effort of redemption: the redemption from the wrong way of reading history and the redemption from corrupt ways of ordering political and military institutions and social life, which are in part the consequence of the wrong way of appreciating history.

Men, he remarks in the Proem to Book 1 of the *Discourses*, hold antiquity in great respect and admiration; they are prepared to buy a bit of an old statue to adorn their house, and the artists endeavour to imitate its perfection. Yet, to my great astonishment and grief, one finds neither prince nor republic who resorts to the examples of the ancients

in constituting republics, in maintaining states, in governing kingdoms, in forming an army or conducting a war, in dealing with subjects, in extending the empire.

This is due, Machiavelli continues, not so much to the enervating effects of Christian religion, or to the widespread ambition and idleness that pervade Christian provinces and cities, but to the fact that modern men are not capable of properly appreciating histories ('non avere vera cognizione delle storie'): they are not capable of grasping their meaning ('senso') nor of savouring their flavour ('gustare di loro quel sapore che hanno in sé'). As a consequence of their inadequate reading of history, they never think of imitating the ancients, for they believe that it is not only difficult, but impossible, to imitate them.[102]

Machiavelli wrote *on* Livy to restore his history's full meaning, thereby making it useful for moderns.[103] He writes *on* those books what he considers necessary for 'the better understanding of them' according to his cognizance 'of ancient and modern events'. He engages in a complex work of interpretation and reflection having in view a rhetorical goal—that is, to offer the readers of the *Discourses* eloquent and useful political lessons.

Machiavelli maintains that, through historical examples, the orator has the power to make the readers 'see' the horrors of corruption, ambition, vainglory, and avarice; he can touch their feelings and their imagination, not just their reason, and almost compel them to flee from vice and follow virtue. If a prince reads ancient histories, Machiavelli writes, he will *see* ('vedrà') the good emperors living in safety among safe citizens, 'a world replete with peace and justice. He will see the senate's authority respected, the magistrates honoured, rich citizens enjoying their wealth, nobility and virtue held in the highest esteem.' He will *see* the absence of any rancour, any licentiousness, corruption, or ambition; he will *see* the 'world triumphant, its prince glorious and respected by all, the people fond of him and secure under his rule'. If he then reads the histories of the bad emperors, he will *see* their times

distraught with wars, torn by seditions, brutal alike in peace and in war, princes frequently killed by assassins, civil wars and foreign wars constantly occurring, Italy abused and ever a prey to fresh misfortunes, its cities demolished and pillaged. He will *see* Rome burnt, its Capitol demolished by its own citizens, ancient temples lying desolate, religious rites grown corrupt, adultery rampant; he will *see* the sea covered with exiles and the rocks stained with blood. He will *see* in Rome countless atrocities perpetrated; rank, riches, the honours men have won, and, above all, virtue looked upon as a capital crime. He will *see* calumniators rewarded, servants suborned to turn against their masters, freed men turning against their patrons, and those who lack enemies attacked by their friends (emphasis added).[104]

The reader can see all that through his imagination set in motion by the words of the rhetorician who draws from history all its meaning and its full flavour. And, if he is just a human being, endowed with the ordinary passions of human beings, his imagination will move his passions: he will be 'frightened' to 'imitate the bad times' and will be inflamed by an ardent desire to 'follow the good'.[105] Through history, rhetoric can attain results that reason alone would never be able to.

As he did in *The Prince*, Machiavelli backs most of his political recommendations with the rhetorical topics of advantage, safety, honour, and praise. When he addresses the fundamental issue whether the republic should be aristocratic, like Sparta or Venice, or popular, like Rome, to cite an obvious example, he frames the discussion in terms of safety, as the title of the chapter indicates: 'Whether the guard of liberty can be more safely entrusted to the people or to the great; and which has greater cause for tumult, he who wishes to acquire or he who wishes to maintain'; and he concludes that it is safer to entrust the guardianship of liberty to the people because tumults and dissensions are 'most often caused by him who possesses, because the fear of losing generates in him the same wishes that are in those who desire to acquire; for it does not appear to men that they possess securely what a man has unless he acquires something else new', because those who possess much 'are able to make an alteration with greater power and greater motion', and, lastly, because the ambitious behaviour of the wealthy 'inflames in the breasts of those who do not possess the wish to possess so as to avenge themselves against them by despoiling them or to be able also themselves to enter into those riches and those honours that they see being used badly by others'.[106]

As he continues his discussion of the relative merits of the Roman and Spartan (and Venetian) republics, he insists again on the issue of security and he explains that, although the constitutions of Sparta and Venice, designed with a view of domestic concord rather then expansion, attained 'the true political life and the true quiet of a city', the example to be followed is that of Rome, because 'when a republic has been ordered so as to be capable of maintaining itself without expanding, and necessity leads it to expand, this would erode its foundations and bring it to ruin sooner'.

Even if having a large body of citizens, and entrusting them with the guardianship of liberty, as well as employing them in war necessarily brings about dissensions and tumult, as was the case in Rome, still the safest advice is to adopt the Roman example. In addition, Machiavelli remarks, to imitate the Roman example is also the 'more honourable part'. As he did in *The Prince*, in offering his counsel on political issues of vital importance for the life of republics, he has in view both security and honour—that is, the two subdivisions of the *utile* as defined by his Roman mentors.

The section of the *Discourses* where Machiavelli uses with impressive mastery the full range of the rhetorical devices of advantage, security, honour, and praise is the chapter which marks the conclusion of the discussion on the virtues and the vices of popular and aristocratic republics—namely, the chapter on the different modes of expansion which republics have adopted.

First, he utterly dismisses the mode of expansion by conquest and subjugation adopted by the Spartans, the Athenians (and the Florentines) as 'entirely useless' ('al tutto inutile'); he then further reinforces his point by remarking towards the end of the chapter that such a mode of expansion is 'useless in armed republics' and 'very useless' in those republics that are unarmed, 'as the republics of Italy have been in our times', as Florence and Venice were.

Secondly, he concludes his oration by recommending the mode of expansion by the formation of a league 'of several republics together in which none was before another in either authority or rank', a mode which was followed by the ancient Tuscans, should the imitation of the Romans seem difficult. The ancient Tuscans' mode of expansion, Machiavelli writes, made them 'secure for a long time', and provided them with 'the highest glory of empire and of arms', as well as 'a very great praise for customs and religion'.[107] His advice is, once again, designed to indicate the pathway to attain security, honour, and praise.

Whereas in the *Discourses* Machiavelli comments on Livy to extract from his history of the Romans all the wisdom and the power of rousing men's passions that they contain, in the *Florentine Histories* he has the chance of writing history in his own way to offer good political advice to his fellow-citizens and stimulate their love of liberty. He treasures once again classical rhetoricians' wisdom and writes the *Florentine Histories* because he knows that, 'if every example of a republic is moving, those which one reads concerning one's own are much more so and much more useful'.[108] Even if the historian cannot narrate and magnify examples of virtue but must instead report examples of corruption and ineptitude, still the history is valuable:

even if in describing the things that happened in this corrupt world one does not tell about the strength of the soldiers, or the virtue of the captain, or the love of the citizen for his fatherland, it will be seen with what deceits, with what guile and arts, the princes, the soldiers, and the heads of republics conducted themselves so as to maintain the reputation they have not deserved. It may, perhaps, be no less useful to know these things than to know the ancient ones, because, if the latter excite liberal spirits to follow them, the former will excite such spirits to avoid and eliminate them.[109]

History, even a history of dark times, is more useful than moral reasoning not only because it arouses emotions, but also because it enters into details and therefore offers materials for refined political wisdom. In the case of the history of Florence, as Machiavelli explains, it offers the rhetorician the opportunity to describe in detail the most crucial problem of republican politics—namely, the problem of civil strife and factions, and offer his compatriot useful advice on the matter:

if nothing else delights or instructs in history, it is that which is described in detail: if no other lesson is useful to the citizens who govern republics, it is that which shows the causes of the hatreds and divisions in the city, so that when they have become wise through the dangers of others, they may be able to maintain themselves united.[110]

While the *Discourses* are a study of the deliberations of the Romans in both domestic and foreign affairs designed to persuade and to move the minds of the young to imitate the Romans and turn them away from the corruption of modern times, the *Florentine Histories* are a study of the deliberations of the Florentine people designed to persuade and move the minds of his fellow-citizens not to repeat the mistakes of their ancestors and instead to deliberate and act according to the true principle of republican politics. In the former work he sets himself the goal of giving advice on the means to attain liberty and greatness; in the latter he intends to teach the path to civic unity and the restoration of a true civil and free way of life. The two works together give us the full picture of Machiavelli's mode of political theorizing based on history and rhetoric. Though in different ways, they are both powerful efforts to write eloquently of politics and they offer an example of a political philosophy based on rhetoric and history— that is, an example of genuine 'civil science', as his Roman mentors understood it.[111]

In the *Florentine Histories* Machiavelli has the chance to make the protagonists speak in their own voices to persuade or dissuade their fellow-citizens to uphold or reject a course of action. He can show deliberative rhetoric in action, and make ancient Florentines speak to the Florentines of his times to urge them with powerful and wise words not to imitate the errors that caused the decline of the city. To achieve that, he makes them speak according to the rules of rhetoric. To persuade or dissuade, all the orators that Machiavelli calls on to perform on the stage of the *Histories* appeal either to the *utile* or to the *honestum* or to necessity, or to combinations of the three of them.[112]

An example of oration based on the topic of *utile* is the speech delivered by one of the Signori before the Duke of Athens to dissuade him from pursuing his ambition of imposing his tyranny over Florence. We have come to you, says the orator

not to oppose your designs with any force, but only to point out to you . . .
how dangerous [*pericoloso*] is the course you are selecting, so that you can
always remember our advice and that of those who counsel you otherwise,
not for your advantage [*utilità*] but to vent their rage.

Having tried to dissolve the Duke's hostility by stressing that they,
unlike other advisers, are advising him to pursue what is really in
his interest, the orator continues by stressing how difficult, indeed
impossible, it would be for the Duke to establish a tyranny over a
city like Florence which has a long tradition of liberty. He would
have to face the hostility of the whole city, and 'amidst universal
hatred one never finds any security, because you never know from
whence evil may spring, and he who fears every man cannot secure
himself against anyone'. Therefore, the most secure course of
action is not to try to become a tyrant of Florence, but to be
content 'with the authority that we have given you', for 'that
dominion is alone lasting which is voluntary'.[113]

The words of the Signore 'did not move the obdurate spirit of the
Duke in any part'. On the contrary he replies with a speech which
is an example of the fundamental rhetorical technique of arguing
'on both sides' ('in contrarias partes'), as Cicero put it.[114] He
remarks that he has no intention of depriving Florence of its liberty, but rather aims to restore it, for if by his authority he could
destroy the sects and fight ambition and enmities, he would in fact
return Florence its liberty. As for the dangers that the Signori have
pointed out to him, the Duke responds that he 'did not consider
them, because it was the duty of an evil man to set aside good for
fear of evil, and of a pusillanimous man not to pursue a glorious
undertaking because the end was doubtful'.[115] His words were not
persuasive either; not because the spirit of the Signori was obdurate
like his, but because the words made a poor attempt to conceal his
wicked intentions. As a result, he was forced to leave Florence
when the people took up arms on behalf of liberty—further evidence of the principle that Machiavelli had laid down in the *Discourses*: unlike the populace, which can be persuaded to return to
the pathway of goodness by the words of a 'good men', there is no
one who can *talk* to a bad prince; therefore 'is there any remedy
except the sword'.[116]

If the goal is to persuade citizens to moderate their requests and
give up the desire of revenge, a wise magistrate should appeal to the
common interest of the city, humanity, honesty, and love of country.

An example of this kind of oration is the speech delivered by the Gonfalonier Luigi Guicciardini on behalf of the Signoria.

If we had believed that during our magistracy our city had to be ruined, either by opposing you or by gratifying you [Machiavelli reports], we would have avoided these honors with flight or exile; but as we hoped to have to do with men who might have in them some humanity [*umanità*] and some love for their fatherland [*ed alla loro patria qualche amore*], we accepted the magistracy willingly, believing that with our humanity we could conquer your ambition by any mode.[117]

After the appeal to humanity and love of country, Machiavelli puts in the mouth of the upright and eloquent magistrate a powerful dissuasion based on the topic of the interest of the city, and framed according to the figure of the *interrogatio*—that is, a question designed not to get information, but 'to emphasize our point' and give our words a 'greater fire'.[118]

What end will these demands of yours have, or how long will you abuse our liberality? Do you not see that we tolerate being conquered with more patience than you tolerate victory? To what will your disunion lead this city of yours? Do you not remember that when it was disunited Castruccio, a vile citizen of Lucca, defeated it? That a duke of Athens, one of your private condottieri, subjugated it? . . . Why, then, do you want your discords to make a slave of a city in peace that so many powerful enemies left free in war? What do you get out of your disunion other than servitude? Or of the goods that you have stolen or would steal from us other than poverty?[119]

In perfect observance of the classical model, the oration ends with an exhortation based upon the themes of decency and moderation:

These Signori and I command you, and if decency permits it, we pray you to still your spirits for once and be content to rest quietly with the things that have been ordered through us, and, if ever you wish something new, be pleased to ask for it with civility and not with tumult and arms. For if they are decent things, you will always be granted them, and you will not give occasion to wicked men, at your charge and to your cost, to ruin your fatherland on your shoulders.[120]

Luigi Guicciardini's oration is a model speech that a 'good citizen' ought to deliver to calm the wicked passion of fellow-citizens: his words, he writes, 'moved the spirits' of the insolent citizens, not only because they were appropriate and eloquent, but also because they 'were true'.[121] It is a speech that evokes the orations composed by earlier theorists of communal self-government for the benefit of the Podestà or other magistrates. By speaking in that way, Machiavelli remarks, Luigi Guicciardini behaved not only as 'a good citizen', but as a 'buon signore', two expressions that reveal the presence in the *Florentine Histories* of the old language of the pre-humanist theorist of republican self-government.[122]

The *Florentine Histories* also provide examples of orations centred around the topics of compassion and fear of God, like the speech delivered by the citizens of Seravezza before the Ten of War. To protest and claim repair for the sack of their city perpetrated by the Florentine commissioner Astorre Gianni, they appealed to the Ten of War's sense of justice. 'We are sure, magnificent Signori,' says their spokesman, that our words will find faith and compassion in your Lordships when you learn the way in which your commissioner seized our country and in what manner we were treated afterwards by him'. After a touching report of the atrocities they endured, the orator ends his speech by appealing to the fear of God: 'And if our countless ills do not move you, may fear of the wrath of God *move* you, for he has seen His churches sacked and burned and our people betrayed in His bosom' (emphasis added). This too was a successful oration, for, as Machiavelli promptly comments, 'the atrociousness of the thing, first learned and then understood from the living voices of those who had suffered it, *touched* the magistrates; and without delay Astorre was made to return and was then condemned and admonished' (emphasis added).

An example of oration based upon the topic of necessity is the speech that the anonymous worker addresses to his fellows who are deliberating whether to continue their revolt or to depose arms and 'to put a quiet poverty ahead of perilous gain'. After a brief Proem, the orator goes at the core of the matter: 'because arms have been taken up and many evils have been done, it appears to me that one must reason that arms must not be put aside and that we must consider how we can secure ourselves from the evils that have been committed. Certainly I believe that if others do not teach us, necessity does.'[123]

To persuade his fellows to continue the revolt and multiply the arsons and robberies, the orator endeavours to counter their sense of inferiority with regard to the Florentine nobility by resorting to a theory of natural equality of men: 'all men, having had the same beginning, are equally ancient and have been made by nature in one mode. Strip all of us naked, you will see that we are alike; dress us in their clothes and them in ours, and without a doubt we shall appear noble and they ignoble, for only poverty and riches make us unequal.'[124] He then tries to overcome their moral scruples by explaining that victory, however obtained, never brings shame, and by stressing that they should not take conscience into account, for 'where there is, as with us, fear of hunger and prison, there cannot and should not be fear of hell', and in a world in which 'men devour one another', only the bold can rise out of servitude.

As he moves towards the final peroration to continue the revolt with renewed determination, the anonymous orator goes back to the theme of necessity and explains that actions performed under the constraints of necessity are judged in a different way: 'I confess this course is bold and dangerous, but when necessity presses, boldness is judged prudence; and spirited men never take account of the danger in great things, for those enterprises that are begun with danger always end with reward, and one never escapes a danger without a danger.'[125] This oration too, Machiavelli reports, was effective. The speaker 'strongly inflamed' spirits that were already hot for evil and persuaded them to deliberate to take up arms. And what made it persuasive was the appeal to necessity, which is most 'useful' in human affairs, as Machiavelli writes in the *Discourses*.[126]

In addition to the oration to the Duke of Athens, Machiavelli presents in the *Florentine Histories* other instances of words that failed to persuade. Among them it is worth mentioning the description of the conspiracy against Maso degli Albizzi, who had established a harsh regime odious even to the good citizens of his own faction.[127] A number of citizens banned by Maso, Machiavelli narrates, resolved to enter Florence secretly, kill Maso degli Albizzi, call the people to rebel, and institute a new and free government. The conspirators, 'all young, fierce, and disposed to try all fortune so as to return to their fatherland', with loud voices exhorted the Florentines to take up arms and free themselves from the regime they hated so much. They proclaimed that the grievances and the malcontents of the city, more that their own injuries, had moved them to risk their lives to free their fatherland. Their words, Machiavelli remarks, 'even though true, did not move the multitude in any way', either because of fear, or because the killing that the conspirators had perpetrated made them odious.[128] Whatever the cause, the political lesson that Machiavelli conveys from this story is that it is very difficult 'to want to free a people who want in every mode to be enslaved'.[129]

The Ambivalent Power of Rhetoric

Though at times it fails, eloquence has the power of making nefarious plans appear inspired by noble and honest goals. The words that Machiavelli uses to describe this practice are 'adonostare'—that is, to give one's intentions and goals the appearance of being honest, and 'colorare'—that is, to colour one's intentions and goals so that they appear in a positive light. In classical rhetoric, 'colour' is a technical term that describes the orator's skill to present the facts in the light that suits the orator's purposes. As Quintilian describes it with reference to Cicero, the orator who knows how to colour or varnish creates the impression that he is doing something on behalf of those very persons against whom he spoke'.[130]

Machiavelli offers examples of the technique of colouring from both foreign and domestic politics. He reports that the Venetians did not think that they could start a war against Florence, as in fact they intended to do as part of their alliance with Alfonso, king of Naples, without first attempting to justify the war 'under some colour'.[131] They attempted to colour their plan by saying that Florence was responsible for a number of acts that had damaged Venice and the friendship between the two republics, and by reminding them lovingly that 'he who wrongfully offends gives cause to others, with reason, to feel offended, and he who breaks the peace may expect war'.[132]

As for domestic affairs, Machiavelli refers to 'colouring' in the oration delivered by a number of citizens 'moved by love of their fatherland' to advise the Signori to pass a reform of the statutes that would end factional strife. What is most pernicious, says the speaker, is to see that the promoters and leaders of the sects that are destroying the republic 'give decent appearance' to their intentions and their ends with pious words. Although they are all enemies of common liberty and oppress it, they do so 'under colour [colore] of fighting for aristocratic or popular government'.[133] Another example that Machiavelli reports is that of Corso Donati, who was rancorous against the popular government because he believed that the city had not given him the honours that were due to him, but 'made the indecency of his intention appear decent by invoking a decent cause', and, because of their ignorance, many citizens believed that Corso was acting for love of his fatherland.[134]

As his reconstruction of Florentine history shows, Machiavelli assigns eloquence a central role in political and social struggle. It has the power of uniting or dividing citizens, of moderating or inflaming emotions, of arousing the passions that destroy civil life, such as avarice, envy, and ambition, or those that sustain it, such as love of common good, love of country, love of justice, magnanimity, courage, and fortitude. It can destroy republics or keep them alive and flourishing.

In his appreciation of the importance of eloquence in politics, Machiavelli reveals once again his debt to Roman authorities. Cicero had stressed the ambivalent character of eloquence and oratory at the very outset of *Of Invention*. No little part of the disasters and misfortunes of our own Republic and of many mighty cities, he remarks, 'was brought about by men of eloquence'.[135] On the other hand, it is also true that 'many cities have been founded, that the flames of a multitude of wars have been extinguished, and that the strongest alliances and most sacred friendship have been formed not only by the use of reason but also more easily by the help of eloquence'.[136] And in *Of the Orator*, through the words of Crassus, he celebrates oratory as the art that has always reigned supreme in all free peoples ('in omni libero populo'), and 'in communities which have attained the enjoyment of peace and tranquillity'. Oratory has the power to hold assemblies of men, to win their minds, to direct their wills wherever the speaker wishes, or to divert them from whatever he wishes ('tenere hominum coetus, mentes allicere, voluntates impellere quo velit; unde autem velit, deducere'). No achievement, Crassus continues, is more glorious than the orator's ability to transform the impulses of a crowd, the conscience of the judges, the austerity of the Senate. Eloquence has not only founded cities, for it was because of the eloquence of some great men that humanity was persuaded to abandon the brutish existence in the wilderness and to accept the laws of a tribunal and civil rights; it also keeps civil society united and upholds the safety of individuals and of the entire state.[137]

This exalted view of rhetoric is challenged in the dialogue *Of the Orator* by Scaevola, who cites examples of men who destroyed the republic 'by use of this eloquence', to which, according to Crassus, civil communities 'still look for their chief guidance'.[138] Quintilian, too, concedes that eloquence has been pernicious not only against individuals, but also against the public good, and has indeed thrown 'ordered commonwealths into a state of turmoil or even brought them to ruin'. But he also remarks that oratory has greatly

contributed to institute cities and to defend republics by exhort-
ing citizens to resist, by denouncing the plans of ambitious men,
and by reviving the courage of demoralized armies. Eloquence has
the power to educate the mind to virtue; therefore, 'although the
weapons of oratory may be used for either good or evil, it is
unfair to regard it as an evil which can be employed for the
good'.[139]

Even if, as we have seen, Machiavelli takes up from Roman
rhetoricians the idea of the ambivalent power of eloquence, he
also believes that eloquence is far from sufficient to found and
preserve states. It is 'easy to persuade peoples', he writes in *The
Prince*, but it is 'difficult to keep them persuaded'. For this reason,
'all armed prophets succeed whereas unarmed ones fail', as happened to Girolamo Savonarola, 'who perished together with his new
order as soon as the masses began to lose faith in him; and he lacked
the means of keeping the support of those who had believed in him,
as well as of making those who had never had any faith in him
believe'. A true political leader must, therefore, be able 'to force
them to believe', as Moses, Cyrus, Theseus, and Romulus did.[140]

His awareness of the limits of eloquence turns into sarcasm
when he comments upon the view that political affairs can be
successfully conducted by means of embellished speeches. Before
they were overcome by the fury of transalpine wars, he writes in
the *Art of War*, Italian princes believed that, in order to demonstrate their own ability as politicians, they need do nothing more
than 'think of a sharp reply in their study, write a fine letter, show
quickness and cleverness in quotable sayings and replies, and
expect their words to be taken as the responses of oracles'.[141]
However, it is precisely in the *Art of War* that Machiavelli stresses
the importance of eloquence and lists rhetorical skills as one of the
essential features of the good general:

To persuade or dissuade a few about a thing is very easy, because if words are
not enough, you can use authority and force; but the difficulty is to remove
from a multitude a belief that is unfavorable either to the common good or to
your belief, when you can use only words proper to be heard by all, since you
are trying to persuade them all.[142]

Held in the greatest respect by ancient generals, oratory has
become in modern times 'completely obsolete' among modern
captains. And yet nothing is more effective than eloquence to
impel an army's will, and to move the soldiers' passions:

For there are countless times when things come up by which an army would be ruined if the general either could not or was not accustomed to speak to it; this speaking lightens fear, sets courage afire, increases determination, uncovers deception, promises rewards, shows perils and the way to escape them, reproaches, begs, threatens, fills with hope, praises, berates, and does everything through which human passions are extinguished or exited.

Hence, Machiavelli concludes, 'any prince or republic intending to set up a new military establishment and bring reputation to such an army must accustom its soldiers to hearing their general speak, and must accustom its generals to speak skilfully'.[143]

In this passage Machiavelli recapitulates all the powers of eloquence in full agreement with the teaching of Roman rhetoricians and of their humanist followers. He continues the tradition of Roman rhetoric also in another important respect—namely, the view that rhetoric is the art that flourishes in free republics.[144] Eloquence plays a central role in deliberative assemblies, the core of the republic, where magistrates and citizens have to be able to persuade a multitude by using only words without using force or fear, as was the case in the Roman republic, where 'a tribune or any other citizens could propose to the people a law, in regard to which every citizen was entitled to speak either in favour of it or against, prior to the deliberation being reached'.[145] This order was good as long as the citizens were incorrupt, because Machiavelli stresses, 'it is always a good thing that anyone anxious to serve the public should be able to propose his plan'; and it is also a good thing that everyone should be at liberty to express his opinion, so that, when the people have heard what the different orators have to say, they may choose the best advice. There is nothing to fear about the use of rhetoric in deliberative assemblies, for, 'when two speakers of equal skill are heard advocating different alternatives, very rarely does one find the populace failing to adopt the better view or incapable of appreciating the truth of what it hears'.[146]

It is, on the contrary, one of the most pernicious effects of corruption that only powerful citizens propose laws and no one dares to speak against them. When this is the case, the people were induced, 'either by deceit or by force', to deliberate their own ruin.[147] Even when the populace has become licentious and turbulent, eloquence can still do some good, for a good man can address it and moderate its exalted passions. But when political orders are corrupt, words are no longer sufficient. Even a wise and good man who knows what should be done to reform the orders of the republic will not be able to 'persuade others' to undertake the necessary reforms. When corruption and fear have attained complete domination over the republic, there is no longer room for eloquence. The power of words must be strengthened by the power of arms.

By placing Machiavelli's political works in the context of the tradition of Roman rhetoric, we can not only gain a better perspective of his interpretation of politics, but also understand the nature of his own theorizing on politics. He practised political theory, not as the work of a philosopher, nor as the work of a scientist, but as the work of an orator. He wrote on politics to offer counsel and advice on the most useful way to found, govern, and redeem a principality or a republic, not to identify political or moral truths, and even less to frame universal laws of politics based upon observation of facts.

The fact that he wrote rhetorically means that he 'should not be chiefly read as a theorist of republicanism but rather as a proponent of a rhetorical politics, one that proceeds topically and dialectically, and that can be used by tyrant and republican alike'.[148] His rhetorical way of writing was perfectly congenial with his republicanism. If one writes to persuade and to move one's fellow-citizens, or political leaders, to adopt the kind of conduct that is conducive to the safety and the greatness of the republic, as republican writers have invariably been doing over the centuries, one must write rhetorically. Machiavelli wrote rhetorically when he was offering advice concerning the security and the liberty of republics and when he was writing to offer his advice on the best ways to secure the state of a prince. This is perhaps the key to the old puzzle of the compatibility of *The Prince* and the *Discourses*: what would be contradictory for a philosopher—namely, to compose a work designed to advise a prince on how to found and preserve a principality and then another one to advise on how to found and preserve a republic—is perfectly permissible, indeed praiseworthy, for an orator.

All his political writings are rhetorical, but not in the sense that he proceeds topically and dialectically and even less because of his 'dichotomizing mode of argument, hyperbolic and theatrical style, apparent contradictions, and deliberately failed example'. They are rhetorical in a broader and yet more specific sense—that he was following the rules of deliberative rhetoric as laid down by Roman rhetoricians. The fact that he wrote rhetorically does not affect his republicanism, except in the sense that it makes it powerful and eloquent. He was an orator in the classical sense—that is, a citizen who is competent 'in justice, in civic duty, and in how cities should be established and ruled', who 'can really play his part as a citizen and is capable of meeting the demands of both public and private business, the man who can guide a state by his counsels, give it a firm basis by his legislation, and purge its vices by his decisions as a judge'.[149]

Taking the image of the classical orator as his model, Machiavelli wrote what he believed a good citizen should write to offer advice on civil affairs to his fellow-citizens and future generations, and he wrote it rhetorically. It is in the light of the Roman interpretation of the duty of the good man counselling on political matters that we must read Machiavelli's own statement of the goals of his political theorizing. It is 'the duty of a good man, ('offizio di uomo buono'), he writes in the Proem to book II of the *Discourses*, to teach others the good that 'you have not been able to carry out' because of the malignity of times.[150] At the end of the *Art of War* Machiavelli restates his commitment to the ideal of the good citizen capable of offering sound advice on political matters in a more melancholic but straight way:

I repine at Nature, who either should have made me such that I could not see this [the corruption of political and military orders in Italy] or should have given me the opportunity of putting it into effect. Since I am an old man, I do not imagine today that I shall have the opportunity to do so. Therefore I have made free with it to you, who, being young and gifted, can, at the right time, if the things I have said please you, aid and advise your princes to their advantage.[151]

He composed all his major political works inspired by the ideal of the classical orator as a good man trained in the art of rhetoric and competent in political and civil affairs. His style of writing is a powerful example of the possibility of practising political theory in an attractive manner, if we abandon, at last, the pretension to cultivate it as a philosophical search for truth or a scientific enterprise. If we want to reinvigorate our political theory and turn it into a useful endeavour, it is time to take Machiavelli's teaching seriously, and to go back to the pursuit of political theory as a rhetorical practice based upon historical knowledge which aims at verisimilitude rather than truth, and endeavours to impel passion and commitment, in addition to conquering reason's consent.

4

The Theory of the Republic

Machiavelli's fame as a republican theorist came relatively late. His contemporary fellow-Florentines did not trust his republican faith, and, when a republican government was restored in 1527, they did not return him to the post of *Secretario* that he had lost in 1512. What damaged him was not so much the fact that he had served the Medici in a few humble affairs and had written the *Florentine Histories* for Giulio de' Medici, but the authorship of *The Prince*: 'Everyone hated him because of the *Prince*'. The rich thought that his *Prince* was a document written to teach the Duke 'how to take away all their property, . . . the Piagnoni regarded him as a heretic, the good thought him sinful, the wicked thought him more wicked or more capable than themselves, so all hated him'. Giovanbattista Busini, the author of this well-known judgement, was notoriously malicious and hostile to Machiavelli, but his words render well the mood of the Florentines, including Florentine republicans, to the old *Secretario*.[1]

The restoration of Machiavelli's reputation as a republican thinker began with Alberico Gentili, a jurist educated at Perugia who fled to England and in 1587 was appointed Regius Professor of civil law in Oxford. In his *De legationibus*, issued in 1585, he wrote an eloquent eulogy of Machiavelli, whom he praises as the author of the golden ('aureas') observations on Livy, and as a man of unique prudence and learning. Those who have written against him, Gentili claims, have not understood Machiavelli's ideas at all, and have indeed slandered him. The truth is that Machiavelli was

a strong supporter and enthusiast for democracy. [He] was born, educated and received public honours in a Republic. He was extremely hostile to tyranny. Therefore he did not help the tyrant; his intention was not to instruct the tyrant, but by making all his secrets clear and openly displaying the degree of wretchedness to the people . . . he excelled all other men in wisdom and while appearing to instruct the prince he was actually educating the people.[2]

Almost a century later, the interpretation of Machiavelli as a champion of liberty was resumed by Spinoza in his *Tractatus Politicus*. The opinions of that 'wise man', wrote Spinoza, seem to me particularly attractive in view of the well-known fact that he was an advocate of freedom ('pro libertate fuisse constat'), and also 'gave some very sound advice for preserving it'.[3] After Spinoza, the idea of Machiavelli as a misunderstood republican was authoritatively endorsed by Pierre Bayle's *Dictionnaire*[4] and by Diderot in the *Encyclopédie*[5] and it received its final sanction in the well-known lines of Rousseau's *Contrat social*: 'While appearing to instruct kings' he has done much to educate the people. Machiavelli's *Prince* is the book of Republicans.'[6]

For us, though we may not believe that *The Prince* is the book of republicans, Machiavelli's reputation as a republican theorist is a solid acquisition. We still debate how the same person could have been a republican citizen and the author of *The Prince*, to borrow the title of the seminal essay by Hans Baron; but contemporary scholars all agree that Machiavelli was an advocate of republican constitution. A number of scholars seem to agree, however, that Machiavelli's republicanism was of a rather special sort, because 'it contained a strain of monarchism, in so far as he believed that even republics could not come into existence without the help of great individual personalities', as Friedrich Meinecke put it;[7] or because it is in truth a 'mixture of republicanism and tyranny', as Harvey Mansfield and Nathan Tarcov have recently written.[8] Others have remarked that the distintive aspect of Machiavelli's republicanism was his commitment to civic and military virtue, even to its most unpleasant manifestations—war and conquest.[9]

I believe that these interpretations of Machiavelli's republicanism are either partial or wrong or both. As I hope to be able to show in this chapter, Machiavelli's republicanism is not a commitment to the value of civic or military virtue, and even less devotion to the pursuit of military greatness and predation, but a commitment to the ideal of a well-ordered republic—that is, a republic which is kept in order by the rule of law and by constitutional arrangements that ensure that each component of the polity has its proper place; it is a commitment to the principles of the political and civil life (*vivere politico; vivere civile*) and to a conception of political liberty understood as an absence of personal dependence, which he inherited from the jurists, the theorists of communal self-government, and the civic humanists of the Trecento and the Quattrocento. It is precisely on this tradition that I shall now focus to set the appropriate context which should permit us to attain a better historical understanding of Machiavelli's republicanism.

Republicanism before Machiavelli

For pre-humanist and humanist political theorists, the republic or *civitas* is an association or federation of individuals bound together by principles of justice ('*iure sociati*').[10] Civil communities, wrote, for instance, Brunetto Latini in his influential *Book of Treasure*, were instituted to live in peace and security under the shield of laws. A civil community ('cité') is, therefore, as Cicero said, an assembly of men living under the same law ('*vivre a une loi*').[11] After the rediscovery of Aristotle's *Politics* in the 1260s, the notion of civil life was equated with that of 'political life'. Aegidius Romanus (Giles of Rome), in the *De regimine principum libri III* (*The Rule of Princes*), composed in 1280, speaks in fact of 'political community or city' ('*communitatem politicam sivi civitatem*') and describes civil or political community in Aristotelian terms as the necessary condition for men to live well—that is, to live the life of virtue. Even when defined in strict Aristotelian language, the fundamental requirement of political life is the rule of law. To live politically ('vivere politicum'), Giles writes, means to live under the laws and under laudable constitutional statutes.[12]

The conception of civil or political life as the life according to the law was also a central feature of the language of the thirteenth and fourteenth centuries' jurists, who provided a fundamental contribution, though often neglected, to the theory of republican self-government. An important source in this respect is the *Digest of Justinian*, where it is stated that the law is 'the common agreement of the *polis* according to whose terms all who live in the *polis* ought to live' and the 'standard of justice and injustice' for political beings. In the same vein, late medieval jurists equated the political man to the man living in a civil community. All stressed that to live politically or civilly means to live under the rules of civil law or justice. Indeed, the very aim of civil justice is to make individuals live the life of the *civitas* or *polis*—that is, civil or political life.[13]

Political or civil life was not the same as political regime—that is, republican government. Advocates of monarchy like Giles of Rome, for instance, claimed that the form of government most apt to sustain political life was hereditary monarchy. Republican theorists, on the contrary, stressed that the form of government best suited to political life is the rule of elective magistrates with limited tenure appointed by the sovereign body of the citizens. Republican government ('politia' or 'principatus politicus'), wrote, for instance, Ptolemy of Lucca, is the regime appropriate for civil communities ('civitates'); and by republican regime he means a form of government in which rulers are elected by the citizens and are bound by the laws of the city.[14]

Understandably, Quattrocento republican theorists equated political and civil life with republican government or with mixed government—that is, a form of government which wisely combines the virtues of monarchy, aristocracy, and popular government. This latter interpretation, whose importance can hardly be overestimated, was endorsed by the theorists who were looking at the Republic of Venice as the model political constitution. The Venetian historian Lorenzo de' Monaci summarized the conventional understanding, saying that a true political constitution is one 'where the laws rule' and the best way to ensure the rule of law is to imitate the mixed government as exemplified by Venice.[15]

Whatever the judgement on the form of government, it was plain to all that political or civil life is the opposite of tyranny. Because the tyrant is above the law; his domination violates the fundamental requirement of political life. While monarchical government may still be called 'political', wrote Coluccio Salutati in the *De tyranno* (*Treatise on Tyrants*), tyranny cannot, because a political government ('principatus politicus') is one in which sovereign authority is limited by the laws ('auctoritate restricta legibus').[16] About thirty years later, in the 1430s, Giovanni Cavalcanti described the practice of taking important political decisions in the private palaces of powerful citizens, which was a patent violation of the statutes of the city, as tyrannical and repugnant to political life ('tirannesco e non politico viver').[17]

This tradition of thought was well alive in Machiavelli's time. In a public oration delivered in 1493—which Machiavelli may well have attended—Alamanno Rinuccini stressed, quoting Cicero, that justice and good laws are the foundations of any humane way of living and particularly of political and civil life ('humano vivere et maxime politico et civile'). He was speaking of the civic militia, which he praised as the necessary defence of the laws which constitute the essence of any good and political life ('fondamento d'ogni buono et polytico viver').[18] And less than a year later, in the *Trattato circa il reggimento e il governo della città di Firenze* (*Tract on the Constitution and the Government of Florence*) that set the ideological and constitutional basis of the republican government that was to employ Niccolò in 1498, Girolamo Savonarola explained at length that a true civil government ('governo civile') is a government of the whole citizenry ('per tutto il popolo'), and as such it is the best shield against tyranny.[19]

Before turning to Machiavelli, another central theme of the tradition that I have been analysing needs to be studied—namely, the connection between civil or political life and political liberty. For fourteenth-century Italian jurists and political philosophers, the essential feature of political liberty is independence—that is, a city's capacity to give itself its statutes and laws, as opposed to its being dependent on the Emperor's will. Cities which 'live in their own liberty' ('que vivunt in propria libertate'), wrote, for instance, Baldus de Ubaldis, 'enjoy absolute self-'government' ('absolute proprio regimine'). Because they use their own laws, they do not require anybody else's assistance, and their status does not change whether they act on the basis of a privilege or on the basis of a statute.[20] Since they are the result of the citizens' explicit consent, argues Bartolus of Saxoferrato, the statutes that city-republics have given themselves have the same force as customary laws ('paris potentia'). Therefore, they do not need the authorization of a higher authority. This means to say that a free city is one which does not recognize any superior power ('civitas quem superiorem non recognoscit'), and for this reason its people is a free people ('populus liber').[21] Having equated the people of a free city with a *populus liber*, Bartolus had laid down all the preliminary steps needed to perform his famous juristic masterstroke: 'being composed of a free people which does not recognize a higher authority, the city can be attributed within its territory the same powers of jurisdiction that the emperor has over the territory of the empire: the city is its own prince ('civitas sibi princeps').[22]

Like the liberty of the city, the individual citizens' liberty is also described as independence from the will of other men, which can exist only in so far as the laws and not men rule. The existence of a true civil and political life in an independent city is therefore the first condition for the individual citizens to be free.

The source of the jurists' interpretation of political liberty as independence was the Roman Law, in which the status of a free person was defined as not being subject to the mastery (*dominium*) of another person, as opposed to the slave, who is an individual dependent on another person.[23] As the individual is free if he has personal and political rights ('sui iuris'), so a people or a city is free in so far as it lives under its own laws ('suae leges').[24] The first implication of this principle is that, if a people or a city receives the laws from a king, it is not free but a serf; it is not at liberty but in servitude.[25] Its position is analogous to that of a slave before his master. Monarchy, which for the Romans meant monarchy in its proper sense—that is, absolute monarchy—was therefore equated with domination, while only the republic was considered to be the form of government and the way of life of a free people. Another equally important consequence of the interpretation of political liberty as being the status of an independent people living under its own laws was the recognition that liberty implies the acceptance of the restraints, (*frenum*) that laws impose on an individual's actions, and, therefore, that political liberty exists only where the law is sovereign.

This conception of political liberty was eloquently described, among other places, in three classical texts which became the core of modern republicanism. The first was Livy's account of the recovered Roman liberty after the expulsions of the kings as consisting in the fact that the laws were more powerful than men.[26] The second was Aemilius Lepidus' statement in Sallust's *Orationes et epistulae* that the Roman people was free because it obeyed none but the laws;[27] the third was the line of Cicero's *Pro Cluentio* destined to be endlessly quoted over the centuries: 'all of us—in short—obey the law in order to be free.'[28]

These pieces of Roman wisdom were echoed and rephrased by Florentine civic humanists. Liberty, wrote Coluccio Salutati, is a 'sweet restraint' ('dulce libertatis frenum') which the laws impose upon all citizens.[29] The same principle is restated by Bruni: true liberty ('mera ac vera Libertas') consists in the equality ensured by the laws.[30] In his *Historiarum florentini populi libri XII* (*A History of the Florentine People*), he attributes to Giano della Bella the idea that, whenever laws are 'more powerful than single citizens', liberty is preserved ('Libertas servatur').[31] In the second half of the Quattrocento, the same principle is eloquently reiterated by the opponents of the Medici. A republic which wishes 'to live in freedom' ('vivere in libertà) must never allow a citizen to become more powerful than the laws ('che egli possa più che le leggi'), wrote Alamanno Rinuccini in his *Ricordi*,[32] and a few years later in the *Dialogus de libertate* (*Dialogue on Liberty*) he restates the same principle quoting Cicero: 'the greatest liberty consists in obedience to the law' ('legibus parere summa Libertas est').[33]

To be able to protect the liberty of the citizens, the laws must be fair—that is, aim at the common good—and not further the particular interest of the prince or of a faction or of a social group. According to republican theorists, this goal can be attained, and therefore true liberty properly secured, only if sovereign power—that is, the power to pass laws and to appoint magistrates—belongs to the citizens. As Leonardo Bruni wrote in his *Laudatio florentinae urbis* (*Eulogy of the City of Florence*) referring to the well-known principle of Roman Law, 'what concerns many ought to be decided by the action of the whole citizen-body acting according to the law and legal procedure', which was an eloquent way of restating the point that only self-governing republics carry out laws that promote the common good and therefore permit the full enjoyment of a true civil life and true liberty.[34]

The consequence of this conception of political liberty was that equality before the law must be accompanied by the liberty to participate in equal terms to the government of the republic. The connection between political liberty and republican government was also stressed by Poggio Bracciolini in a letter of 1438 to the Duke of Milan: 'neither individual citizens nor the aristocrats rule the city, but the entire people are admitted with equal right to public office; as a result of which high and low, noble and non-noble, rich and poor alike are united in the service of liberty, for whose preservation they do not shun any expenses, or fear any labours.'[35]

For theorists of republican self-government, an essential dimension of political liberty was therefore the liberty to participate in public deliberations and to be appointed to public posts as a recognition of one's virtue and services to the common good. This liberty, they maintained, is very dear to citizens of the republics because it gives them the chance to satisfy their legitimate ambition and to develop their best moral and intellectual qualities.[36]

A well-instituted republic must encourage citizens 'participation by rewarding civic virtue, and be sure to entrust the highest public posts to the citizens who have displayed outstanding talents in serving the common good. As stated in the declaration which opens the law introducing election by lot, 'the citizens who have shown to be fit to hold public posts' should be allowed 'gradually to ascend to and to attain public office'; on the other hand, 'those whose life does not render them worthy of it, should not climb up to government posts'.[37] A good political and civil order must therefore have a hierarchy of honour based upon virtue; that is, it must be just, if liberty has to be effectively preserved.

Last, to ensure that participation in public deliberations is a real exercise of political liberty, citizens must be allowed freely to express their ideas. As a participant to the debates on the reform of the city's statutes of November 1458 put it, the liberty of freely speaking in deliberative councils is a most valuable good, and difference of opinion which normally arises in deliberative bodies is not at all to be considered a sign of civic discord, but is in fact the best way to discover truth.[38] A republic cannot be said to be free, wrote Alamanno Rinuccini in his *Dialogue on Liberty*, if, because of fear, or corruption, or any other cause, citizens are forced not to say what they sense openly and freely. Whereas in a free republic citizens engage in open discussions in all public councils, under a tyrant a cold silence reigns everywhere.[39]

Machiavelli's Theory of the Well-Ordered Republic

If we now analyse Machiavelli's works, the first point that needs to be stressed is that Machiavelli's republicanism is above all else a commitment to the *vivere civile*. Any form of government, including republican or popular government, which does not fulfil the requirements of civil and political life is either a tyranny or a corrupt republic—that is, the two worst calamities that can befall a people.

In full agreement with the tradition that I have outlined, Machiavelli regards the rule of law as the basic feature of civil and political life. In the *Discourses*, he in fact contrasts political life ('vivere politico') with tyranny, understood as authority unbound by laws ('autorità assoluta'), and opposes armed violence to 'civil modes and customs'.[40] In the *Florentine Histories* he contrasts civil life ('vivere civile') with 'sole authority' ('unica autorità').[41] Elsewhere, he opposes political life to corruption: in order to obtain glory, he writes, a man must use different methods in a corrupt city ('città corrotta') from those he would use in one which lives politically ('politicamente').[42] A corrupt city, he explains, is precisely one where laws are disobeyed ('le leggi bene ordinate non giovano'),[43] where 'are found neither laws nor institutions which will suffice to check widespread corruption'.[44]

When he speaks of rule of law, Machiavelli means, first of all, observance of the principle of legality—that is, the principle which prescribes that men's actions are to be judged on the basis of general rules which apply equally to all actions of the same type and to all individuals of the group concerned. Like the jurists, he sees the generality and the impartiality of the law as the basis of civil life. The laws, he says, 'make [men] good'—that is, compel them to serve the common good and refrain from harming their fellow-citizens, as civil and political life demands.[45] A wise legislator must frame the laws assuming that 'all men are wicked', and that they will always behave with malignity, if they have the opportunity. The law is therefore necessary, and, once it is in place, it must be obeyed without allowing for privileges or discriminations. As he strongly asserts, crimes have to be punished regardless of the personal and public merits of the criminal. No well-ordered republic ('republica bene ordinata'), he writes, 'allows the demerits of its citizens to be cancelled out by their merits; but, having prescribed rewards for a good deed and punishments for a bad one and having rewarded someone for doing well, if the same person afterwards does wrong, it punishes him, regardless of any of the good deeds he has done'. Should this principle of legal justice be disregarded, he concludes, and the wording is important, 'civil life will soon disappear' ('si risolverà ogni civilità').[46]

Machiavelli's commitment to the principle of legality is apparent also in his strong admonition that to remain well ordered, and to prevent corruption, a republic must be sure that punishments are always inflicted according to the law by legitimate public authorities, never by private citizens acting outside the law. Coriolanus, who commanded not to distribute corn to the people in order to diminish their political power, was saved from popular fury by the tribunes, who summoned him to appear in court. Had the mob lynched him, Machiavelli remarks, his death would have been a wrong inflicted by private citizens on a private citizen ('offesa da privati a privati'). This violation of legality would have caused fear and mistrust in the efficacy of the law to provide for adequate protection. As a result, citizens would have formed factions to protect themselves, thereby causing the downfall of the republic.[47] But, since the whole matter was settled by public authorities in full respect of the law—that is, in an orderly way ('ordinariamente'), the Roman Republic did not suffer serious consequences.[48]

When he speaks of rule of law, Machiavelli always means rule of just laws—that is, laws and statutes that aim at the common good. It is the law understood in this sense which is the foundation of true civil life and of the liberty of the citizens. As the anonymous speaker of the *Florentine Histories* eloquently explains, to restore a 'free and civil life' ('vero vivere libero e civile'), Florence needs new laws and statutes that will protect the common good and replace the rule of factions, which imposes 'orders and laws made not for the public but for personal utility', 'not in accordance with free life' but by the ambition of that party which is in power'.[49] In the *Discourses* he stresses that, when the Roman Republic became corrupt, 'only the powerful proposed laws, not for the common liberty, but to augment their own power'.[50]

The best government is that which is more apt to secure the rule of law and the common good. It is precisely from this angle that Machiavelli discusses the comparative merits of different forms of government. A political life can be ensured either through a republican government or through a monarchy, provided that, whoever the sovereign is, is bound by laws. Between the government of a people 'chained' ('incatenato') by the laws and that of a prince 'bound by the laws' ('obbligato dalle leggi'), Machiavelli firmly believes that the former is better than the latter; but the fundamental requisite in order to have a political life is that the sovereign, be it one or many, is under the law, because a prince 'who can do what he pleases is mad' and a people 'which does what it likes is unwise'.[51]

In his defence of the superiority of republican government over monarchy, Machiavelli restates the classical argument that, if deliberations on matters of general interest are entrusted to the many, it is more likely that the common good will prevail over particular interest. 'I claim', he writes in the *Discourses*,

that the populace is more prudent, more stable, and of sounder judgement than the prince. Not without good reason is the voice of the populace likened to that of God; for the opinion of the people is remarkably accurate in its prognostications, so much so that it seems as if the populace by some hidden power discerned the evil and the good that was to befall it.[52]

And in Book II of the same *Discourses*, he puts the point even more forcefully: only in republics is the common good 'looked to properly', because only in republics are the deliberations that are conducive to the common good carried out no matter if they hurt this or that private person. In a principality just the opposite is true, for what the prince does in his own interest usually harms the city, and what is done in the interests of the city 'harms him'.[53]

The protection of the rule of law is also Machiavelli's main concern in his discussion of the issue of the guardianship of liberty—that is, the institution of a specific magistracy with the power of supervising the legality of the decisions of governing bodies modelled after the Spartan ephors and Rome's tribunes.[54] The issue being discussed, as Machiavelli clearly indicates from the beginning, is security ('più sicuramente')—that is, whether the usurpation of the constitution of the republic and the imposition of factional interests can be better prevented, and therefore liberty better secured, by entrusting the guardianship of liberty to the populace or to the nobility.

Following the rhetorical method of arguing from both sides, he first presents the argument in favour of popular government: if we consider the goals of the nobility and of the common people, it will be clear that the nobility desires to dominate, whereas the ordinary people desire only not to be dominated and consequently to live free ('vivere liberi'); it is, therefore, reasonable to believe that the ordinary people will take greater care to protect liberty: 'since it is impossible for them to *usurp* power, they will not permit others to do so' (emphasis added). He then presents the reasons of the advocates of aristocratic government, who claim that it is safer to give a predominant role to the nobility because in this way they are satisfied and contented while at the same time the people are deprived of the opportunity of causing endless squabbles and trouble in the republic, as the examples of Sparta and Venice amply prove.

After he has admitted that, 'if due weight be given to both sides, it still remains doubtful which to select as the guardians of liberty', he settles the issue by reframing it in more general terms—that is, by posing the question who are more harmful in a republic: those who wish to have more or those who are afraid to lose what they already possess. Both can cause great turbulence, but the nobles who are afraid of losing what they possess are more dangerous, for 'men are inclined to think that they cannot hold securely what they possess unless they get more at the expense of others', and they have more means than the people to alter the constitution. Everything considered, then, it is wiser to entrust sovereign power in the hands of the ordinary citizens, if one wants to establish and preserve a true civil and free way of living.[55]

Machiavelli's republicanism is a commitment to a well-ordered popular government. By a well-ordered, or moderated, republic he means, in accordance with Cicero's concept of orderliness or moderation, a republic in which each component of the city has its proper place.[56] As examples, he cites Sparta, where Lycurgus introduced a constitution which 'assigned to the kings, to the aristocracy, and to the populace each its own function, and thus introduced a form of government which lasted for more than eight hundred years to his very great credit and to the tranquillity of that city', and Rome, which became a perfect republic ('repubblica perfetta') when, after the institution of the tribunes, 'all three estates now had a share' in the government.[57]

As an example of a badly ordered republic Machiavelli points to Florence, which never had a constitution capable of recognizing the place of each social group and therefore oscillated in its history between governments that were either too popular or too aristocratic. In the former case, the people deprived the nobility of the magistracies, with the result that the city became 'ever more humble and abject'; in the second, the people did not have a share in the government.[58] Because of its constitutional weaknesses, Florence has never had a republic that was capable of satisfying the humours of the different groups, and has therefore never been a stable republic.[59]

Machiavelli severely chastises the nobility's arrogance; but he also bitterly reproaches the ambition of the populace. Not content with having secured their position in regard to the nobles, Machiavelli remarks, the Roman people 'began to quarrel with the nobles out of ambition [per ambizione] and also to demand a share in the distribution of honours and of property'. This, he concludes, grew into a disease, which led to the dispute over the Agrarian Law and in the end caused the destruction of the Republic.[60] The ambition of the nobility would have ruined Rome's liberty much earlier, had not the people kept them in check for 300 years. In several cases, however, it was necessary to restrain the tribunes of the people too, because their ambition was harmful to the common good and the safety of the fatherland.[61]

Even more eloquent than the example of Rome was that of Florence, where the people wanted completely to exclude the nobility from the government in order to 'be alone in the government' ('essere solo nel governo'). Whereas the desire of the Roman people to share the highest honours with the nobles was reasonable, that of the people of Florence was 'injurious and unjust' ('ingiurioso e ingiusto').[62] With their exaggerated requests, the people of Florence compelled the nobility to resist with all their force, with the consequence that social conflict often degenerated into armed confrontations. Moreover, as long as the people were sharing the highest posts in the government with the nobles, they acquired 'the same virtue' that was typical of the nobility; but when the nobility was excluded from government, Florence could no longer avail itself of that 'virtue in arms and that generosity of spirit that were in the nobility', and became more and more 'humble and abject'.[63]

In the *Discourses* Machiavelli praises social conflict between the people and the nobles in Rome as a major cause of the preservation of liberty. Those conflicts, he remarks, led to laws and statutes in favour of public liberty—that is, laws that satisfied, at least to some extent, the people's and the nobles' interests. From Roman history he derives a general piece of advice for modern republics—namely, that 'in every republic there are two humours, that of the populace and that of the nobility, and that all legislation favourable to liberty is brought about by the clash between them'.[64]

Heterodox as it was, however, his praise of social conflict is consistent with his commitment to the principles of civil life. When he stresses the good effects of social conflicts, he refers in fact to conflicts that did not, or very rarely, exceed the boundaries of civil life and were settled 'by disputing' ('disputando'), as in Rome, not 'by fighting' ('combattendo'), as in Florence.[65] He condemns social conflicts which degenerate into armed confrontations as the most lethal danger for a republic, and he praises the conflicts that do not end with laws that imposed the domination of one group over the others, as was the case in Florence, but with laws that incorporated the claims of both, thereby preserving the common good, as was the case in Rome. Social conflicts, therefore, help to sustain common liberty only in so far as they do not violate the main prerequisite of civil life—that is, the rule of law and the common good.

Even though he remains loyal to the ideals of civil and political life, Machiavelli does not endorse the conventional wisdom which identifies true political life with the Republic of Venice. According to the prevailing understanding, the constitution of the Republic of Venice was considered to be the true model of political life, because it was a mixed constitution that ensured the rule of law, a remarkable stability, and social quiet. For Machiavelli, civil and political life does not need to be quiet. If the cost of social quiet and civic concord is to have a constitution that does not permit the republic to expand and to protect its own independence, the honourable advice to offer is for the republic to renounce social peace in order to put itself in the position of being capable of expansion.[66]

Venice, Machiavelli remarks, was able to preserve its much vaunted social peace by restricting the number of citizens with full political rights, and by not employing its people in war. This constitutional arrangement is rational as long as the city is powerful enough to discourage potential aggressors, and is able to remain free without expansion. But it may well be that the city needs to expand its territory, for instance, to weaken a powerful and aggressive neighbour. In this case, a constitution designed to preserve above all social peace turns out to be an obstacle to the city's liberty. For this reason Machiavelli urges the abandonment of what his contemporaries regarded as the model of the 'true political life and true quiet of a city' ('il vero vivere politico e la vera quiete d'una città'), and tries to persuade them that even a tumultuous republic with a large population and a civic army can be a *vivere politico*, if it respects the principles of the rule of law and the common good—with the additional advantage of being more secure and more honourable.[67]

However, the aspect of Machiavelli's republicanism which shows the greatest debt to the Roman legacy and the Florentine civic humanists is his analysis of political liberty. Like the civic humanists, and in a language similar to that of the jurists' and of the Roman republican authorities, he defines free men ('uomini liberi') as men who do not depend on others ('dependono da altri'),[68] and contrasts the status of a free citizen with that of a serf ('nascono liberi e non schiavi').[69] Accordingly, he defines free states as states 'accustomed to living under their own laws and in freedom' ('consueti a vivere con le loro legge et in libertà').[70] He maintains that individual citizens enjoy their liberty securely in an independent republic in which civil life is properly preserved. If the rule of law is restored and if the laws that promote the interest of factions are replaced with laws that aim at the common interest, Florence, says a good citizen in the *Florentine Histories*, will enjoy a 'true, free and civil life' ('vero vivere civile e libero').[71] On the contrary, as he explains in the *Discourses*, a city cannot be said to be free if there is a citizen 'whom the magistrates fear'.[72]

As he clarifies in the *Florentine Histories*, a city can be said to be free ('si può chiamar libera') if it has good laws and good orders which restrain the bad humours of both the nobles and the people—that is the desire of the former not to be subject either to the laws or to men, and the licence of the latter.[73] Free republics must be capable of moderating the citizens' passions and desires so that they do not transgress the boundaries of civil laws. One example is the Roman Republic, where the populace 'was never servilely obsequious, nor yet did it ever dominate with arrogance: on the contrary, with its own institutions, it honourably kept its own place'.[74] Another example, in Machiavelli's times, can be found in the German free cities, which 'enjoy freedom and observe their laws in such a way that neither outsiders nor their own inhabitants dare to usurp power there'.[75] And in an earlier chapter of the *Discourses*, he forcefully restates the fundamental connection between law and liberty by remarking that the dissolution of the republic initiates when 'one begins to corrupt a law which is the nerve and the life of the free way of living'.[76]

A monarch or a prince can satisfy the individual's desire to live securely, if he introduces orders and laws which aim at protecting both his power and the security of the people, and if he obeys the laws and does not permit others to violate them. If a prince does that, Machiavelli writes, the people will feel secure and content, as in the case of France, 'in which the people live in security simply because its kings are pledged to observe numerous laws on which the security of all their people depends'.[77]

However, political liberty is secure and can be enjoyed in its fullest extent only under a republican government, because, in addition to security, a good republic allows the citizens to enjoy a liberty which is precluded under monarchies and principalities— that is, the equal liberty to participate in public deliberations and to be called to sit in office and even to attain the highest honours— a dimension of political liberty which Florentine republicans praised, as we have seen, as a most precious good.

In a republic, Machiavelli writes in the *Discourses*, citizens are confident that their children 'will have the chance to become rulers', if they are virtuous; in a principality, on the contrary, this chance is precluded, because the prince 'cannot bestow honours on valiant and good citizens over whom he tyrannizes, since he does not want to have any cause to suspect them'.[78] Moreover, a republic ('vivere libero') rewards citizens 'only for honest and determinate reasons, and apart from this rewards and honours no one'.[79] A prince, on the contrary, can be easily persuaded to bestow public honours upon corrupt men.[80] Finally, and for Machiavelli this is a consideration of the greatest importance, in a good republic poor citizens have the same chance to attain public honours as anybody else: in Rome 'poverty did not bar you from any office or from any honour, and virtue was sought out no matter in whose house it dwelt'.[81] If the citizens appoint the magistrates, there are better chances that the positions of highest responsibility and prestige are filled by most eminent citizens. This is yet another reason why a republican government is the most fit to preserve a true 'political order'. As Machiavelli writes in the *Discourse on Remodelling the Government of Florence*, it is against any political order ('contro ad ogni ordine politico') not to appoint distinguished and honoured citizens to the highest offices of the republic.[82]

Machiavelli fully endorses yet another principle of political liberty which both Roman theorists and their Florentine admirers had pointed as a distinctive feature of a free city—namely, freedom of speech. Under a republican government, the citizens can govern themselves and freely express their opinions in public deliberations. Machiavelli offers as an example the Roman Republic, where 'a tribune or any other citizen could propose to the people a law, in regard to which every citizen was entitled to speak either in favour of it or against it, prior to a decision being reached'. It is a good thing, Machiavelli comments, 'that everyone should be at liberty to express his opinion', so that, 'when the people have heard what each has to say, they may choose the best plan'.[83]

Because it makes possible the secure enjoyment of all aspects of political liberty, Machiavelli literally identifies republic with liberty and opposes it not only to tyranny and licence but to monarchy and principality as well. *Pace* Meinecke and the other scholars who have described Machiavelli's republicanism as a republicanism with a monarchical or even tyrannical bent, Machiavelli maintains that principality, or monarchy, and liberty are antithetical, and liberty in its fullest expression can be enjoyed only in a republic. The much quoted opening of *The Prince* is eloquent in this regard: 'All the states, all the dominions that have held sway over men, have been either republics or principalities'; and a few lines later he reiterates the same distinction but replaces the word 'republic' with 'being free': 'states thus acquired are either used to living under a prince or used to being free ('usi a essere liberi').[84] In Chapter 5 he writes that 'when cities or countries are accustomed to living under a prince . . . the inhabitants are used to obey . . . and they do not know how to embrace a free way of life [vivere liberi]'; and in the chapter on 'Civil Principality', he mentions three mutually exclusive possibilities: 'a principality, a republic or licence' ('o principato o libertà o licenzia').

In the *Discourses* the examples of the identification between republican government and liberty are, of course, more abundant. A few references will do. In Book I, Chapter 16, he distinguishes between to govern a multitude 'through freedom' ('per via di libertà') or 'through a principality' ('per via di principato'). And in Book II, Chapter 2, he remarks that in ancient times the peoples of Italy 'were all of them free', and among them 'one never hears of there being any kings'; Tuscany, in particular, was free, and it enjoyed its freedom very much, and very much hated the very name 'prince'. Lastly, in Book III, Chapter 12, speaking of the towns around Venice, he remarks that 'they are accustomed to living under a prince [*use a vivere sotto uno principe*] and are not free [*e non libere*]'.

To live under a monarch or a prince, as the passages quoted above show, means to be unfree, not only in the sense that the citizens are precluded from the enjoyment of political liberty—that is, the participation in sovereign deliberations and the appointment of the magistrates—but also in the sense that they are in a condition of dependency on the will of a man. They are not a *populus liber* which lives under its own laws; they are in servitude. Under a monarch, subjects may enjoy a modicum of security, which, however, is always precarious because of their dependency on the monarch's will. Since subjects have no power to prevent the monarch from passing laws that serve his own or others' particular interest, they are at any moment liable to be oppressed. The constant possibility of being oppressed which comes from the subjects' condition of dependency generates feelings of fear which in turn stimulate servile habits utterly incompatible with the status and the duties of a free people. As Machiavelli puts it in a well-known passage from the *Discourses*, the distinctive sign of republican liberty is the absence of the fear of being oppressed: the common advantage which results from republican self-government 'vivere libero' is 'the possibility of enjoying what one has, freely and without incurring suspicion, for instance, not to fear for the honour of women, and of one's children, not to fear for oneself'.[85] Absence of fear keeps away servility, as was the case with Rome, as long as 'the Republic lasted uncorrupt', where the Roman people 'never served humbly'.[86]

Political Corruption and its Remedies

The analysis of Machiavelli's theory of the republic and of republican liberty can be repeated in specular terms by looking at the matter from the opposite side—that is, from the side of corruption. And if we study Machiavelli's republicanism from the angle of corruption, it is even clearer that its essence is the ideal of civil and political life. Machiavelli himself speaks in various instances of political life as the opposite of corruption and he contrasts a 'civil and free way of living' ('uno vivere civile e libero') with tyranny ('vivere assoluto e tirannico').[87] Elsewhere, speaking of German free cities, he positively connects political life with non-corrupt life ('vivere politico e incorrotto').[88] While in the 'vivere politico' the law rules over men, in the corrupt republic laws are disobeyed. When the citizens are corrupt, he writes, 'good laws are of no avail'.[89] A 'most corrupt city' ('città corrottisima'), he explains, is one in which 'there will be found neither laws nor institutions which will suffice to check widespread corruption'.[90]

The corruption that destroys civil and political life is the corruption of the customs, of the habits of the citizens, their unwillingness to put the common good above private or factional interest. Corruption also is an absence of *virtù*, a kind of laziness, of inaptitude for political activity, or lack of the moral and physical strength that is necessary to resist tyranny and to stop ambitious and arrogant men from imposing their domination over the polity.

Corruption is a disease that penetrates the deepest fibres of collective life, permeates the manners, and perverts the citizens' judgement on honour and glory. Machiavelli's clearest portrait of the corrupt republic is to be found in the *Florentine Histories*, where an anonymous citizen describes the state of the city at the times of the struggle between the Ricci and the Albizzi:

the young are lazy, the old lascivious; both sexes at every age are full of foul customs, for which good laws, because they are spoiled by wicked use, are no remedy. From this grows the avarice that is seen in our citizens and the appetite, not for true glory, but for the contemptible honours on which hatreds, enmities, differences, and sects depend; and from these arise deaths, exiles, persecution of the good, exaltation of the wicked.[91]

In the corrupt republic there is no true civic friendship, as citizens gather only to do evil against the fatherland, or against other citizens; there is no mutual trust, as oaths and faiths are respected only as long as they are useful or deceive. The citizens' judgement on persons and actions is perverted: harmful men ('uomini nocivi') are praised as industrious ('industriosi') and good men are blamed as fools.[92] The perversion of language, whereby evil men are called industrious and the good fools, is for Machiavelli, who restates once again a classical view, one of the clearest signs of the corruption of customs.[93]

The contrast between civil and political life and corruption is also evident from Machiavelli's treatment of religion. Religiosity and fear of God, two fundamental foundations of political life, are not to be found in corrupt cities. In his description of Rome under the emperors, he mentions 'the ancient temples lying desolate' and 'religious rites grown corrupt'.[94] The same holds true for Florence at the height of its corruption, where 'religion and fear of God have been eliminated in all'.[95] Neglect of divine worship and the lack of fear of God causes the ruin of republics or requires the presence of a prince to instil fear in the hearts of the subjects.[96] Without fear of God citizens are not only unable to perform great deeds of courage and resistance when the liberty of their country is at stake, but are also incapable of obeying the laws and living with civility.[97]

Along with a careful diagnosis of corruption, Machiavelli devotes large sections of the *Discourses* to investigate its causes. He points first to the servile origin of the cities. A city which 'at the outset was in servitude to another', he remarks, 'would find it not merely difficult, but impossible, ever to draw up a constitution that will enable it to enjoy tranquillity in the conduct of its affairs'.[98] The example is Florence, which was founded under the emperors and, having always lived under foreign rule, remained for a time 'abject' and incapable of taking care of itself. When it attained some liberty, it attempted to give itself good political orders, but since the new ones were mingled with the old ones that were unfit for free government, they turned out not to be good. For this reason, Florence has never had a political regime 'such as would entitle it rightly to be called a republic'.[99]

Another cause of corruption is princely or monarchical rule. As I stressed when I discussed Machiavelli's conception of political liberty, peoples who have been living for a long time under a prince acquire servile habits; they do not know how to govern themselves, how to deliberate on public matters, or how to defend themselves from external enemies. If, by chance, they become free, they soon fall under the domination of another prince.[100] It was, therefore, a great fortune for Rome that the kings 'quickly became corrupt, with the result that they were expelled before their corruption had penetrated to the bowels of that city'.[101] When the Roman people was not corrupt, it was capable of preserving the liberty that it had attained after the expulsion of the kings; but when it became 'extremely corrupt', it was unable to preserve the liberty it had regained when Caesar was killed, and even less when Gaius Caligula and Nero were killed, and 'the whole of Caesar's stock was exterminated'.[102]

Princely government had eroded the citizens' moral and physical strength: instead of learning how to serve the common good, they had learnt to serve powerful men and had got used to depending on somebody's will.[103] Whether we focus on Machiavelli's theory of the good republic, or on his portrait of the corrupt republic, we isolate the idea that political liberty is incompatible not only with arbitrary and absolute power, but also with monarchy.

Personal dependence and therefore corruption are also caused by 'absolute power' and by exaggerated wealth. Absolute power ('autorità assoluta'), says Machiavelli, can very soon corrupt even a virtuous city, because whoever has such a power can have friends and partisans—that is, citizens who are loyal to him, and not to the constitution.[104] Exaggerated wealth is a source of corruption for similar reasons. Wealthy citizens can easily obtain an outstanding power incompatible with civic equality and the rule of law by doing private favours, such as lending money, paying for dowries, protecting felons from the magistrates. Through favours, they form powerful cohorts of partisans and friends who feel even more encouraged to become 'corrupters of public morals and law breakers'.[105]

Another cause of personal dependence and therefore of corruption is the 'gentry' ('gentiluomini')—that is, people who live 'in idleness on the abundant revenue derived from their estates, without having anything to do either with their cultivation or with other forms of labour essential to life'.[106] The gentry are pernicious to civil life, not only because of their idle and corrupt way of life, but also, and above all, because they have subjects who are 'under their obedience' and therefore are dependent on them. For this reason, no republic and no political life ('alcuna republica, né alcuno vivere politico') has ever lasted for long in the Kingdom of Naples, in Rome, in Romagna, and in Lombardy, where the gentry are numerous and powerful. Rightly, therefore, German free cities which want to preserve their 'political and uncorrupted' way of life do kill the gentry, whenever they have the chance, as causes of corruption ('causa di corruttela').[107]

Lastly, a powerful cause of corruption is Christian religion, or, more precisely, the interpretation of it 'according to laziness and not according to virtue'.[108] As it has been taught by the Roman Catholic Church, Christian religion has rendered the world weak and made it an easy prey for 'wicked men', because it has 'glorified more humble and contemplative men than men of action' and 'has assigned as man's highest good humility, abnegation, and contempt for mundane things'. Unlike pagan religion, which placed the highest good in the greatness of soul and in the strength of the body, Christian religion exhorts men to be strong, not in order to accomplish great deeds, but in order to suffer. No longer educated to perform virtuous deeds, men became an easy prey for tyrants.[109]

Whatever the causes, corruption destroys the fundamental principle on which civil life rests—namely, the rule of law and the priority of the common good over particular interests. Which means that corruption destroys political liberty and puts a people in a state of servitude. It is for this reason, and not because of his alleged commitment to the ideal of *virtù*, that Machiavelli devotes so much effort to investigating the institutional and political measures that have to be adopted to preserve the civil and free form of life and successfully to repeal tyranny and corruption, as well as to prevent the republic from falling under yet another form of lack of freedom and dependence—that is, under foreign domination. Whereas in his outline of the essential features of true civil community and his account of political liberty Machiavelli follows the conventional wisdom that humanist political theorists had built upon Roman political philosophy and Roman Law, his investigations of the constitutional and political devices that are needed to preserve and recover a civil and free community diverge in important aspects from traditional views. However, as I hope to be able to clarify, the precise content of his revisions of the conventional wisdom on civil and political life can be perceived only if we also take seriously his intellectual and ideological debt to that tradition.

For Machiavelli, to avoid tyranny or licence, a free and civil community must be well ordered, which means, first of all that it must respect with the utmost intransigence the principles of legal order. Even if the culprit is the most wicked man, even if he has perpetrated the most nefarious crimes against the republic, still his legal rights must be protected, if civil life has to be preserved. Machiavelli illustrates this point with the utmost briskness in his comment on the death of Appius Claudius, the chief of the Decemviri who imposed a tyranny in Rome, who was denied the right to appeal to the people [*appellatio ad populum*]. Because of the gravity of his crimes, Appius Claudius no doubt merited the severest punishment; however, Machiavelli writes, and again his wording has to be noticed, 'it scarce accorded with civil life [*fu cosa poco civile*] to violate the law, especially a law that had just been made'.[110]

Machiavelli's advocacy of legal order as the fundamental basis of civil life is even more eloquent in his judgements of momentous cases that occurred under the Republic of Florence in his own times. It was a frequent practice in Florence to violate legality either by passing *ad hoc* statutes designed to protect the power of ruling groups and families, or by openly disregarding existing legislation. The most recurrent considerations that were put forth to justify the violation of laws and statutes were arguments based on the classical *topos* of necessity and expediency. In 1501, for instance, the lawyer Domenico Bonsi, a moderate Savonarolian, urged the Signoria not to be too rigorous in the observance of the laws: 'the Signoria should be trusted, that to want certitude in everything is impossible, that affairs must be conducted according to accident and circumstance, and that one should not will the ruin of the city by [always] insisting on the observance of the laws'.[111]

An eloquent example of the Florentine republican élite's attitude on legality was the trial of Paolo Vitelli, a captain of Florentine troops in the war against Pisa. Accused of treason, he was brought to trial on 1 October 1499 and sentenced to death. The mood of the jury which led to the death sentence was well summarized by the words of Niccolò Altoviti, a doctor in civil and canon law: 'under no circumstances should Paolo Vitelli be let off with his life: first because of his contacts with your rebels [the Pisans], which he denies not and for which he deserves by law to die.' Next, Altoviti remarked that, in view of the man's rank, place, and what he could do to hurt the Republic, [we] should not proceed according to legal forms [*secondo e'termini di ragione*], for this is not the way things are usually done in the affairs of states [*chè cosí non si suole nelle cose delli stati*]'.[112]

But the most significant debate on legality which took place in Machiavelli's times was surely that which occurred on the occasion of the trial and subsequent death sentence against five leading Florentine citizens—Bernardo del Nero, Niccolò Ridolfi, Lorenzo Tornabuoni, Giannozzo Pucci, and Giovanni Cambi—accused in August 1497 of conspiring to restore the Medici's regime. According to a law in part inspired by Savonarola and passed in March 1495, any citizen condemned to death, or exile, or the payment of more than 300 large florins had the right to appeal to the Signoria, and the Signoria was obliged to present the appeal before the Grand Council.

To the above-mentioned citizens, however, that right was denied. We have records of the opinions of some of the lawyers who supported the decision to oppose the appeal, and two of them, in particular, resorted to the argument of necessity. Domenico Bonsi, for instance, noted that the appeal law allowed for exceptions, 'above all when such delay threatens to put the city into an imminent danger'. Luca Corsini, speaking on behalf of the committee called the Eight on Public Safety, remarked that, since the Republic had been restored, 'the city has been besieged and hated by those who want to live tyrannically', and concluded that 'the law appears to grant the right of appeal, but if this [exposes] the city to an obvious danger, then such appeal must be denied to avoid a danger which would bring ruin to the city'.[113]

Whereas Machiavelli seems to have agreed with the Florentine authorities on Vitelli's case,[114] he strongly disagreed with them on the trial against the five citizens sentenced to death on charge of conspiracy against the Republic. Against the opinion of the Republic's authorities and a number of eminent lawyers, he judges the matter in exactly the same way he judged the conduct of the Roman Republic in the case of Appius—namely, as yet another violation of the principles of civil life and as a grave political error. He qualifies such mistakes as the worst example that a republic can set ('non credo che sia cosa di più cattivo esemplo'), and remarks that the fact that Savonarola did not speak up against the decision to deny the five citizens the right to appeal to the Grand Council lessened his reputation more than anything else. Both in the case of Appius and in that of the five Florentine citizens, Machiavelli sides in favour of the respect of legality, even if in both cases the death sentences were passed against enemies of liberty to secure the interest of the state ('per conto di stato'). The lawyers had crafted fine arguments to justify the violation of the law on behalf of the Republic's safety; Machiavelli, the alleged champion of the priority of politics over the law, stands for legality.

To protect a republic from corruption, magistrates must be inflexible in defending the rule of law, particularly in the case of eminent or famous citizens who threaten the statutes of the republic. Capital sentences executed against prominent citizens such as the sons of Brutus, the Decemviri, Maelius, Manlius Capitolinus, and the action taken by Papirius Cursor against Fabius and the charge brought against the Scipios were so noteworthy and sufficiently close to one another in time that they kept the fear of punishment well alive in people, thereby compelling them to respect the laws. When memorable executions became less frequent, men began to break the laws and to be corrupt ('corrompersi'). It is, therefore, always useful, Machiavelli remarks, to remember the severity of Brutus, the father of Roman liberty, who not only sat on a tribunal and condemned his own sons to death, but attended the execution.[115]

The republic must count on very severe and intransigent citizens who are 'wholly devoted to the common good' ('amando solo il bene comune') and are 'in no way affected by private ambition' ('e non risguarda in alcuna parte all'ambizione privata').[116] In addition to the virtue of the magistrates, republics demand the virtue of the whole citizenry, if corruption and tyranny are to be successfully repealed. As I shall be discussing in the next chapter, Machiavelli describes the virtue that republics need as love of country. At this stage of the argument, however, it has to be stressed that the virtue he praises is always linked with a respect of the rule of law, and he praises it as a means to keep the republic well ordered.

Machiavelli's own examples illustrate well his conception of a virtuous citizenry. As long as the Roman Republic was incorrupt ('incorrotta'), he writes, the Roman people honourably kept its own place, obeyed the consuls and the dictators when the public safety so required ('per la salute pubblica'), and resisted against powerful citizens when they were attempting to destroy public liberty. The same is true also for his favourite example of virtuous citizenry in modern times—that is, the German free cities. Their civic virtue, he remarks, consists above all in the fact that they 'observe their laws' and do not permit anyone to 'usurp them', and in the fact that they dutifully discharge their civic obligations, beginning with paying taxes in proportion to their income as determined by the city's magistrates.[117]

The civic virtue which Machiavelli extols is an everyday virtue which translates into orderly fulfilment of civic obligations and abiding by the law more often then expressing itself as military valour. The republic is not the embodiment of virtue, nor is it instituted to affirm and enhance virtue; it is a civil order which needs virtue. The difference must be noticed, for it cast the right light on the republic and civic virtue, as Machiavelli understood them both.

In addition to these precepts, Machiavelli issues another fundamental piece of advice to protect the republic from corruption—namely, to uphold religion and respect, and encourage religious worship. Those princes and those republics which 'desire to remain free from corruption', he remarks, should above all else maintain the ceremonies of their religion incorrupt and should always hold them in veneration; there can be no surer indication of the decline of a country than to see divine worship neglected. Even if the rulers of the republic or a prince do not believe at all in God, they must none the less be sure that citizens practise religious worship. As long as their republic remains religious, it will also be 'good and united' ('buona e unita')—that is, incorrupt.[118]

Where there is religion, it is easy to form good armies and train men to military discipline, which is the other fundamental shield against the spread of corruption. Machiavelli states this principle in *The Prince*: 'The main foundations of all states (whether they are new, old, or mixed) are good laws and good armies, since it is impossible to have good laws if good armies are lacking, and if there are good arms there must also be good laws.'[119] In the *Art of War* he carries the argument further, stressing that, against the conventional view which holds that military and civil life are incompatible to one another, the classics rightly teach us that in fact the two are compatible and in fact that one requires the other:

because all the arts that are provided for in a civil community are for the sake of the common good of men, all the statutes made in it so that men will live in fear of the laws and of God would be in vain if for them there were not provided defenses, which when well ordered, preserve them, even though they themselves are not well ordered. And so, on the contrary, good customs, without military support, suffer the same sort of injury as do the rooms of a splendid and kingly palace, even though ornamented with gems and gold, when, not being roofed over, they have nothing to protect them from the rain.[120]

Republics which train the citizens to military discipline without, however, ever allowing them to practise warfare as their profession succeed in warding off corruption. As long as Rome maintained its military orderings incorrupt, the whole Republic also 'remained immaculate' ('visse immacolata'): 'no great citizen ever presumed, by means of such an activity, to retain power in time of peace, so as to break the laws, plunder the provinces, usurp and tyrannize over his native land and in every way gain wealth for himself.'[121] A well-ordered republic should, therefore, 'decree that this practice of warfare shall be used in times of peace for exercise and in times of war for necessity and for glory'.[122] If the practice of the art of war is firmly under the control of the laws, the republic should not fear at all that its armed citizens might become seditious; instead, it should value its armed citizens as the safest foundation of its civil life and its liberty.[123]

Machiavelli's advocacy of military discipline and virtue certainly does not entail that his republicanism is inspired by a fascination for conquest and predation, as has been claimed. Like that of the earlier theorists of communal self-government, his republicanism is informed by the commitment to the ideals of liberty and greatness, and he surely identifies civic greatness with, among other things, territorial expansion. However, for him territorial aggrandizement does not mean conquest and predatory expansionism. The ancient Tuscans, he writes, attained a remarkable greatness [*grandezza*], not through conquest, but by forming a league consisting of several republics in which no one of them had preference, authority, or rank above the others; and 'when other cities were acquired, they made them constituent members in the same way as the Swiss act in our times, and as the Acheans and the Aetolians acted in Greece in olden times'.[124] He highly praises their method of attaining greatness as one which resulted in the greatest glory of empire and of arms and sustained most laudable customs and religiosity, and warmly recommends it to his fellow-Florentines as being the best one, if the imitation of the Romans should appear 'difficult'. At the same time, and not just in the *Discourses* but in all his writings on the subject, he condemns the policy of expansion through conquest and subjection, as being 'completely useless' ('al tutto inutile'), in general, and 'most useless' ('inutilissima') for unarmed republics.

Even the Roman method of expansion, which he ranks as the best of all, is not, at least in the way he presents it, predatory at all, since it consisted in forming alliances 'in which you reserve yourself the headship, the seat in which the central authority resides, and the right of initiative', and in granting Roman citizenship to conquered or allied peoples. One of the aspects of Roman expansionist policy which he exalts in the most eloquent manner was their practice of letting 'those towns they did not demolish live under their own laws, even those that surrendered not as partners but as subjects', and of not leaving in them 'any sign of the empire of the Roman people', but obliging them 'to some conditions, which, if observed, kept them in their state and dignity'.[125]

With equal eloquence he praises the Florentines' protective and benevolent policy towards Pistoia and blames their predatory policy towards Pisa, Siena, and Lucca. The result of the former was that the Pistoiese were so quick and so willing to accept the Florentine's rule; the result of the latter was that 'the others have exerted and exert all their force so as not to come under it'.[126] Hence his exhortation to pursue expansion either by leagues or by providing protection and to employ armed violence only as a last instance: 'I do not mean to say that armed forces should not have been used, but that they should be used only as a last resort, where and when other means are not enough'.[127]

Machiavelli's hostility to predatory expansionism is also apparent in other comments on his own Republic's foreign politics. In the *Florentine Histories*, for instance, he praises the deliberation to try to regain authority over Arezzo and the other Tuscan cities that had rebelled against Florence during the tyranny of the Duke of Athens by recognizing their liberty instead of using force:

[The Florentines] sent spokesmen to Arezzo to renounce the dominion they had over that city and to sign an accord with them, so that, since they could no longer have them as subjects, they might profit from them as friends of their city. With the other towns they also made agreements as best they could, provided that they keep the Florentines as friends, so that, being free, the other towns could help maintain the Florentines' own freedom.

This policy, Machiavelli comments, was 'prudent', and led to felicitous results. In many cases greatness and security can better be attained by providing cities and peoples with protection instead of oppressing them.[128] For this reason he criticizes Florence's policy towards the subjects of the dominion for not being sufficiently just and for failing to gain their loyalty by providing them with adequate protection against external aggression and against wrongdoers.[129]

Machiavelli's most eloquent dismissal of predatory expansionism is to be found in his account of the war that Florence, under Lorenzo the Magnificent's leadership, waged against Volterra in 1472. To settle a controversy over the proprietorship of a alum mine, Machiavelli reports in the *Florentine Histories*, the Volterrans sent their spokesmen to Florence. Florentine authorities deliberated that the mine belonged to its owners, who, however, should have paid to the people of Volterra a sum of money every year. Volterra being a subject city, it was obliged to abide by the Florentines' verdict. Instead violent tumults arose in Volterra which ultimately led to open rebellion against Florence's domination.

Two different positions were discussed in Florence as to how to deal with Volterra's rebellion. On the one hand, Tommaso Soderini advocated a peaceful agreement that would have at least partially satisfied the Volterrans' claims; a lean truce, he stressed, is better than a fat victory. On the other hand, Lorenzo de' Medici wanted to undertake a military campain against Volterra to demonstrate, as Machiavelli put it, 'how much his advice and prudence were worth, especially as he was being encouraged by those who were envious of the authority of Messer Tommaso'. As Machiavelli's narration makes clear, the conflict with Volterra was for Lorenzo the occasion to affirm his own leadership over the city.

Attacked by overwhelming forces, poorly defended by fickle mercenaries, politically isolated, the Volterrans had no other choice but to surrender to the Florentine commissioners. Once inside Volterra, the Florentine commissioners ordered the magistrates of Volterra to abandon their posts, and to return home. But, Machiavelli, narrates, on the way, one of them was plundered, in contempt, by a soldier:

from this beginning, as men are more ready for evil than good, arose the destruction and sacking of the city. For a whole day it was robbed and over-run; neither women nor holy places were spared, and the soldiers—both those who had defended it badly and those who had fought against it—stripped it of its property.

What makes Machiavelli's account truly remarkable is not only the fact that he openly points to the Florentines' responsibility for the sack; but also his unequivocal condemnation of Lorenzo's predatory expansionism.[130] The chapter on Volterra does in fact end, not with a celebration of Lorenzo's prudence, but with Tommaso Soderini's words: 'to me it [Volterra] appears lost; for if you had received it by accord, you would have had advantage and security from it; but since you have to hold it by force, in adverse times it will bring you weakness and trouble and in peaceful times, loss and expense.' Yet another restatement of the political principle he had amply elucidated in the *Discourses*—namely, that predatory expansionism is most useless, indeed damaging.

For Machiavelli, lust for conquest from a mere desire to increase one's own power is not a virtue, but a nefarious vice. It does not lead to greatness, but to ruin. The most frequent cause of the fall of kingdoms and republics, he writes in *The Golden Ass*, is that the powerful with their power ('potenza') 'are never satisfied'. The desire of conquering, 'destroys the states', and, even if all recognize the error, 'none flees from it'. And a few lines later, he contrasts Venice, Sparta, and Athens, which fell in ruin after they had conquered the powers around them, with the German free cities, which live 'secure', even if their dominion does not extend more than six miles round about.[131]

When he urges the Florentines to provide themselves with good armies, he does not allure them with prospects of conquest and predation, nor does he evoke the commonplace of Florence's superiority and its claim to dominate over other peoples, as Bruni and other Quattrocento Humanists did. On the contrary, he employs rhetorical devices to persuade Florentine authorities that the republic needs an army to avoid finding itself in a condition of dependency and therefore to protect its own liberty.[132] As he explains in the oration he composed to persuade the Great Council to authorize new taxes to levy a civic militia, no wise king or republic has ever put its state at the mercy of other powers or has considered itself to be secure when it had to count on others' help. He offers on this matter a precise rule: each city, each state, must regard as enemies all those powers which can occupy its territory and against which it cannot defend itself.[133]

From this it follows that, if a republic wants to secure its freedom, it must attain that greatness which permits it to defend itself without being dependent on somebody else's help. A republic, or a principality, must then pursue territorial greatness as a means to attain security. And it must pursue it, not through conquest and predation but through appropriate alliances, through leagues, and by protecting and treating with justice subject cities and peoples, and by using military might only as a last resort.

Redemptive Politics

Even if they can count on good laws and good armies, however, republics will not be able to last for long, if they do not provide themselves with specific constitutional devices which allow them to deal successfully with situations of emergency, when rapid decisions are needed and extraordinary measures must be taken. If a republic does not have constitutional procedures to face situations of emergency, it is bound either to stand by the constitution and ruin, or to violate the constitution in order to save itself.

In his analysis of this delicate issue of statecraft Machiavelli reveals once again his commitment to the principles of legality which constitute the basis of civil and political life. He does not recommend a reliance on a redeemer or on a man of exceptional virtue who is capable of saving the republic by using extraordinary means. On the contrary, he urges republics to predispose legal procedures to face situations of necessity. Even though extraordinary measures may do good in some cases, yet 'the precedent thus established is bad, since it sanctions the usage of dispensing with constitutional orders for a good purpose, and thereby makes it possible, on some plausible pretext, to dispense with them for a bad purpose'. Therefore 'no republic is ever perfect, unless by its laws [con le leggi sue] it has provided for all contingencies, and for every eventuality it has provided a remedy and determined the method of applying it'. The example which Machiavelli points to is, this time, Venice—a detail worth noticing since Machiavelli is not at all keen to praise Venice. In this case, however, he cannot avoid a word of praise for that republic which has provided itself with legal means to face situations of emergency.[134]

However, if a republic lacks constitutional arrangements that permit it to face situations of emergency, its leaders must take upon themselves the burden of violating the laws and use extraordinary powers. Pier Soderini, the lifetime Gonfaloniere of the Republic of Florence, was clearly told that the Medici's partisans were plotting to destroy the republican government, but, Machiavelli reports, he refused to assume extraordinary powers and break civil equality because he believed he would be able to extinguish the malevolence of the enemies of the republic 'by patience and goodness', and he thought that, had he assumed extraordinary powers, the Florentines would have been alarmed and would 'never again agree to appoint a Gonfaloniere for life'.

Soderini's concerns were 'wise and good', Machiavelli comments. However, he adds that 'an evil should never be allowed to continue out of respect for a good when that good may easily be overwhelmed by that evil'.[135] Moreover, Soderini did not consider that, if he had assumed extraordinary powers, the Florentines would have understood that he did it for his country's safety and not for his own ambition. The outcome of his patience, goodness, and respect for the laws at all costs was that he lost 'his country, his status, and his reputation'.[136]

Situations of emergency are severe tests that only well-ordered republics can pass. But an even more prohibitive and almost impossible achievement is to redeem a corrupt republic and restore in it a political life. Machiavelli describes the redemption of a corrupt republic as the most glorious task of all:

should a prince seek worldly glory, he should most certainly covet possession of a city that has become corrupt, not, like Caesar, to complete its corruption, but, like Romulus, to reorder it. Nor in very truth can the heavens afford men a better opportunity of acquiring glory; nor can men desire anything better than this.[137]

Recovery and redemption of a corrupt republic can be attempted either by peaceful means through the reform of the existing orders, or by violence and absolute authority. Of the two, *pace* the commentators who have insisted on Machiavelli's propensity to recommend extraordinary over ordinary means, Machiavelli strongly urges the former. To use extraordinary means to institute a republic in a corrupt city, one must become prince of the city and be able to dispose of it as one thinks fit. To reorder a city to political life, therefore, a good man is needed, whereas to gain absolute power presupposes a bad man. Therefore, Machiavelli concludes, 'very rarely will there be found a good man ready to use bad methods in order to make himself prince, though with a good end in view; nor yet a bad man who, having become a prince, is ready to do the right thing and to whom it will occur to use for good that authority which he has acquired by bad means'.[138] A similar warning to try to reform the republic's institutions through legal rather than violent means is also repeated in the *Florentine Histories*, where a patriot ends his exhortation to the Signoria to restore a 'true free and civil life' in Florence by stressing that it is better 'to do now, with the benignity of the laws, [*con la benignità delle leggi*] that which, after deferring, men may be required by necessity to do with the support of arms [*con il favor dell' armi*]'.[139]

Certainly, Machiavelli also insists on the difficulty of restoring political life in a corrupt city through a peaceful reform of its orders. The reform could be peacefully carried out if a prudent man sees the weaknesses of the existing orders and persuades his fellow-citizens to change them. But prudent men rarely arise, and even more rarely do they manage to persuade the citizens to change the mode of life which they are accustomed to in order to prevent an evil that they do not yet see. Hence, the reform of the city through ordinary means is, like that through violence and absolute authority, also almost impossible.

What makes the work of a redeemer truly glorious is the fact that the goal of redemption is the restoration of the rule of law; and the most glorious redemption is that which is accomplished through the laws. Of the two most important celebrations of redeemers that Machiavelli composed, one refers to a prince who should liberate Italy with the armies; the other, to be found in the *Discourse on Remodelling the Government of Florence*, refers to a wise and powerful citizen who peacefully carries out the restoration of the republic. In both cases, what makes the achievement glorious is the institution of new orders and new laws. War and armies, he says in the 'Exhortation to Liberate Italy', quoting Livy, are just because they are necessary, and arms become holy when there is no other hope but in them; but, he adds, and the qualification is important, 'nothing brings so much honour to a new ruler as new laws and new orders that he has devised'. It is the restoration or the institution of laws and orders that 'will make him revered and admired'.[140] In the peroration that ends the *Discourse on Remodelling the Government of Florence*, he restates the same concept:

no man is so much exalted by any act of his as are those men who have with laws and with institutions remodeled republics and kingdoms; these are, after those who have been gods, the first to be praised. And because there have been few who have had opportunity to do it, and very few of those who have understood how to do it, the number who have done it is small. And so much has this glory been esteemed by men seeking for nothing other than glory that, when unable to form a republic in reality, they have done it in writing, as Aristotle, Plato, and many others, who have wished to show the world that, if they have not founded a free government, as did Solon and Lycurgus, they have failed not through their ignorance but through their impotence for putting it into practice.[141]

To say that the restoration of a political life is almost impossible does not mean to say that it should not be attempted. It means rather that only extraordinary men will be able to carry it through. By their outstanding virtue and courage, they will give life to new orders that will restrain men's ambition and insolence. These exceptional citizens must not hesitate to use almost regal power ('una mano quasi regia') in order to check men's insolence. Machiavelli's wording is important; he speaks of shifting the republic towards monarchical government, and to use almost regal powers; he means that, of the three elements that ought to form a well ordered government—namely, the monarchical, the aristocratic, and the popular—one, the monarchical or executive, has for a while to have predominance over the other.[142]

The argument that the restoration of political life can only be accomplished, if at all, by one man alone who uses an almost regal authority does not contradict at all the fact that Machiavelli's republicanism is a commitment to the principles of the civil and political life, and to a mixed government which includes an almost monarchical element in the *persona* of the Gonfaloniere or a Doge who must, when corruption threatens civil life, assume extraordinary powers to impose the rule of law.

Nor is Machiavelli's emphasis on the extraordinary virtue of founders and redeemers incompatible with his advocacy of the rule of law which is the core of his republicanism. In the formative moments of the republic, when the laws are not in place, and in the moments of crisis, when the laws are in place but are not respected because of the omnipresent corruption, it is necessary for a founder or redeemer to use his outstanding virtue to institute the laws, or to make the laws obeyed again. The restoration of liberty in a corrupt city is the work of the virtue of one man alone, not of the laws; it is due, as Machiavelli remarks, to the 'simple virtue of one man alone independently of any law'.[143] It is a 'simple virtue', however, which does not supplant the rule of law at all, but in fact founds or restores it.

Rule of law and rule of men are both essential components of Machiavelli's republican theory. One cannot exist, or continue to exist, without the other: when the rule of law has not yet been instituted or when it has been spoiled by corruption, it is time for men's virtue to come forth to institute the rule of law or give laws and statutes a new life.[144] Once the foundational or redemptive work is completed, the care of the republic must be entrusted to the many, and the many must have it dear, if it is to last, as he puts it in the *Discourses*.[145] Where the virtue of founders, redeemers, and ordinary citizens comes from, when it comes, is the subject of next chapter.

5

The Passion of Liberty

A theorist who composed the 'Exhortation to Liberate Italy' and declared 'I love my country more than my soul' can hardly be doubted to have been a fervent patriot. His reputation as a patriot in part redeemed him from the sinister fame as adviser of tyrants and perfidious teacher of corrupt politics. Writing in 1827, Lord Macaulay stressed that although it is scarcely possible to read *The Prince* 'without horror and amazement', 'we are acquainted with few writings which exhibit so much elevation of sentiment, so pure and warm zeal for the public good . . . as those of Machiavelli'. His 'patriotic wisdom', Macaulay concludes, offered an oppressed people 'the last chance of emancipation and revenge'.[1] When Macaulay was writing these lines, that oppressed people was beginning to recognize Machiavelli as the prophet of its independence and national unity. Carlo Cattaneo, one of the best minds of the Italian Risorgimento, wrote that Machiavelli, who had been for three centuries the 'remorse of the conscience of unarmed Italy', had become the symbol of a people who at last are resolved to recover their dignity.[2]

Yet, other scholars have not only openly questioned the view of Machiavelli as a forerunner of Italian national consciousness, but have claimed that it is a plain anachronism to place him among modern theorists of the principle of nationality. Luigi Russo, writing in 1936 against nationalist rhetoric of the time, remarked that the famous 'Exhortation to Liberate Italy' is just another version of the late medieval cry against the barbarians, and that Machiavelli regarded the unification of Italy as the political act of a prince or a monarch, not as the necessary completion of the cultural unity of the Italian people. Since he lacked the romantic view of the nation as a moral ideal, he could not be the 'prophet of Italian unity', but only an unrefined patriot.[3]

Russo was right: Machiavelli was not a theorist of the nation nor an advocate of the value of nationhood; but surely he was a patriot, or, more precisely, a republican patriot. This distinction may sound to us a pedantic point, used as we are to believing that patriotism and nationalism are the same. On the contrary, it is essential to grasp the meaning of Machiavelli's patriotism.[4] As I hope to be able to elucidate in this chapter, love of country was for him a synonym of what we call civic virtue—that is, love of the common good of the citizens which translates into acts of service and care for the republic. It is a passion which makes the individual's soul both generous and strong. As such, it gives ordinary citizens the motivation to discharge everyday duties, and resist tyranny and corruption; it inspires magistrates and rulers in their commitment to justice; it sustains legislators in their wisdom; and it gives redeemers and saviours the strength to restore liberty.

Machiavelli's interpretation of patriotism is a refinement of Roman republican ideas which had been reworked by late-medieval scholastic thinkers and by Quattrocento humanists; it is also, however, remarkably different, for a number of relevant aspects, from Florentine patriotic rhetoric. A study of these traditions will help us to identify the content of his patriotism and thereby better understand an aspect of his political thought which has received almost no attention from scholars.

The Tradition of Republican Patriotism

By Machiavelli's times, the language of patriotism was a recognizable ideological tradition derived mainly from the works of Roman republican theorists. For these authors, love of country was a component of justice. It belongs, as Cicero puts it in *Of Invention*, to *pietas*, which he defines as 'the feeling which renders kind offices and loving service to one's kin and country'.[5] Being a component of justice, love of country obeys the general principle of giving every man his due ('suam cuique . . . dignitatem') and preserving the common interest ('communi utilitate'). Although it respects the general principles of justice, it is more a natural affection than a rational principle: 'there is no social relation among them all more close, none more dear, than that which links each one of us with our republic (*re publica*). Parents are dear; dear are the children, relatives, friends; but one *patria* embraces all our loves (*caritates*).'[6] As Cicero's wording indicates, love of country is a compassionate affection sustained by the sense of belonging to the republic—that is, the community of citizens. He distinguishes in fact the strong sense of closeness that comes from belonging to the same 'people, tribe, and tongue' from the even more intimate ('interius') sense of closeness that unites citizens of the same republic who have so much in common: 'forum, temples, colonnades, street, statutes, laws, courts, rights of suffrage, to say nothing of social and friendly circles and diverse business relations with many.'[7]

Love of country was interpreted as being a charitable love which unites the citizens of a free republic; it presupposes a sense of belonging and commonness which only equal and free citizens can experience and cherish. It is an attachment not to abstract institutions and rights, but to the institutions and the rights that citizens feel as being theirs because they preserve and enjoy them through their service. It is an inward feeling that at times expresses itself as an attachment to places that are meaningful for the citizen (even if they are places that have been the stage of conflicts and defeats) and nurtures itself with symbols and narratives. As Livy aptly put it, it is a compassionate love which embraces all citizens, and gives them, in moments of danger for the common liberty, the moral and physical strength to accomplish arduous tasks.[8]

The classical Roman interpretation of love of country as compassionate love of the republic (*caritas reipublicae*) and of citizens (*caritas civium*) was partly lost in Scholastic treatments of the subject. In the *Summa theologiae*, Aquinas in fact defines *patria* not as republic but as 'the place in which we were born and nurtured'. However, he fully accepts the idea that love of country is a form of compassionate love which translates into 'acts of loving care and benevolent service for fellow-citizens and friends of the country',[9] and remarks, in full agreement with Cicero's analysis, that *pietas* for one's country aims at the common good and is therefore identical with justice.[10]

The interpretation of love of country as a compassionate love which moves men to put the common good before particular interests was condensed in an important passage of the *Of Princely Government* most probably written by Ptolemy of Lucca:

Amor patriae in radice charitatis fundatur—Love for the fatherland is founded in the root of charity which puts, not the private thing before those that are common, but the common things before the private, as beatus Augustin says elucidating the words of the Apostles on charity. Deservedly, the virtue of charity precedes all other virtues because the merit of any virtue depends upon that of charity. Therefore the *Amor patriae* deserves a rank of honour above all other virtues.[11]

The reference to Augustine is an important one, because it allows Ptolemy to stress the empowering effect of love of country. In Psalm 121: 12 Augustine was in fact exalting the moral strength of charity (*fortitudo charitatis*)—that is, the power of love to generate a new soul, a new human being which puts public things before private things and longs for sharing and unity with his fellow-men. The new soul is not only nobler and more perfect than the old one attached to private goods, but also challenges death by making the individual part of the larger community of the *patria* which outlives him.[12]

In Ptolemy of Lucca's analysis, the idioms of Roman republican patriotism are fused with the language of Christian theology. Not only does he describe love of country as a compassionate love which moves citizens to serve the common good, but he also restates the classical identification of *patria* with republic. Because love of country is 'zeal for the common good', it tends towards the same end as God's command to love one's neighbour as oneself. This is why Cicero says, in reference to the *respublica*, that 'nothing which prevents you from answering the summons of your country must be permitted to stand in your way'. In Ptolemy's analysis, love of country maintains the classical feature of a political love of fellow-citizens; of citizens who are dear to us—even though we do not personally know them—because they are citizens like us. At the same time, he presents it as a noble virtue in perfect tune with Christian theology and ethics.[13]

For Remigio de' Girolami, a dominican friar who preached and taught theology at Santa Maria Novella, love of country is love of the common good. In a free republic, the common good is the source of all the most valuable goods that civil life provides to all; and above all else, it provides the possibility of living in security protected by the shield of fair laws. Love of country, remarks Remigio, is a rational love, because it pushes citizens to pursue the common good—that is, a good which it is in the interest of each of them to defend.[14] He does not go so far as to say that a citizen ought to be prepared to sacrifice his soul to save his country, but he stresses that the individual's good ought to be sacrificed for the common good of peace.[15]

Florentine patriotism assumed a marked secular and anticlerical connotation during the war of 1376–8 against Pope Gregory XI, which was recorded in the histories as the war of the Eight Saints, after the eight magistrates who bravely defended common liberty, defying both the temporal and the spiritual powers of the Church of Rome. It was at that time that the idea that a good citizen ought to be prepared to sacrifice even his soul to defend his country's liberty entered in the language of Florentine patriotism. When, according to an anonymous diary of the time, the ambassadors of the Florentine Republic reported before the Signori and the Consiglio that Pope Gregory XI told them 'Either I will completely destroy Florence, or Florence will destroy the Church', the *Consiglio del Popolo* decided to fight with the greatest determination and vigour and declared that they were prepared to sacrifice their properties, their persons, and even their souls and God.[16]

By the early fifteenth century, the expression 'to love the Comune more than one's own good and one's own soul' was part of Florentine political language, as we can see from *The Ricordi of Gino di Neri Capponi*, composed in 1420. The Florentines, writes Poggio Bracciolini in his *History*, had to chose between love of country ('la carità della patria'), on the one hand, and fear of religion ('el timore della religione'), on the other. They resolved to put fear of religion aside, and not to fear the condemnations of men who pretended to be religious and to serve God but for the sake of ambition were in fact violating all human and divine law.[17] When Machiavelli wrote to Francesco Vettori 'I love my country more than my soul', his correspondent surely did not find Machiavelli's phrase extravagant.

Yet, in spite of their hostility against the papal court, Florentine patriots considered the defence of their own *patria* as perfectly compatible with, indeed as commanded by, Christian religion, as the Trecento Scholastics had claimed in their orations. Our faith, wrote Salutati in a letter of 1396, commands us to defend our country and our republic ('imperat patriam rempublicamque defendi'). Even though the bonds of Christian community are higher and more suave than all other bonds, including civic bonds ('patrie glutinus'), it is a supreme duty of a good Christian and a good citizen to serve the common good of the republic with all his energies.[18] All human beings, he writes, are brothers in Christ, regardless of their race and nationality; but it is also true, as Cicero teaches us, that our affections and our obligations are proportioned to the degree of closeness and sameness.[19] This means that although we have obligations to humanity, we have to care more for our fellow-citizens than for foreigners.

Salutati identifies *patria* with 'republic' and stresses, again in full agreement with the Ciceronian tradition, that love of country is a charitable love that encompasses all our affections for our parents, our children, our relatives and friends.[20] For this reason, love of country is the passion which must inform the conduct of every good citizen and above all the magistrates of republics, who must devote all their energies to protect and to educate, with the help of civil law, the citizens of their *patria*. The *patria* comes before the individual citizen, but cannot exist without citizens; hence the interest and the good of the former cannot possibly be separated from that of the latter.

Salutati's Christian and republican patriotism also embodies a strong civic pride. Florence is for him a glorious *patria* and a regal city ('regiam urbem') adorned with the most splendid palaces, among which excels the palace of the people ('palatium populi'), and the most beautiful dome. The Florentines, he remarks, excel all other peoples for their intelligence, wit, eloquence and virtue. Moreover, the city was founded by the Romans when Rome was still a free republic; they can, therefore, rightly claim to be the direct descendants of that most glorious and powerful people of antiquity and to be entitled to attain a comparable greatness.[21] However, he also describes love of country as a passion that translates into inhuman ferocity and cruelty, and claims that love of country is a sweet passion that justifies crimes perpetrated for one's country's defence and expansion and renders the most cruel acts 'neither burdensome nor difficult'.[22]

The text which better combines the two main themes of Florentine patriotism—love of common liberty and civic pride—is the *Eulogy of the City of Florence* composed by Leonardo Bruni in 1403–4. Florence, he remarks, is a republic devoted to justice and liberty, because without justice 'there can be no city, nor would Florence even be worthy to be called a city', and without liberty a great people like the Florentines 'would not even consider life worth living'.[23] The principles of justice and equality that inform the institutions of the republic also affect the citizens' way of living, encouraging habits of toleration and humanity: as all citizens are equal, no one can be 'proud or disparage others'.[24] Florence is just towards its citizens, and fair to the foreigners who come to live therein. All those who have been exiled from their country either by seditious plots or by the envy of their compatriots can find another homeland in Florence: 'as long as Florence continues to exist, no one will ever really lack a homeland.'[25] Hence, Florence is not only a true *patria* for the Florentines; it is also a *patria* for all victims of misfortune and injustice.

Along with the celebration of republican political principles, the *Eulogy of the City of Florence* exalts Florence's superiority based on its unique splendour: 'Florence is of such a nature that a more distinguished or more splendid city cannot be found on the entire earth.'[26] The city's extraordinary splendour is a claim for domination. Everyone, stresses Bruni, would surely recognize that she is 'worthy of attaining dominion and rule over the entire world'.[27] Moreover, Florence's origin was nobler than any other city, as it was founded by the Romans when Rome was still a republic.

Since Florence has as its founders those who by their skill and military prowess dominated the entire world, and since it was founded when the free and unconquered Roman people flourished in power, nobility, virtues, and genius, it cannot be doubted at all that this one city not only stands out in its beauty, architecture, and appropriateness of site, but also greatly excels beyond all other cities for the dignity and nobility of its origin.[28]

The combination of republican values and civic pride that characterizes Bruni's patriotism appears also in the *Oration for the funeral of Nanni Strozzi*, a Florentine citizen who died in 1427 in battle against the forces of the Duke of Milan. Our *patria*, he remarks, deserves the foremost honour, even above our parents, because it is 'the first and prerequisite basis of human happiness'.[29] And by *patria* he means, in full agreement with the republican legacy, the free republic. Florence, he remarks, has a popular constitution designed to protect the liberty and equality of all citizens. She deserves the citizens' devotion because it allows each and all of them to live 'free from the fear of men' and to pursue the highest public honours.[30]

To the Florentines gathered for the funeral of Nanni Strozzi, Bruni not only says that they ought to love their republic because it allows them to live free. He also stresses that they ought to be proud to belong to the most noble of all cities which possesses a

wide dominion and commands universal respect. They are descendants from the Etruscans and the Romans, two of the most glorious
peoples of antiquity; no city can claim a nobler origin, no people
have more illustrious ancestors. They are not only entitled to live
free; they are also entitled to dominate the other cities of Tuscany.

Other Florentine scholars writing in the same period stressed
that the essence of patriotism is civic virtue—that is, the desire
and the capacity to serve the common good and the laws of the
republic, not the ambition to dominate other peoples. Leon Battista
Alberti, for instance, contrasts the corrupt citizen who covets and
seeks the good of others and 'thirsts after and usurps the public
wealth', with the good citizen who accepts the burdens that its
country (*patria*) imposes on him.[31] Through the words of the young
Lionardo, he remarks that the good citizen is he who loves his own
private leisure, but also that of his fellow-citizens; who cares for
the unity, peace, and tranquillity of his own family, 'but much
more for his country [*patria sua*] and the republic'. Good citizens
must 'care for the republic' and 'toil at the tasks of their country' to
sustain the public good, and, more importantly, to prevent the
wicked from taking advantage of the indifference of the good citizens and pervert 'both public and private well-being'.[32]

In Alberti's interpretation, therefore, to serve the public good is
not only the best way to secure one's own private tranquillity, but
also the right path to fame and glory: let us endeavour, concludes
Lionardo, 'to earn some praise and fame by our excellence, zeal,
and skill, and so prepare ourselves to be of service to the republic,
to our country'.[33] The prospect of attaining the love and the respect
of one's fellow-citizens in one's own country shall give the good
citizen the strength to face the enmity of the wicked and punish
them with necessary severity. Severity in imposing the public
good, writes Alberti, and the choice of words is significant, is 'a
most pious act' ('cosa piissima').[34]

An even more complete summary of republican patriotism is to
be found in Matteo Palmieri's *Vita Civile (Of Civil Life)*, composed
between 1435–1440. He presents service to the republic as the
completion of a life inspired by the ideal of civil virtues,[35] and
praises love of country as the most upright and honest thing,
indeed as one of the duties of justice prescribed by natural law.[36]
He equates *patria* with republic, and—a detail worth noticing—he
speaks of compassion for the country ('pietà della patria') as a
synonym for 'civil compassion' ('civile pietà') to indicate the moral

strength of citizens who perform extraordinary deeds to defend the common liberty.[37] Of all men's deeds, he remarks, none is more praiseworthy than serving one's country—that is, to labour to preserve civic union and concord.[38] Only those citizens who have deferred their private whims to public honour, interest, and glory and have sacrificed their patrimony, endured exile, and even offered their lives for the common good of their countries, he remarks at the end of the work, attain true and perennial glory.[39]

Machiavelli's Patriotism

If we now turn to Machiavelli, we can see that he endorsed and kept alive some important features of the conventional language of patriotism, particularly the interpretation of love of country as a charitable love of the common good of the republic. He explicitly affirms the equation between common good and *patria* in the *Discourse*, where he writes that a prudent founder who intends to serve not his own interest but the common good, not the interests of his own successors but the common fatherland, must be alone in his authority. He uses here the expressions 'common good' ('bene comune') and 'common fatherland' ('comune patria') as equivalent terms opposed to 'oneself' ('sè') and 'one's own lineage' ('la propria successione') respectively.

Machiavelli not only endorses the conventional republican understanding of love of country as the passion which drives citizens to put the common good before personal and particular interests, but follows Roman authorities and their admirers in describing the conduct of those who labour to serve their country as the proper conduct of the *vir virtutis*. The deeds of kings, captains, and lawgivers who have laboured for their country ('*per la patria loro affaticati*'), he writes at the very outset of the *Discourses*, are 'most virtuous' ('virtuosissime').[40]

He also equates, again in complete agreement with republican tradition, fatherland (*patria*) with republic as opposed to principality and tyranny. Machiavelli uses this distinction, for instance, in the chapter on conspiracies in the *Discourses*, where he discusses conspiracies 'against the fatherland' ('contro alla patria'), on the one hand, and 'against a prince' ('contro ad uno principe'), on the other, even though he devotes the chapter almost entirely to the discussion of the latter.[41] As he clarifies towards the end of the chapter, to conspire against the fatherland does in fact mean to conspire against a republic in order to become prince or tyrant of it, in the sense of absolute sovereign and usurper of legitimate political authority as established by the city's constitutional orders.[42] *Patria*, here, stands therefore, and the detail is important, for republic in the sense of constitutional political order.

In all the examples of patriotism he takes from Roman history, Machiavelli emphasizes that love of country is a moral force that makes the citizens capable of understanding what the common good of the republic consists of and pursuing it. It is a passion that makes them wise and virtuous: because they can see beyond the boundaries of their family or of their social group, they act in the way that is most apt to secure their own and the republic's interest. Machiavelli eloquently describes these effects of patriotism in the *Discourses*, where he comments upon Livy's account of the story of Manlius Capitolinus, who was cited by the tribunes of the people to appear before the Roman people to respond for the tumults he raised against the Senate and the laws of the country ('leggi patrie').

In Machiavelli's description of the episode, both the nobles and the tribunes behaved in a remarkably virtuous way: the former did not support Manlius at all, even though he was one of them and they 'were usually very keen to defend one another'; the latter referred him to the judgement of the popular assembly, even if Manlius had been inimical to the Senate and they were always looking favourably to citizens who opposed the nobles. But the most noteworthy feature of the whole story is the behaviour of the Roman people, who, in spite of their greatest desire to promote their particular interest ('grandissimo desiderio dell'utile proprio') and their hostility towards the nobles, sentenced him to death.

What made that verdict possible? 'With all of them', is Machiavelli's answer, 'love of country [*lo amore della patria*] weighed more than any other consideration, and they looked upon the present dangers for which he was responsible as of much greater importance than his former merits; with the result that they chose he should die in order that they might remain free.'

It was, however, a painful decision. After they had sentenced Manlius to death, Machiavelli tells us in another chapter of the *Discourses*, the Roman people missed him, and the memory of his virtues moved everyone's compassion.[43] Yet, had Manlius come back to life, Machiavelli notices, the Roman people would have 'passed the same sentence on him', not because they were heartless, and not even because they were wise and rational, but because their love of the republic was more powerful than their compassion and their admiration for the individual.

The true patriot is a citizen who stands for constitutional legality. In the *Discourses* Machiavelli points to the oration that Livy puts in the mouth of the tribune of the people Publius Sempronius against the censor Appius Claudius as an example of 'the goodness and humanity of many citizens and of their willingness to obey the laws and the auspices of their fatherland'.[44] The oration is an eloquent defence of constitutional legality against the attempt of an insolent citizen to impose an abuse of power. The whole issue, as Livy remarks, was a matter of justice, and Publius' argument is essentially a legal one. Against Appius' effort to justify his refusal to relinquish his post after eighteen months, as the Aemilian law disposed, Publius invokes the fundamental legal principle whereby 'in a conflict of two laws the old is ever superseded by the new' and remarks that Appius' pretention was an unacceptable privilege: 'or will this be your contention, Appius, that the people is not bound by the Aemilian law? Or that the people is bound, but that you alone are exempt?'[45]

Machiavelli's endorsement of the conventional theme that love of country is a compassionate love of the common good is also evident in his comment on Livy's narration of the episode of Fabius Massimus Rullianus in the chapter of the *Discourses* which he entitles 'That a Good Citizen out of Love of his Country [*per amore della patria*] ought to ignore Personal Affronts'. The Roman Senate, says Machiavelli, sent ambassadors to beseech Fabius Massimus Rullianus to put his resentment aside and, for the common good ('per beneficio pubblico'), to appoint Papirio Cursore dictator. Fabius accepted the Senate's appeal 'moved by love of country' ('mosso da carità della patria'), even though he made it clear, by his silence and in other ways, that the nomination was for him very painful. Machiavelli not only uses the term *carità* to describe love of country, but also uses *patria* and 'public good' as interchangeable terms to indicate the goals which inspire the patriot's conduct. For him, in perfect agreement with the classical view, love of country is a form of strength which permits good citizens to accomplish painful, but virtuous deeds.[46]

Love of country, in the republican sense, is an important political passion also in modern times. Although the history of Florence is the triumph of ambition, factionalism, greed, and envy, Florence also has examples of good citizens standing against tyranny and corruption for love of country, and citizens appealing to love of country to move other citizens to join them in the resistance. The orations that Machiavelli attributes to Florentine citizens in the *Florentine Histories* are to be treated not as historical documents, but as texts that reveal how Machiavelli believed a patriot should speak and act in momentous occasions of the life of the republic. An example is Farinata degli Uberti, who opposed his Ghibelline friends' resolution to raze Florence to the ground to destroy forever the strength of the Guelphs, saying that 'he had not undergone so many perils with so much trouble not to be able to live in his fatherland'. Unlike the other Florentine Ghibellines, his love of country was stronger than his desire to punish his enemies and gave him the energy 'to oppose so cruel a sentence given against so noble a city'.[47]

For Machiavelli, love of country is the passion of magnanimous souls, like Cosimo Rucellai, of whom he wrote that 'I do not know what possession was so much his (not excepting, to go no further, his soul) that for his friends he would not willingly have spent it—I do not know of any undertaking that would have frightened him, if in it he had perceived the good of his country [*patria*]'.[48]

Cosimo Rucellai is not the only example of the empowering effects of love of country. In the *Florentine Histories* Machiavelli illustrates the same effects when he describes anonymous citizens who gathered together to stop the factional strife that was about to destroy the republic. At the time when the whole city was living in 'very great suspicion, each fearing every sort of ruin for himself', Machiavelli reports, many citizens, 'moved by love of their father-land' ('mossi dall'amore della patria') convened in the church of S. Pietro in Scheraggio, and after much discussion, resolved to meet the Signoria. One of them of greater authority addressed the Signori, saying at the very opening of his oration that it was 'the love that we bear for our fatherland' ('l'amore che noi portiamo alla patria nos-tra') that made them resolve to gather and to offer themselves to help to eliminate factional strife. And he ends the oration urging the Signori to introduce the political reform that would put an end to sects and restore 'the free and civil life'. The final exhortation, which Machiavelli presents as the appeal of men 'moved by charity for [their] fatherland, not by any private passion', deserves to be quoted, as it exemplifies Machiavelli's view of the model patriot.

To this we urge you, moved by charity for our fatherland, not by any private passion. And although its corruption be great, eliminate now the evil that affects us, the rage that consumes us, the poison that kills us; and credit the ancient disorders not to the nature of men but to the times, which have now changed, so that you can hope for better fortune for our city through better orders. The malignity of fortune can be overcome with prudence by putting a check on the ambition of those ambitious citizens, by annulling the orders that nourish sects, and by adopting those that do in truth conform to a free and civil life.[49]

Machiavelli wants the reader to believe that the anonymous orator said those words sincerely. In other cases, he openly says that declarations of love of country were just pretensions to cover up malignant intentions. Speaking of Corso Donati, for instance, he remarks that he convinced many citizens that he was denouncing the Republican officers out of love of country, but he was in fact making 'the indecency of his intent appear decent with a decent cause'.[50] Whereas Corso Donati was just covering the true motivation of his actions, the anonymous speaker spoke as a citizen who sincerely loves his fatherland and urged the Signori to introduce the political reforms that Florence needed to attain civil peace.

Because it is a compassionate love that gives the citizens the strength to serve the common good, and because it is a love of the republic and of the way of life inspired by the values of liberty and civic equality, love of country is the antidote to corruption and tyranny. This does not imply that *patria* is identical with republic and that love of country is only love of liberty. As Guicciardini wrote in the *Dialogue on the Government of Florence*, the *patria* embraces many sweet affections, such that even those who live under princes love their country ('*amano la patria*') and have endured many perils for it.[51] Machiavelli also admits that there have been kings and princes who have laboured for their country.[52] In the *Florentine Histories*, for instance, he recognizes that Lorenzo the Magnificent 'exposed his very life to gain peace for his fatherland', and was therefore honoured by his fellow-citizens 'with the joy that his great qualities and merits deserved'.[53]

What exactly is the object of love of country, if it is not only love of the republic and of liberty? His friend Vettori wrote to him that it is a love of 'all its men, its laws, its customs, its walls, its houses, its streets, its churches and its countryside'.[54] Vettori's words echo the humanist commonplace that *patria* is a most sweet name ('*dulcissimum*'), and particularly sweet is the *patria* in which one lives free. Memories and place become particularly meaningful and stimulate stronger attachments when they remind the citizens of their liberty. Even if their fathers did not keep alive in the citizens the memory of liberty, says an anonymous orator of the *Florentine Histories*, 'the public palaces, the places of the magistrates, the ensigns of the free orders recall it'. They remind the citizens of the 'sweetness of a free way of life' ('dolcezza del vivere libero'), Machiavelli comments.[55] The *patria* always inspires love and attachment, but, when the *patria* is joined with republican liberty, citizens love it in a special manner. Peoples and places acquire a special beauty which stimulates feelings of closeness and sharing. The very aesthetic perception of the city's beauty changes according to the significance of places with respect to the life and the history of the republic.

For Machiavelli, love of country is not just love of political institutions. Something else is involved: it is a love of the republic instituted and kept alive by a particular people in a particular place, with its specific culture and history, with its prophets, martyrs, heroes, and villains. Still, there is an important difference between the love of country by subjects of monarchs and princes, and the love of country by citizens of republics. The former, like the latter, are attached to places, to memories, and to a culture, but they lack the spirit of equality, solidarity, and responsibility which grows only among individuals who have shared as equal citizens the pains and the joys of republican liberty and self-government. And the spirit of equality, solidarity, and responsibility is a culture which gives places, buildings, and memories a particular significance.

Civic humanists, as we have seen, had defined the specific character of love of country of citizens of republics by describing it as particularly sweet (*dulcis*). Their choice of words does not indicate a mere difference in the intensity of the affection, but a difference in its quality. Machiavelli's words—'the sweetness of free life' ('la dolcezza del vivere libero')—are even more eloquent. They convey the idea of a love of country which is love of a concrete way of living under particular republican institutions in places filled with memories, culturally dense, historically situated. It is love not just of republican political institutions and laws, but of republican institutions and laws, and the political and social practices they permit and encourage.

Machiavelli asserts that the individual highest moral obligation is to the country. He justifies his claim with the Ciceronian and

Platonic topic that, since we owe our country not only our life, but also the most precious goods that fortune and nature bestow upon us, we must pay back our debt by serving it with all our energies. From the recognition that we owe our country every good, it follows, as he writes in the outset of the *Discourse on our Language*, that we are never entitled to offend it, however great is the harm that we have received. To offend one's country is therefore a nefarious act, more nefarious than battering one's father and one's mother.[56]

Elsewhere, however, he describes the citizen's moral obligation to his country in a much less intransigent way. To be sincerely loved by its citizens, the country has to deserve its citizens' love, and to deserve it, it must love them equally, it must be just to them. If it is not, a good citizen is excused if he resolves to fight against the government or the institutions, even if his conduct can be seen as treason.

Rinaldo degli Albizzi, who persuaded the Duke of Milan to levy a war against Florence to destroy Cosimo de Medici's regime, is not treated by Machiavelli as a wicked man and a parricide. We know that in the *Florentine Histories* Machiavelli tends to present Cosimo's enemies in a good light to belittle Cosimo's fame; still, he could have presented Rinaldo's appeal to the Duke of Milan as the request of a resentful man glad to see his city defeated by a foreign prince to enjoy the fall of his enemy's regime—that is, as another example of the triumph of envy. On the contrary, he makes him speak as a good patriot. Rinaldo opens his oration with an *excusatio* in which he stresses that, since he and his friends are in fact defending the liberty of their country oppressed by Cosimo, they deserve to be excused: 'no good man will ever reprove anyone who seeks to defend his fatherland in whatever mode he defends it.' Florence cannot complain that they are taking up arms against it, whereas in the past they defended it, 'because that fatherland deserves to be loved by all its citizens that loves all its citizens equally, not that, having overlooked all others, adores a very few'.[57]

Having explained that what he was doing was honourable, Rinaldo, following a classical rhetorical scheme, reinforces his argument by stressing that his resolution to invoke the support of the Duke of Milan is also necessary. Florence, he says, suffers from the worst of all diseases—servitude. It needs a radical cure, and it is the duty of a good citizen to administer the required treatment. A war against Cosimo's Florence would then be just and laudable:

What therefore can be a greater disease in the body of a republic than slavery? What medicine is it more necessary to use than that which will relieve it from this infirmity? Only those wars are just that are necessary, and those arms pious where there is no hope outside them. I do not know what necessity is greater than ours, nor what piety can exceed that which takes our fatherland out of slavery.[58]

As he did in other cases, Machiavelli could have told the reader that, with these noble words, Rinaldo was simply covering his nefarious intentions with pretensions of honesty, justice, and piety. He could have said that he was in fact redescribing his actions to appear as a redeemer, and not a traitor. Instead, he adds no comment to Rinaldo's words. A few pages later, when he narrates Rinaldo's death, he presents him as a sincere patriot. Having seen that all hopes of returning to Florence were lost, Machiavelli remarks, Rinaldo chose to settle in Ancona; later he went to the Sepulchre of Christ 'so as to earn a celestial fatherland for himself, since he had lost his earthly one'.

Machiavelli presents Rinaldo as a man who loved his country: he tried first in many ways to return to Florence, and then to find a new country in heaven. He describes him as a man who was not of a malignant temper but rather the victim of the bitter factional strife in which he happened to live.[59] Speaking of Rinaldo's archenemy Cosimo, instead, he says that people accused him of loving 'himself more than his fatherland', his power more than his country—a subtle indirect way of telling the reader that he was not a good citizen at all.[60] Machiavelli's benevolent treatment of Rinaldo invites the reader to believe that it is plausible for a patriot to maintain that only that country which loves all the citizens equally deserves the citizens' love. For love of country a citizen should forget harms or injustices done to him; but he should not forget or forgive an oppressive regime.

Love of country does not make citizens docile and passive. It instils commitment to the institutions and the laws which protect the common liberty, while at the same time disposes the citizens to resist against tyranny and corruption. When he extols the Roman people as an example of virtuous citizenry, he remarks that 'when it was necessary to take action against some powerful person, it did so, as is seen in the case of Manlius, of the Ten, and in the case of others who sought to oppress it'.[61]

The kind of virtue which a republic needs is, for Machiavelli, a love of country which drives each citizen to do his share of service and makes him intransigent with the arrogant and the enemies of common liberty. It is not a virtue of saints and martyrs, but just the virtue of good citizens. It is more the consequence of the expansion of a particular passion over others and the recognition of one's own self-interest as citizen more than the result of the sacrifice of passions or individual interests.

When he offers examples of patriotic peoples, he does not mention peoples capable of sacrificing their personal interest, but rather citizens who serve the common good to be able to enjoy their private lives safely. Except for a small number of citizens who desire liberty in order to obtain authority over the others, the greatest majority of the citizens 'desire liberty to live in security'.

The attachment to republican government which was so strong in ancient peoples, Machiavelli writes, was largely due to the fact that free republics serve the private interests of citizens well and permit them to enjoy their private lives and private affections safely and happily: 'all towns and all countries that are in all respects free profit by it enormously. For, wherever increasing populations are found, it is due to the freedom with which marriage is contracted and to its being more desired by men.'

This comes about where every man is ready to have children

since he believes that he can rear them and feels sure that his patrimony will not be taken away, and since he knows that not only will they be born free instead of into slavery, but that, if they have virtue, they will have the chance to become princes. One observes, too, how riches multiply and abound there, alike those that come from agriculture and those that are produced by the trades. For everybody is eager to acquire such things and to obtain property, provided he is convinced that he will enjoy it when it has been acquired.[62]

Because the citizens compete among themselves to serve the common good, *both* private and public welfare ('privati e publici commodi') increase marvellously. On the contrary, corrupt citizens who do not want to serve the common good bring about their own ruin, as occurred to the subjects of Constantinople who refused to give the Emperor the money he needed to defend them and as a result were conquered by the Turks.[63] Machiavelli told the poignant story of the subjects of Constantinople in the oration he composed to persuade his fellow-Florentines to give the Republic the money necessary to institute a reliable army. A few years later, in the *Discourses*, he offers an equally powerful example of how a virtuous citizenry pays its taxes in order to preserve its freedom and its security. In free German cities, he writes, when the republic needs

to spend any sum of money on public account, it is customary for their magistrates or councils, in whom is vested authority to deal with such matters, to impose on all the inhabitants of a town a tax of one or two per cent of the income. The decision having been made, each person presents himself to the tax collectors in accordance with the constitutional practice of the town. He then takes an oath to pay the appropriate sum, and throws into a chest provided for the purpose the amount which he conscientiously thinks he ought to pay.

Whereas the subjects of Constantinople lost their properties and their lives, the citizens of German free cities, thanks to their 'goodness', enjoy their liberty in safety and prosper.[64]

To serve the common good of one's country is for Machiavelli a moral obligation; but he knows that citizens are not moved to virtuous deeds by an appeal to philosophical principles. For this reason he always connects patriotism with security, prosperity, self-interest, and liberty. Love of country and love of liberty are for him hardly distinguishable. In some instances, Machiavelli seems to suggest that peoples who are not taught properly to love and honour their country cannot love liberty either. But other passages suggest a causal relationship: if people do not properly love their country and do not train themselves to defend it, they cannot hope to keep alive their republican institutions for long, and once the republic is dissolved, love of liberty evaporates from their hearts.[65]

When love of country is not sufficient to defend common liberty, it needs the help of religion. Machiavelli's patriotism is not irreligious and not even antichristian; it is just anticlerical, as Florentine patriotism had been since the end of fourteenth century. As he explains in the *Discourses*, in moments of grave danger for the liberty of the republic, fear of God comes to give the strength that love of country by itself is not able to provide. After the disastrous defeat at Cannae, Machiavelli narrates, 'many of the citizens got together and, despairing of their fatherland, decided to abandon Italy and to transfer themselves to Sicily. When Scipio heard of this, he forced them to swear that they would not abandon their country.' This episode shows, Machiavelli comments, that those citizens whom 'neither love of country nor the laws' sufficed to restrain from abandoning Rome were restrained 'by an oath which they had been forced to take'.[66]

In this case it was pagan religion which came in support of patriotism; but for Machiavelli Christian religion also, if correctly interpreted, can reinforce a love of country. Roman religion integrated love of country with the fear of God; Christian religion could stimulate patriotism in so far as it exhorts us to cultivate compassion and to serve the common good, as Aquinas himself had written and later Christian theorists of republican patriotism had preached in the churches of Florence. When Machiavelli writes that our religion 'permits us to exalt and defend the country' and 'wishes us to love and to honour [our country], and to train ourselves to be such that we may defend it', he was upholding a tradition of Christian patriotism which had old roots in Florentine intellectual and political life.[67]

He also restates another distinctive theme of Florentine patriotism—namely, the idea that our obligation to our country comes before our obligations to the Church's commands. In the *Florentine Histories* he openly praises the magistrates who governed the city during the war against Pope Gregory XI. They were called saints, he writes, 'even though they had little regard for censures, had despoiled the churches of their goods, and had compelled the clergy to celebrate the office'. So much more, he concludes, 'did those citizens then esteem their fatherland than their souls' ('tanto quelli cittadini stimavano allora più la patria che l'anima').[68] For him obligations to one's country also come before moral principles. When the republic's liberty is in danger, Machiavelli remarks,

no attention should be paid either to justice or to injustice, to kindness or to cruelty, or to its being praiseworthy or ignominious. On the contrary, every other consideration being set aside, that alternative should be wholeheartedly adopted which will save the life and preserve the freedom of one's country'.[69]

Love of country should give the strength to deliberate on the course of action which will save the life and liberty of one's country, in spite of its high moral costs; but it does not have the power to turn a tragic choice into a cheerful one.

Unlike that of the Trecento and Quattrocento humanists, Machiavelli's patriotism did not translate into celebrations of the superiority of Florence. The magnificent palaces that Bruni had mentioned in the *Eulogy* as signs of the city's splendour are for him 'proud and regal' symbols of the power and wealth of the great families. To build his magnificent palace, he writes in the *Florentine Histories*, Luca Pitti did not refrain from using illegal means, and, once the palace was completed, it became the centre of seditious gatherings of the enemies of the Republic.[70] Moreover, the theme of the origins of the city, which had received so much attention from Florentine historians, is for him of little interest. In the *Florentine Histories* he settles the issue with a few words: '[Florence] was born under the Roman Empire; and in the times of the first emperors it began to be recorded by historians.'[71] Its origins were, therefore, servile—a mark that affected the subsequent history of the city. In the *Discourses*, he remarks that the case of Florence is similar to that of other cities which were not at the outset free, and therefore could not make great progress.[72] Whether it was founded by the soldiers of Sulla or by the inhabitants of Fiesole, 'it was built under the Roman Empire, and could at the outset make no addition to its territory save such as was allowed by the courtesy of the emperor'.[73]

During his political career, he was more a critic of, than an apologist for, the Florentine Republic. He was devoted to it, he served it with all his energies and with impeccable honesty, but he did not fail to remark upon its meanness, injustice, and imprudence. As he himself admitted, he was contrary to the opinion of the Florentines.[74] His love of country does not make him blind or cowardly; he sees his country's crimes and he openly denounces them, even when he is writing as the official historian of Florence. Unlike Bruni, who had claimed in the *Eulogy* that all the wars that Florence fought were justified because the Florentines were the descendants of the Romans and therefore the heirs of the territories that belonged to the Roman Republic, Machiavelli remarks in the *Florentine Histories* that the wars against King Ladislao and Duke Philip 'were made to fill the citizens [with riches and power], not for necessity'.[75]

The Florentines had not only fought unjust wars, they had also been unjust in war, as in the case of the war against Lucca in 1429, when Astorre Gianni, a commissioner of the Republic of Florence,

had his troops seize all the passes and strongholds of the valley and had the men assemble in their principal church; and after he had taken them all prisoners, he had his troops sack and destroy the whole country, in a cruel and avaricious example, and sparing neither holy places nor women, whether virgin or married.[76]

Another equally shameful atrocity was perpetrated against Volterra in 1472, when for a whole day the city 'was robbed and overrun' and 'neither women nor holy places were spared, and the soldiers [. . .] stripped it of its property'.[77]

Whereas he rejects the belief in Florence's superiority, he makes fun of the pompous parochialism which was the other side of the coin. The best example of Machiavelli's irony on this matter is surely the dialogue between Ligurio and Nicia in *Mandragola*, Act I, Scene II:

LIGURIO. Yet what you spoke first is bound to worry you, for you aren't in the habit of letting the Cupola [the Dome] out of your sight.

NICIA. You are wrong. When I was younger, I was a great gadabout. Why, they never held the fair at Prato without my going there, and there isn't a single town all around where I haven't been. And I can say more too; I have been at Pisa and at Livorno—think of that. . . .

LIGURIO. At Livorno did you see the sea?

NICIA. You know I did.

LIGURIO. How much bigger than the Arno is it?

NICIA. Than the Arno? It's four times, more than six, more than seven, you'll make me say; and you don't see anything but water, water, water.

LIGURIO. I wonder, then, since you have pissed in so many snowbanks, that you make such a fuss about going to the baths.

Unlike Nicia's, Machiavelli's horizons were larger than Florence and the neighbouring cities. In his travels to foreign countries he observed the institutions and the way of life of different peoples, and often he found them more laudable than those of his own republic and of Italy as well. He describes the defensive provisions of the German free cities a 'most beautiful order' ('uno ordine bellissimo') and highly praises their simple and free way of life.[78] To the French he reserves severe criticism, but in *The Prince* he does not fail to call their monarchy 'well ordered and well governed', and in the *Discourses* he praises their constitutional laws as being suitable to guarantee the security of 'all the peoples' of the kingdom.[79]

Machiavelli also recognizes Florence's excellence. In the *Discourse on Our Language*, composed around 1524, he writes that, since Florence is nobler ('più nobile') than other countries, its citizens have a greater obligation to it. But his remarks on Florence's excellence do emphasize a potentiality rather than a fact: Florence could become a great republic, if its citizens and its magistrates were pervaded by civic virtue; if it had been capable of providing itself with good political and military institutions; if it had adopted a wiser policy of expansion.[80] Had Florence had institutions that had kept her united and peaceful, he writes in the *Florentine Histories*, 'I know no republic either modern or ancient that would have been its superior, so full of virtue, of arms, and of industry would it have been'. But the potentiality for greatness was rarely actualized; more often it translated into arrogant policies.[81]

Really to attain greatness, Florence should try to incorporate and integrate alien peoples and cultures instead of celebrating its own uniqueness and preserving its purity. Machiavelli considers the integration of alien and heterogeneous elements as a strength, not as a weakness or a loss of aesthetic beauty. As he remarks in the *Discourse on our Language*, languages cannot be simple, but have to mingle with others. For a language to remain itself, however, it must be sure that alien words do not alter its order and are assimilated well—like the Romans, who admitted alien peoples in the Republic and used many foreign soldiers in their armies without losing their good political and military orderings.[82]

If a republic, or a language, does not need help from alien peoples or alien idioms, it is most laudable, but since no republic and no language can remain pure, it must know the right way to become stronger and more beautiful through integration. Like Scholastic thinkers, Machiavelli praises unity over multiplicity, but also recognizes that, since purity is not possible, variety can bring strength and beauty to the body of the republic and to language.[83]

The theme of a linguistic or cultural unity of a people or a nation is not part of Machiavelli's patriotism. While *patria* is a central word of Machiavelli's language, he rarely uses the word 'nation' at all.[84] In the *Discourses* he speaks in fact of nation—with reference to France, Spain, Italy—to indicate common customs, and specifically corrupt customs.[85] In the same chapter he uses as a synonym for *nazione* the old roman term *provincia* that indicated in origin the administrative subunits of the empire. A few lines earlier, he stresses the same point regarding the corruption of France, Spain, and Italy—calling them this time 'provinces' instead of nations.[86]

The distinctive characters of provinces or nations are for Machiavelli customs and forms of life. The title of Chapter 43 in book III of the *Discourses*, for instance, reads: 'That Men who are born in the same Country [*provincia*], display throughout the Ages much the same Characteristics.' He means, as he promptly clarifies, that each province has its own mode of life.[87] In addition to customs and forms of life, other distinctive features of provinces or nations are tongues and political orderings:

I say, then, that the territories a conqueror annexes and joins to his own well-established state [*stato antiquo*] are either in the same country [*provincia*] with the same language, or they are not. If they are, it is extremely easy to hold them, especially if they are not used to governing themselves [*usi a vivere liberi*] . . . But considerable problems arise if territories are annexed in a country [*provincia*] that differs in language, customs and institutions.[88]

The customs of nations are to be studied and understood, as they are of fundamental political importance. But they are not to be loved, at least not in the same way in which one's *patria*, understood as the political institutions and the particular way of life of the republic, is. For him political institutions and political values cannot be separated from customs and ways of life. He speaks in fact of '*vivere* libero', or '*vita* libera' [emphasis added]—that is, a particular way of life, a culture—as opposed to the 'vivere servo'—that is, another way of life and culture. *Patria*, like nation, is a way of life and a culture; it is a particular way of life inspired by liberty. In the famous sentence that Machiavelli wrote to his friend Vettori in one of his last letters—'I love my *patria* more than my soul'—one could replace 'patria' with 'vivere libero' without altering the meaning of the sentence; to replace 'patria' with 'nazione' would make it absurd.[89] What characterizes love of country and makes it noble even when it requires us to put the country before the soul is the fact that the country is a common good, whereas the soul, important as it is, is individual. It makes men subordinate their attachment to a good which is distinctively their own to goods that they have in common with others. No good can be more individual than one's soul; yet love of country makes us subordinate it to the common liberty—that is, to a liberty which is ours as much as anyone else's.

Occasionally, a patriot who succeeds in defending common liberty obtains the citizens' gratitude and reward, like Romulus and other founders who were most honoured and most happy in their lifetimes, and after death enjoyed perennial glory. In most cases, however, patriots are neglected or even mistreated. In the *Florentine Histories* Machiavelli reports the example of Benedetto Alberti, 'a very rich man, humane, severe, a lover of the liberty of his fatherland, a man to whom tyrannical modes were very displeasing', who led the struggle against the regime of Giorgio Scali and was later sentenced to exile.[90] The words that Machiavelli attributes to Benedetto are yet another example of his conception of patriotism as a compassionate love of common liberty. His farewell speech expresses no resentment or anger against his country; only sadness and concern for the loss of common liberty, and for the sufferings that his beloved and other citizens will have to endure:

> For myself, I do not sorrow, for the honors that my fatherland gave to me when it was free, it cannot take away when enslaved, and the memory of my past life will always give me greater pleasure than the unhappiness that will accompany me in my exile will give me displeasure. It does pain me much that my fatherland must remain the prey of a few and be subjected to their pride and avarice. I am pained for you because I fear that the evils that today are ending for me are beginning for you and will pursue you with greater harm than they have pursued me. I urge you therefore to steady your spirits against all misfortunes and to conduct yourself in such a way that should any adversity come to you—for many will come—everyone will know that they came to you who were innocent and without blame.[91]

Like Rinaldo degli Albizzi, Benedetto Alberti went to Palestine to fight for Christ's Sepulchre, 'in order not to live a lesser opinion of his goodness abroad than he might have left in Florence'. After his death his bones were brought back to Florence, and the same people who had persecuted him in the most ignominious way, attributed him the highest honour. For him, like many other patriots, recognition and glory came too late.

By telling the stories of eminent Florentines like Benedetto Alberti, Machiavelli wants to exhort his fellow-citizens to imitate their example; to stand for common liberty, even if the reward they get in their lifetime is their fellow-citizens' ingratitude. For Machiavelli a good citizen should loyally serve his country, even when he feels that his merits and his qualities are not recognized. He has to be prepared to serve without resentment, even if he is entrusted with positions of lesser responsibility, nor should he consider it a humiliation to be under the orders of people who had in the past been his subordinates. As a good example, he points to the Romans, who, 'though they had a great esteem for glory, yet they did not deem it an unworthy thing to obey one who had previously been under their command, nor serve in an army of which they had formerly been commanders in chief'.[92] As a negative example there is Venice, 'which makes the mistake of thinking that a citizen who has held high office should be ashamed to accept a lower; and the state is content that he should decline to accept it'.[93] The reason for Machiavelli's judgement is once again the priority of the common good: to refuse to serve in a lower position is wrong because, even if it is honourable from the standpoint of the individual citizen, it damages the republic.[94]

In the later years of his life, Machiavelli had the opportunity to put into practice the principles he had preached. In May 1521, he was sent to Carpi as orator of Florence to the General Assembly of the Franciscan Order to transact a minor business for the Medici. As he arrives in Carpi, he receives a request from the Officer of the Guild of Woollen Cloth Makers to carry out an even more inglorious mission—that is, to find a Lenten preacher. The humiliating and yet comic situation in which Machiavelli found himself at the age of 52 is brilliantly appreciated by Guicciardini in a letter of 17 May 1521, in which he remarks that to give Machiavelli the task of finding a preacher was as clever an idea as to charge Pacchierotto, a famous pederast in Florence, 'to find a beautiful and gallant wife for a friend'.[95]

Machiavelli's reply and the subsequent epistolary exchange with Guicciardini, is a revealing document of Machiavelli's own way of looking at one's obligations to one's country. As he had preached in the *Discourses*, he responds to his friend that he intends to serve his country to the best of his abilities, even if the mission he had to accomplish would have brought him no honour and was surely an insult to his talents and his reputation:

I was sitting on the toilet when your messenger arrived, and just at that moment I was mulling over the absurdities of this world; I was completely absorbed in imagining my style of preacher for Florence: he should be just what would please me, because I am going to be as pigheaded about this idea as I am about my other ideas. And because never did I disappoint the republic whenever I was able to help her out—if not with deeds, then with words; if not with words, then with signs—I have no intention of disappointing her now.[96]

This was his patriotism: a patriotism based upon a sincere

commitment to one's obligations, however unrewarding they are, joined with a deep conviction of the absurdity of the world and with a healthy irony towards the world, himself, and patriotism too.

Obligations are serious matters, but the world is not. One has to discharge one's obligations without becoming rancorous or resentful when one's country treats one poorly. 'When I read your titles as orator of the republic and of friars', Guicciardini wrote to him two days later, 'and I consider how many kings, dukes and princes you have negotiated with in the past, I am reminded of Lysander, to whom, after so many victories and trophies was given the task of distributing meat to those very same soldiers whom he had so gloriously commanded.'[97]

Compelled by malignant fortune to discharge a humble task, Machiavelli accepts his fate with irony and loyalty. He tries to make the best out of it: he sleeps, reads, keeps quiet, eats 'for six dogs and three wolves', organizes, with Guicciardini's complicity, the most hilarious burlesque at the friars' expenses, makes fun of the friars, and even tries to learn something useful for his political and moral investigations.[98]

Unconventional, irreverent, extravagant, ironic, opinionated, deceitful, unpretentious, keen to enjoy the pleasures of life, when they are available; and yet capable of serving his republic because he believes it is his duty, because he does not want to lose face, and because he hopes that in one way or another some reward might come.[99] This is the image of the model patriot that Machiavelli offered his contemporaries and us in his life even more eloquently than in his works.

Even if he knows by experience and by reading history that patriots' prize is often their fellow-citizens' ingratitude, Machiavelli promises great rewards to princes who commit themselves to noble deeds for love of country. To move a new prince to liberate Italy, Machiavelli appeals first to his sense of compassion: he mentions the 'ravaging of Lombardy', the cruelties, and the insolences, and 'the sores that have been festering for so long'; and then he allures him with the prospect of the grand honour and perennial fame that he will attain.[100] In another exhortation, less famous, which he put at the end of a discourse composed to persuade Cardinal Giulio de' Medici to pass a constitutional reform that would gradually have restored a republican government in Florence, he remarks that the highest honour that a man can hope to attain is that which his country freely bestows on him in recognition of his service to the common good. In addition to that, he assures that the greatest good that a man can accomplish, the one which God esteems most of all, is the good done to one's country: 'I believe the greatest honor possible for men to have is that willingly given them by their country [patria]; I believe the greatest good to be done and the most pleasing to God is that which one does to one's country [patria].'[101]

For rhetorical purposes he resorts once again, as he did in *The Prince*, to the image of God, friend of founders and redeemers, which classical antiquity had passed to modernity. He needed it to persuade his readers that, even if men's reward was highly uncertain, another and higher reward was destined to founders and redeemers of republics. Perhaps he also needed this illusion to continue to believe in the possibility of a true civil and free way of living, his most passionate ideal, and the soul of his patriotism.

Patriotism was for him the soul of politics. When love of country does not inform it, political action turns into the mean pursuit of personal or particular interest, or into vain search for fame. Only patriotism gives the motivation, the strength, the wisdom, and the restraint that true politics requires.

The kind of political action that Machiavelli glorifies is not the implementation of moral truth, or search for power, and even less the astute manoeuvering within a changing and insecure world. It is the extraordinary achievement of founders and redeemers of civil communities; it is the grand and momentous work of rulers and magistrates; it is the citizens' ordinary willingness to serve the common good and their strength to resist the ambition of the powerful. He sees politics as the perfection of human intelligence made possible by one passion alone—that is, by love of country.

This is the conception of political action of which he can rightly be considered the founder. And this is the only ideal of political action which is still appealing even in our times, if we accept, at last, that there is no moral or political truth, that 'each man behaves according to his own intellect and imagination',[102] that 'there are nothing but crazy people here',[103] and yet we want to enjoy the 'sweetness of liberty'—with a Machiavellian smile.

Notes

Introduction

1. See Quentin Skinner, *Reason and Rhetoric in the Philosophy of Hobbes*, (Cambridge, Cambridge University Press, 1996).

2. *Il Principe*, ch. 18; *The Prince*, 63.

3. 'andare drieto alla verità effettuale della cosa' (*Il Principe*, ch. 15; *The Prince*, 54).

4. 'Buttado a mare l'unità dello spirito medievale', wrote Federico Chabod, Machiavelli 'diveniva uno dei fondatori dello spirito moderno'. By focusing on politics and by identifying the pure nature of political action, he brought to completion the process of emancipation 'che nel campo dell'arte s'era già affermato, da Giotto in poi, e nel campo della scienza stava trionfando con Leonardo'. (Federico Chabod, *Scritti su Machiavelli* (Turin: Einaudi, 1964), 100).

5. 'questa provincia pare nata per risuscitare le cose morte' (*Arte della guerra*, 519; Gilbert, i. 726).

6. 'Machiavelli's Political Science', *The American Political Science Review*, 75 (1981), p. 295. An equally misleading interpretation of Machiavelli's intellectual relationship with the ancients is to be found in Hanna Pitkin, book *Fortune is a Woman* (Berkeley and Los Angeles: University of California Press, Berkeley, 1984; paperback edn., 1987) 45–6: 'What makes Machiavelli worthy to speak with them, of course, is his intelligence and experience, his *furbo* insight into the realities of political affairs. . . . He does not merely know the ways of the fox; he *is* one. Confronting the ancient leaders, he feels like a mere mortal among gods, a clever little fox among real men'. As the letter of 10 December 1513 to Vettori amply shows, Machiavelli believed himself to be worthy to speak with them because he shares with them the same vocation for the study of politics. He is not talking to them to 'outsmart' them or to manipulate them as a little fox, but to learn and discuss with them as an equal (Machiavelli to Vettori, 10 Dec. 1513, in *Lettere*, 423–8; MF 262–5).

7. 'Né so quello si dica Aristotile delle republiche divulse; ma io penso bene quello che ragionevolmente potrebbe essere, quello che è, e quello che è stato' (Machiavelli to Vettori, 26 Aug. 1513, in *Lettere*, 417; MF 258).

8. The most off the mark of all are Leo Strauss's comments. He writes: 'Patriotism, as Machiavelli understood it is collective selfishness' ('Introduction', in *Thoughts on Machiavelli* (Glencoe, Ill.: Free Press, 1958), 11). As I shall illustrate in Chapter 5, for Machiavelli patriotism is the opposite of selfisheness, whether collective or individual.

9. 'E se ogni esemplo di republica muove, quelli che si leggono della

propria muovono molto piú, e molto piú sono utili' (*Istorie*, bk. I, Proem; *FH* 6).

10. To believe that Machiavelli was a misanthrope is simply yet another example of the prejudices, and the ignorance, of many commentators. We have a wealth of documents from different peoples and different periods of the life of Niccolò which amply demonstrate that he was a human being of exceptional warmth and sympathy, a true source of joy for all his friends (see, for instance, the letter of Agostino Vespucci of October 1500 (*MF* 32) and the letter of Filippo de' Nerli of 6 September 1525 (*MF* 366)). It is surprising that even a superb scholar like Judith Shklar has embraced and refined the view of Machiavelli's misanthropy. See Judith N. Shklar, *Ordinary Vices* (Cambridge, Mass.: Harvard University Press, 1984), 206.

1 *Machiavelli's Philosophy of Life*

1. 'Motivi tutti di limitatezza spirituale aggravati finalmente per quella disposizione fondamentale dello spirito del Machiavelli che poco risente la commozione di ogni movimento spirituale, non contenuto nella pura politica; che ignora non soltanto l'eterno e il trascendente, ma anche il dubbio morale e l'ansia tormentosa di una coscienza che si ripieghi su se stessa' (Federico Chabod, *Scritti su Machiavelli* (Turin: Einaudi, 1964), 80–1; Eng. trans., David Moore, *Machiavelli and the Renaissance*, (London: Bowes & Bowes, 1958), 93).

2. A noteworthy exception is Anthony J. Parel's excellent essay *The Machiavellian Cosmos* (New Haven: Yale University Press), 1992. Important remarks are also to be found in Eugenio Garin's seminal essay 'Aspetti del pensiero di Machiavelli', in Garin, *Dal Rinascimento all'Illuminismo* (Pisa: Nistri-Lischi, 1970), 43–77. See also Gennaro Sasso, *Studi su Machiavelli*, (Naples: Morano, 1967), 81–110.

3. 'E quanto al volgere il viso alla Fortuna, voglio che abbiate di questi miei affanni questo piacere, che gli ho portati tanto francamente, che io stesso me ne voglio bene, e parmi essere da più che non credetti; e se parrà a questi patroni nostri non mi lasciare in terra, io l'arò caro, e crederrò portarmi in modo che gli aranno ancora loro cagione di averlo per bene; quando e' non paia, io mi viverò come io ci venni, che nacqui povero, et imparai prima a stentare che a godere' (*Lettere*, 363; *MF* 222).

4. 'Fu d'Avarizia figlia e di Sospetto: | nutrita ne le braccia de la Invidia, | de' principi e de' re vive nel petto'; 'trionfa nel core | d'ogni potente, ma piú si diletta | nel cor del popul quando egli è signore' (*Dell'ingratitudine*, in *Il teatro*, 305, 307; Gilbert, ii. 740).

5. 'La prima de le tre che vien da essa, | fa che l'uom solo il benefizio allega | ma sanza premiarlo lo confessa, | e la seconda che dipoi si spiega, | fa del ben ricevuto l'uom si scorda | ma senza iniuriarlo solo il niega; | l'ultima fa che l'uom mai non ricorda | né premia il ben ma che iusta sua possa | il

suo benefattor laceri e morda' (*Il teatro*, 306; Gilbert, ii. 741. (revised)).
Machiavelli's source here is Seneca, *De benefitiis* 3.1.

6. *Discorsi*, III. 30, *Discourses*, 486.

7. *Parole da dirle sopra la provisione del danaio, facto un poco di proemio et di scusa* (1503), in *I primi scritti*, 413.

8. See the letter of Agostino Vespucci of 8 June 1509 and the letter of Fillipo Casavecchia of 17 June 1509, in *Lettere*, 306–9; *MF* 180–2.

9. *Lettere*, 428; *MF* 265.

10. See the letter of Pier Soderini to Machiavelli, 13 Apr. 1521, in *Lettere*, 516; *MF* 334.

11. 'la cognizione delle azioni delli uomini grandi, imparata con una lunga esperienza delle cose moderne et una continua lezione delle antique' (*Il Principe*, Nicolaus Machiavellus ad Magnificum Laurentium Medice; *The Prince*, (Dedicatory Letter, 3).

12. 'Onde io, per non incorrere in questo errore, ho eletti non quelli che sono principi, ma quelli che per le infinite buone parti loro meriterebbono di essere . . . Perché gli uomini, volendo gudicare dirittamente, hanno a stimare quelli che sono, non quelli che possono essere liberali; e cosí quelli che sanno, non quelli che, sanza sapere, possono governare uno regno' (*Discorsi*, Dedicatory Letter to Zanobi Buondelmonti and Cosimo Rucellai, 121–2).

13. 'Nè considerorono come le azioni che hanno in sé grandezza, come hanno quelle de' governi e degli stati, comunque lele si trattino, qualunque fine abbino, pare sempre portino agli uomini più onore che biasimo' (*Istorie*, bk. I, Proem; FH 8).

14. *Arte della guerra*, 518; Gilbert, ii. 568, 724 (revised).

15. It is, however, an exaggeration to claim that ambition, understood as 'impulse toward mastery and domination' is the central factor of politics, as Wendy Brown, (*Manhood and Politics: A Feminist Reading in Political Theory* (Totowa, NJ: Rowman & Littlefield, 1988), 79). Other passions—such as love of country (*Istorie*, III. 5), love of liberty (*Discorsi*, II. 2), love of the common good (*Discorsi*, I. 58), and desire not to be dominated (*Discorsi*, I. 5)—are equally important and, if properly sustained and encouraged, can be stronger than ambition.

16. 'O mente umana insaziabil, altera, | subdola e varia e sopra ogni altra cosa | maligna, iniqua, impetuosa e fera' *Dell'ambizione*, in *Il teatro*, 320).

17. 'L'empio e crudel martoro | de' miseri mortali, | il lungo strazio e 'nrimediabil danno, | il pianto di costoro | per li infiniti mali | che giorno e notte lamentar gli fanno | con singulti e affanno, | con alte voci e dolorose strida, | ciascun per sé merzé domanda e grida' ('Degli spiriti beati', in *Il teatro*, 332).

18. 'Dirò solo che vi morirno meglio che quattromila uomini, e li altri rimasono presi e con diversi modi costretti a riscattarsi; né perdonarono a vergini rinchiuse ne' luoghi sacri, i quali riempierono tutti di stupri e di

sacrilegi' (*Lettere*, 357; *MF* 216 (revised)). As I shall further illustrate at the end of this chapter, for Machiavelli politics is above all else intended to provide a shelter against men's ambition and ferocity. Therefore, to claim, as Hanna Pitkin does, that 'human autonomy and civility are male constructs painfully won from and continually threatened by corrosive feminine powers' *Fortune is a Woman* (Berkeley and Los Angeles: University of California Press, 1984; paperback edn., 1987), 136 is a misinterpretation of Machiavelli's conception of political action. For him the greatest threat against civil life is not feminine power, but men's ambition, and by 'men' he means males. It is their desire to dominate which has always destroyed and always threatens civil and political life.

19. Felix Gilbert, 'Machiavelli: The Renaissance of the Art of War', in P. Paret (ed.), *Makers of Modern Strategy* (Princeton: Princeton University Press, 1986) 24. The following verses from the poem 'On Ambition' certainly do not describe war as a grandiose event:

> Turn your eyes whoever wishes to see
> the troubles of others, and look again whether yet
> the sun ever saw so much cruelty.
> One weeps for the dead father and one for the husband,
> that wretched other, from under his own roof,
> is to be seen dragged out beaten and naked.
> O how many times, the father holding close
> in his arms the son, with a single blow alone,
> the breast has been sundered of one and the other.
> That one abandons his paternal soil,
> accusing the cruel and ungrateful Gods;
> within, his family full of grief.
> O examples never having existed in the world!
> Because one sees every day many births
> born out of the wounds of their womb.
> Behind her daughter full of troubles
> the mother says, 'To what an unhappy wedding,
> to what a cruel husband have I brought you!'
> The ditches and water are dirty with blood,
> full of skulls, legs, and hands,
> and other limbs torn and cut off.
> Rapacious birds, forest animals, dogs
> are then their paternal graves:
> O sepulchers crude, ferocious and strange! . . .
> Wherever you turn your eyes, you see
> the land full of tears and blood,
> and the air of shrieks, sobs, and sighs.

I am quoting from Sebastian De Grazia's translation in *Machiavelli in Hell* (Princeton: Princeton University Press, 1989), 165–6. For an excellent account of Machiavelli's position on war and peace see pp. 164–73.

20. *Istorie*, II. 37; *FH* 98–9.

21. 'Sol nasce l'uom d'ogni difesa ignudo, | e non ha cuoio, spine o piume o vello, | setole o scaglie che li faccian scudo. | Dal pianto il viver suo comincia quello, | con tuon di voce dolorosa e roca, | tal ch'egli è miserabile a vedello' (*Dell'asino d'oro*, in *Il teatro*, 302; Gilbert, ii. 772).

22. 'nudus humi iacet, infans, indigus omni | vitali auxilio, cum primum in luminis oras | nixibus ex alvo matris natura profudit, | vagituque locum lugubri complet, ut aequumst | cui tantum in vita restet transire malorum' (Lucretius, *De rerum natura* 5. 223–7). See also 5. 953–7: 'necdum res igni scibant tractare neque uti | pellibus et spoliis corpus vestire ferarum', and the description of the primitive man's death in 5. 990: 'unus enim tum quisque magis deprensus eorum | pabula viva feris praebebat, dentibus haustus, | et nemora ac montis gemitu silvasque replebat.'

23. 'Nessuno altro animal si truova ch'abbia | piú fragil vita, e di viver piú voglia, | piú confuso timore o maggior rabbia. | Non dà l'un porco a l'altro porco doglia, | l'un cervo a l'altro: solamente l'uomo | l'altr'uom amazza, crocifigge e spoglia' (*Dell'asino d'oro*, in *Il teatro*, 302; Gilbert, ii. 772).

24. 'E' si conosce facilmente per chi considera le cose presenti e le antiche, come in tutte le città ed in tutti i popoli sono quegli medesimi desideri e quelli medesimi omori, e come vi furono sempre. In modo che gliè facil cosa a chi esamina con diligenza le cose passate, prevedere in ogni republica le future e farvi quegli rimedi che dagli antichi sono stati usati, o non ne trovando degli usati, pensare de' nuovi per la similitudine degli accidenti' (*Discorsi*, I. 39; *Discourses*, 207–8 (revised)).

25. 'Donde nasce che infiniti che le leggono pigliono piacere di udire quella varietà degli accidenti che in esse si contengono, senza pensare altrimenti di imitarle, iudicando la imitazione non solo difficile ma impossibile; come se il cielo, il sole, li elementi, li uomini, fussino variati di moto, di ordine e di potenza da quello che gli erono antiquamente' (*Discorsi*, II, Proem, 124; *Discourses*, 98–9).

26. If we want to understand modernity, Harvey Mansfield has argued, 'one must look to its *beginnings*, when progress was first set in motion'. And at the beginnings of modernity we find Niccolò Machiavelli: 'only Machiavelli, a single man soaked in the Renaissance, and steeped in Humanism, seems, of those in his times, to have declared himself for progress in terms we recognize.' Hence, 'unless one dissolves Machiavelli's arguments into phrases and reduces his design to vulgar office-seeking, one cannot find another thinker or statesman who reminds us so vividly and profoundly of the realism and dynamism of modernity' ('Machiavelli's Political Science', *American Political Science Review*, 75 (1981), 294–5).

27. *Il teatro*, 365; Gilbert, iii. 1464.

28. 'Vedi le stelle e 'l ciel, vedi la luna, | vedi gli altri pianeti andare errando |

or alto or basso sanza requie alcuna' (*Dell'asino d'oro*, in *Il teatro*, 280; Gilbert, ii. 757–8).

29. 'Di quivi nasce la pace e la guerra, | di qui dipendon gli odi tra coloro | ch'un muro insieme e una fossa serra' (*L'Asino d'oro*, in *Il teatro*, 280; Gilbert, ii. 758).

30. 'La virtú fa le region tranquille; | e da tranquillità poi ne risolta | l'ocio: e l'ocio arde i paesi e le ville. | Poi, quando una provincia è stata involta | ne' disordini un tempo, tornar suole | virtude ad abitarvi un'altra volta. | Quest'ordine cosí permette e vuole | chi ci governa, acciò che nulla stia | o possa star mai fermo sotto 'l sole. | Ed è, e sempre fu e sempre fia, | che'l mal succeda al bene, il bene al male, | e l'un sempre cagion de l'altro sia' (*Dell'asino d'oro*, in *Il teatro*, 289; Gilbert, ii. 763).

31. 'Io canterò l'italiche fatiche | seguite già ne' duo passati lustri | sotto le stelle al suo bene inimiche' (*Decennale primo*, in *Il teatro*, 236; Gilbert, ii. 1445).

32. 'Forsitan et ambos excusabis: illam necessitudine fati, cuius vis refringi non potest' (*Decennale primo*, in *Il teatro*, 235; Gilbert, iii. 1444).

33. *Discorsi*, I. 56.

34. Ibid.

35. 'La cagione di questo, credo sia da essere discorsa e interpretata da uomo che abbi notizia delle cose naturali e soprannaturali: il che non abbiamo noi. Pure potrebbe essere, che sendo questo aere, come vuole alcuno filosofo, pieno di intelligenze, le quali per naturali virtú preveggendo le cose future ed avendo compassione agli uomini, acciò si possino preparare alle difese gli avvertiscono con simili segni' (*Discorsi*, I. 56; *Discourses*, 250).

36. 'Non ha cangiato il cielo opinione | ancor, né cangerà mentre che i fati | tengon ver te la lor dura intenzione | E quelli umori i quali ti sono stati | cotanto avversi e cotanto nimici, | non sono ancor, non sono ancor purgati. | Ma come secche fien le lor radici | e che benigni i ciel si mostreranno, | torneran tempi piú che mai felici' (*Dell'asino d'oro*, in *Il teatro* 280–1; Gilbert, ii. 758 (revised)).

37. 'perché la natura, come ne' corpi semplici quando e' vi è ragunato assai materia superflua, muove per se medesima molte volte e fa una purgazione la quale è salute di quel corpo; cosí interviene in questo corpo misto della umana generazione, che quando tutte le provincie sono ripiene di abitatori, in modo che non possono vivervi né possono andare altrove per essere occupati e ripieni tutti i luoghi; e quando la astuzia e la malignità umana è venuta dove la può venire, conviene di necessità che il mondo si purghi per uno de' tre modi: acciocché gli uomini, sendo divenuti pochi e battuti, vivino piú comodamente e diventino migliori' (*Discorsi*, II. 5; *Discourses*, 290 (revised)).

38. Parel, *The Machiavellian Cosmos*, 63–7.

39. *Di fortuna*, in *Il teatro* 312–18; Gilbert, ii. 745–9.

40. 'Questo per la sua patria assai sostenne: | e di vostra milizia il suo decoro | con gran iustizia gran tempo mantenne; | avaro de lo onor, largo de l'oro, | e di tanta virtú visse capace | che merita assai piú ch'io non lo onoro. | E or negletto e vilipeso iace | ne le sue case, pover, vecchio e cieco: | tanto a fortuna chi ben fa dispiace!' (*Decennale secondo*, in *Il teatro*, 259; Gilbert, iii. 1458 (revised)).

41. 'E veramente chi fussi tanto savio, che conoscessi e tempi e l'ordine delle cose et accomodassisi a quelle, arebbe sempre buona fortuna o e' si guarderebbe sempre da la trista, e verrebbe ad esser vero ch'l savio comandassi alle stelle et a' fati. Ma perché di questi savi non si truova, avendo li uomini prima la vista corta e non potendo poi comandare alla natura loro, ne segue che la fortuna varia e comanda a li uomini e tiegli sotto el giogo suo' (*Lettere*, 244; *MF* 135).

42. *Discorsi*, II. 29; *Discourses*, 369–72.

43. *Il Principe*, ch. 25; *The Prince*, 85. See also the peroration which ends the oration composed in March 1503: 'perché io vi dico che la fortuna non muta sententia dove non si muta ordine, né e' cieli vogliono o possono sostenere una cosa che voglia ruinare ad ogni modo' (*Parole da dirle sopra la provvisione del danaio*, in *I primi scritti*, 416).

44. *Dell'ambizione*, in *Il teatro* 319–20; Gilbert, ii. 735–6 (revised). He mentions the occult power which governs men's state also in *Of Fortune*: 'ma perché poter questo ci è negato | per occulta virtú che ci governa, si muta col suo corso il nostro stato' (*Di Fortuna*, in *Il teatro*, 316; Gilbert, ii. 747).

45. On this subject see the very precise remarks of Parel, *The Machiavellian Cosmos*, 54–9.

46. 'Ma Iddio, che sempre in simili estremità ha di quella avuta particolar cura, fece nascere un accidente insperato, il quale dètte al re ed al papa ed ai Vineziani maggiori pensieri che quelli di Toscana' (*Istorie*, VIII. 19; *FH* 341).

47. 'il quale, come vollero i cieli, che al mal futuro le cose preparavano, arrivò in Firenze in quel tempo appunto che l'impresa di Lucca era al tutto perduta' (*Istorie*, II. 33; *FH* 90).

48. 'E benchè fusse la nobilità distrutta, nondimeno alla fortuna non mancarono modi di far rinascere per nuove divisioni nuovi travagli' (*Istorie*, II. 42; *FH* 104).

49. *Discorsi*, II. 5. See also the important remarks by Gennaro Sasso in *Machiavelli e gli antichi e attri saggi*, 3 vols.; (Naples, Riccardo Ricciardi, 1987–8), i, 167–376.

50. *Il Principe*, ch. 26; *The Prince*, 88.

51. 'è piuttosto miracolo che io sia vivo, perché mi è suto tolto l'uffizio, e sono stato per perdere la vita, la quale Iddio e la innocenzia mia mi ha salvata; tutti gli altri mali, e di prigione e d'altro ho sopportato: pure io

sto, con la grazia di Iddio, bene, e mi vengo vivendo come io posso, e così mi ingegnerò di fare, sino che i cieli non si mostrino più benigni' (*Lettere*, 387–8; *MF* 239).

52. 'Ma non sia alcun di sí poco cervello | che creda, se la sua casa ruina, | che Dio la salvi sanz'altro puntello; | perché e' morrà sotto quella ruina' *(Dell'asino d'oro*, in *Il teatro* 290; Gilbert, ii. 764).

53. *La vita*, 104; Gilbert, ii. 555.

54. In *Il Principe*, he mentions God twice in ch. 6: 'benché di Moisè non si debba ragionare, sendo suto uno mero esecutore delle cose che li erano ordinate da Dio, *tamen* debbe essere ammirato *solum* per quella grazia che lo faceva degno di parlare con Dio'; once in ch. 8: 'coloro che osservano el primo modo, possono con Dio e con li uomini avere allo stato loro qualche rimedio'; once in ch. 11: 'sendo esaltati [ecclesiastic principalities] e mantenuti da Dio, sarebbe offizio di uomo prosuntuoso e temerario discorrerne'; once in ch. 25: 'che le cose del mondo sieno in modo governate dalla fortuna e da Dio.'

55. 'né fu a loro Dio piú amico che a voi' (*Il Principe*, ch. 26; *The Prince*, 88). See also De Grazia, *Machiavelli in Hell*, 50–6.

56. 'Dio non vuole fare ogni cosa, per non ci tòrre el libero arbitrio e parte di quella gloria che tocca a noi' (*Il Principe*, ch. 26; *The Prince*, 89).

57. 'piú grato a Dio' (*Discursus florentinarum rerum post mortem iunioris Laurentii Medices*, in *Arte della guerra*, 275; Gilbert, i. 113–14. A few lines later Machiavelli describes the occasion of restoring a republic in Florence as a present of heaven: 'non dà, adunque, il cielo maggiore dono ad uno uomo.' In *Discorsi*, i. 10, he speaks again of 'heavens' offering great men the occasion to accomplish glorious deeds: 'e veramente i cieli non possono dare agli uomini maggiore occasione di gloria, né gli uomini la possono maggiore desiderare.'

58. Macrobius, *Commentary on the Dream of Scipio*, ed. William Harris Stahl (New York: Columbia University Press, 1952), 120. For the Latin text, I have used the *Commento al Somnium Scipionis*, ed. Mario Regali (Pisa: Giardini, 1983).

59. 'Coloro che osservano el primo modo, possono con Dio e con li uomini avere allo stato loro qualche rimedio, come ebbe Agatocle; quelli altri è impossibile si mantenghino' (*Il Principe*, ch. 8; *The Prince*, 33).

60. 'voleva essere scusato con Dio et con li uomini se cercassi assicurarsi dello stato vostro per qualunque modo e' possessi' (*Legazioni*, i. 261).

61. 'quando che no, lui veniva con lo esercito per questo effetto, e li incresceva avere ad offendere altri, ma che se ne scusava con Dio, con gli uomini e con loro, come colui che era vinto dalla necessità' (ibid. 520).

62. *Discorsi*, ii. 1.

63. Roberto Ridolfi, *Vita di Niccolò Machiavelli*, 2 vols.; Florence: Sansoni,

1969), i. 380 and n. 2; Eng trans. *The Life of Niccolò Machiavelli*, trans. Cecil Grayson (London: Routledge and Kegan Paul, 1963), 242.

64. Ridolfi, *Vita di Niccolò Machiavelli*, 379–80; *The Life of Niccolò Machiavelli*, 242.

65. Machiavelli to Francesco Guicciardini, 17 May 1521, in *Lettere*, 519–22; *MF* 336–7.

66. 'Da l'altro canto, el peggio che te ne va è morire e andarne in inferno; e' son morti tanti degli altri! e sono in inferno tanti uomini da bene! Ha'ti tu a vergognare d'andarvi tu?' (*La Mandragola*, Act IV. Sc. i, in *Il teatro*, 92; Gilbert, ii. 805 (revised)).

67. 'Credo gli servirete secondo la espettazione che si ha di voi, e secondo che ricerca lo onore vostro, quale si oscurerebbe se in questa età vi dessi all'anima, perché, avendo sempre vivuto con contraria professione, sarebbe attribuito piutosto al rimbambito che al buono' (*Lettere*, 518–19; *MF* 335).

68. 'E se questa materia non è degna, | per esser pur leggieri, | d'un uom che voglia parer saggio e grave, | scusatelo con questo, che s'ingegna | con questi van pensieri | fare el suo tristo tempo piú suave, | perch'altrove non have | dove voltare el viso: | ché gli è stato interciso | mostrar con altre imprese altra virtute, | non sendo premio alle fatiche sue' (*La Mandragola*, Prologue, in *Il teatro*, 57–8; Gilbert, ii. 776 (revised)).

69. *La Mandragola*, Prologue, *Il teatro*, 57; Gilbert, ii. 777.

70. *Clizia*, Prologue, in *Il teatro*, 117; Gilbert, ii. 824.

71. See the letter to Vettori of 25 Feb. 1514, and the letter to Luigi Guicciardini of 8 Dec. 1509, in *Lettere*, 441–4, 321–3; *MF* 276–8, 190–1.

72. See Ridolfi, *Vita di Niccolò Machiavelli*, 378–91; *The Life of Niccolò Machiavelli*, 242–50.

73. Ridolfi, *Vita di Niccolò Machiavelli*, 390–1; *The Life of Niccolò Machiavelli*, 249–50.

74. On Machiavelli's dream, see the very pertinent remarks by Sasso, *Machiavelli e gli antichi e altri saggi*, iii. 269–74.

75. The verse is from a short poem which deserves to be quoted because it offers us the possibility to know Machiavelli's inward feelings, as he himself perceived them. Unfortunately, no date of composition can be suggested for this text.

> Io spero, e lo sperar cresce 'l tormento
> io piango, e il pianger ciba il lasso core,
> io rido e il rider mio non passa drento,
> io ardo e l'arsion non par di fore;
> io temo ciò che io veggo e ciò che io sento,
> ogni cosa mi dà nuovo dolore:
> cosí sperando, piango, rido e ardo,
> e paura ho di ciò che io odo e guardo.
>
> (*Il teatro*, 357)

76. 'Però se alcuna volta io rido o canto, | Follo perché io non ho se non questa una | ia da sfogare il mio acerbo pianto' (*Lettere*, 371; *MF* 228).

77. 'e vedresti che le furono reti d'oro, tese tra fiori, tessute da Venere, tanto soavi e gentili, che benché un cuor villano le avesse potute rompere, nondimeno io non volli, et un pezzo mi vi godei dentro, tanto che le fila tenere sono diventate dure, e incavicchiate con nodi irresolubili' (Letter to Vettori, 3 Aug. 1514, in *Lettere*, 465; *MF* 293).

78. *La Mandragola*, Act IV, Sc. i; Gilbert, ii. 805.

79. *Clizia*, Act I, Sc. ii; Gilbert, ii. 829.

80. 'mi si lascia qualche volta baciare pure alla sfuggiasca' (*Lettere*, 444; *MF* 278).

81. 'S'a la mia immensa voglia | fussi il valor conforme | si desteria pietà la dove or dorme. | Ma perché non uguali | son le forze al desío, | ne nascon tutti e mali | ch'io sento, o signor mio, | né doler mi poss'io | di voi ma di me stesso, | poi ch'i' veggio e confesso | come tanta beltade | ama piú verde etade' (*Il teatro*, 360).

82. See Vettori's comment in the letter to Machiavelli of 16 Jan. 1515: 'Ma voi mi dite cosa che mi fa stare ammirato: d'avere trovato tanta fede e tanta compassione nella Riccia che, vi prometto, li ero per amor vostro partigiano, ma ora, li son diventato stiavo' (*Lettere*, 487; *MF* 311).

83. 'il più delle volte le femmine sogliono amare la fortuna e non li uomini, e quando essa si muta mutarsi ancor loro' (*Lettere*, 487; *MF* 311); 'Machiavelli's writings', remarks Pitkin, 'never transcended the conventional misogyny of his time' (*Fortune is a Woman*, 305). In comparison with Vettori, at least in this case, he certainly did.

84. 'e quel piacere che voi piglierete oggi, voi non lo arete a pigliare domani' (*Lettere*, 450; *MF* 282).

85. Letter to Vettori, 10 Dec. 1513, in *Lettere*, 425; *MF* 264.

86. 'io credo, credetti, e crederrò sempre che sia vero quello che dice il Boccaccio: che gli è meglio fare e pentirsi, che non fare e pentirsi' (Letter to Vettori, 25 Feb. 1514, in *Lettere*, 450; *MF* 282).

87. Pitkin, *Fortune is a Woman*, 21.

88. 'e di necessità bisogna ridursi a pensare a cose piacevole, né so cosa che diletti più a pensarvi e a farlo, che il fottere. E filosofi ogni uomo quanto e' vuole, che questa è la pura verità, la quale molti intendono così ma pochi la dicano' (*Lettere*, 487–8; *MF* 311).

89. 'tanto mi paiono or dolci, or leggieri, or gravi quelle catene, e fanno un mescolo di sorte, che io giudico non potere vivere contento senza quella qualità di vita' (*Lettere*, 489; *MF* 312).

90. 'E benché mi paia essere entrato in gran travaglio, tamen io ci sento dentro tanta dolcezza, sì per quello che quello aspetto raro e suave mi arreca, sì etiam per avere posto da parte la memoria di tutti e mia affanni,

che per cosa del mondo, possendomi liberare, non vorrei' (Letter to Vettori, 3 Aug. 1514, in *Lettere*, 465; *MF* 293). 'When Machiavelli expounds on the perils of love, it is not the power of women *qua* women that is so deeply threatening but the passions a man feels toward them, his experience of being in thrall to his needs, that make ruins of the rest of his life and undermine his institutional power over women' (Brown, *Manhood and Politics*, 89–90). The lines quoted above illustrate well just how fiercely Machiavelli was in fact expounding on the perils of love and how resolutely he was fighting against feminine powers.

91. Pitkin, *Fortune is a Woman*, 5, 7

92. 'Questi savi, questi savi, io non so dove si stanno a casa; a me pare che ognuno pigli le cose al contrario' (*Lettere*, 444; *MF* 278). 'Like other men in Renaissance Florence', writes Hanna Pitkin, Machiavelli 'had virtually no experience of women as citizens or peers' (*Fortune is a Woman*, 305).

93. See De Grazia, *Machiavelli in Hell*, 20–1.

94. Pitkin, *Fortuna is a Woman*, 123–4

95. See *Lettere*, 354–60; *MF* 216.

96. See *Legazioni*, i. 23–45.

97. See *Discorsi*, iii. 6; *Istorie*, viii. 34.

98. 'bella donna, savia, costumata e atta a governare un regno' (*La Mandragola*, Act I, Sc. iii, in *Il teatro*, 66; Gilbert, ii. 783).

99. 'Voi mi dilegiate, ma non n'avete ragione, ché più rigollio arei se voi fussi qui: voi che sapete bene come io sto lieta quando voi non siete qua giù; e tanto più ora che m' è stato detto costassù è si gran morbo, pensate come io sto contenta, che e' non trovo riposo né dì né note' (*Lettere*, 182; *MF* 93).

100. *Lettere*, 625; *MF* 413.

101. *Lettere*, 630; *MF* 417.

102. 'Ma egli è impossibile che io possa stare molto così, perché io mi logoro, e veggo, quando Iddio non mi si mostri più favorevole, che io sarò un dì forzato ad uscirmi di casa, e pormi per ripetitore o cancelliere di un connestabole, quando io non possa altro, o ficcarmi in qualche terra deserta ad insegnare leggere a' fanciulli, e lasciare qua la mia brigata, che facci conto che io sia morto; la quale farà molto meglio senza me, perchè io le sono di spesa, sendo avvezzo a spendere, e non potendo fare senza spendere' (*Lettere*, 462; *MF* 290 (revised)).

103. 'ché vedi quanto onore fa a me un poco di virtù che io ho; sì che, figliuolo mio, se tu vuoi dare contento a me, e fare bene et onore a te, studia, fa bene, impara, ché se tu ti aiuterai, ciascuno ti aiuterà' (*Lettere*, 625; *MF* 413).

104. 'parlo con quelli che passono, dimando delle nuove de' paesi loro,

intendo varie cose, e noto varii gusti e diverse fantasie d'uomini' (*Lettere*, 425; *MF* 264).

105. *Lettere*, 436–7; *MF* 273; for the letter from Vettori, see *Lettere*, 432–5; *MF* 268.

106. *Lettere*, 437; *MF* 273 (revised).

107. *Istorie*, VII. 28

108. 'El mulettino, poiché gli è impazato, si vuole trattarlo al contrario degli altri pazi: perché gl'altri pazi si legano, et io voglio che tu lo sciolga. Dara'lo ad Vangelo, e dirai che lo meni in Montepugliano, e dipoi gli cavi la briglia et il capestro, e lascilo andare dove e' vuole a guadagnarsi il vivere et a cavarsi la pazia. Il paese è largo, la bestia è piccola, non può fare male veruno' (*Lettere*, 625; *MF* 413).

109. Brown, *Manhood and Politics*, 91.

110. 'Chi vedesse le nostre lettere, onorando compare, e vedesse la diversità di quelle, si maraviglierebbe assai, perché gli parrebbe ora che noi fussimo uomini gravi, tutti vòlti a cose grandi, e che ne' petti nostri non potesse cascare alcuno pensiere che non avesse in sé onestà e grandezza. Però dipoi, voltando carta, gli parrebbe quelli noi medesimi essere leggieri, incostanti, lascivi, vòlti a cose vane. Questo modo di procedere, se a qualcuno pare sia vituperoso, a me pare sia laudabile, perché noi imitiamo la natura, che è varia; e chi imita quella non può essere ripreso' *(Lettere*, 489–90; *MF* 312).

111. See Cicero, *Pro Sestio* 139; *Philippics* 1. 29; *Tusculanae Disputationes* 3. 2. 3.

112. 'Non in mezzo agli otii privati, ma intra le publiche experienzie nasce la fama: nelle pubbliche piazze surge la gloria; in mezzo de' popoli si nutrisce la lode con voce et iudicio di molti onorati; fugge la fama ogni solitudine et luogo privato, et volentieri siede et dimora sopra e teatri presente alle contioni et celebrità; ivi si collustra et alluma il nome di chi con molto sudore et assiduo studio di buone cose sé stessi tradusse fuori di taciturnità et tenebre, d'ignorantia et vizii' (Leon Battista Alberti, *I primi tre libri della famiglia*, in *Opere volgari*, ed. C. Greison (Bari: Laterza, 1966), 281–2; Eng. trans., *The Alberti of Florence: Leon Battista Alberti's Della Famiglia*, ed. Guido A. Guanno (Lewisburg: Bucknell University Press, 1971), 186).

113. For a different interpretation, see De Grazia, *Machiavelli in Hell*, 378–9. See also Victor Santi, '"Fama" e "laude" distinte da "gloria" in Machiavelli', *Forum Italicum*, 13 (1978), 206–15; Russell Price, 'The Theme of Gloria in Machiavelli', *Renaissance Quarterly*, 30 (1977), 588–631.

114. *Discorsi*, II. 1.

115. Ibid. 1. 10.

116. Ibid.

117. Ibid.

118. 'E cosí arà duplicata gloria, di avere dato principio a uno principato nuovo, et ornatolo e corroboratolo di buone legge, di buone arme, di buoni amici e di buoni esempli; come quello ha duplicata vergogna, che, nato principe, lo ha per sua poca prudenzia perduto' (*Il Principe*, ch. 24).

119. Ibid., ch. 26.

120. *Discursus Florentinarum Rerum*, in *Arte della Guerra*, 275–6; Gilbert, i. 114.

121. *Discorsi*, I. 10.

122. 'ingannati da uno falso bene e da una falsa gloria' (ibid.).

123. 'quello appetito non di vera gloria, ma di vituperosi onori, dal quale dipendono gli odj, le inimicizie, i dispiaceri, le sètte, dalle quali nascono morti, esilj, afflizioni dei buoni, esaltazioni dei tristi' (*Istorie*, III. 5; *FH* 110).

124. *Discorsi*, I. 10.

125. *Il Principe*, ch. 8.

126. 'e dico che Pompeo e Cesare, e quasi tutti quegli capitani che furono a Roma dopo l'ultima guerra cartaginese, acquistarono fama come valenti uomini, non come buoni; e quegli che erano vivuti avanti a loro, acquistarono gloria come valenti e buoni' (*Arte della guerra*, 337; Gilbert, ii. 575).

127. *Arte della guerra*, 337; Gilbert, ii. 575.

128. 'E per questo ei volevano che il Consolo per sé facesse e che la gloria fose tutta sua; lo amore della quale giudicavano che fusse freno e regola a farlo operare bene' (*Discorsi*, II. 33).

129. On the distinction between fame and glory in Roman republican political theory, see Donald Earl, *The Moral and Political Tradition of Rome* (Ithaca, NY: Cornell University Press, 1967), 30.

130. *Discorsi*, I. 27; *Discourses*, 178.

131. *Il Principe*, ch. 18.

132. Ibid., ch. 21.

133. Ibid., ch. 18.

134. *Discorsi*, III. 40; *Discourses*, 512. Fraud used in dealing with an enemy 'who has not kept faith with you' in war is, on the contrary, 'glorious', as the title of the chapter states: 'That it is a glorious thing to use fraud in the Conduct of War'.

135. *Discorsi*, I. 58; *Discourses*, 254.

136. *Istorie*, VIII. 19.

137. Ibid. I. 39.

138. *Arte della guerra*, 332; Gilbert, ii. 572.

139. 'Iddio ama la giustizia e la pietà', *Allocuzione fatta ad un magistrato*, in

Arte della guerra, 136; Machiavelli, 'Allocution Made to a Magistrate', ed. Anthony Parel, *Political Theory*, 18, (1990), 527.

140. *Discorsi*, III. 1; *Discourses*, 385–6 (revised).

141. 'Onorare e premiare le virtù, non dispregiare la povertà, stimare i modi e gli ordini della disciplina militare, costringere i cittadini ad amare l'uno l'altro, a vivere sanza sètte, a stimare meno il privato che il pubblico e altre simili cose che facilmente si potrebbono con questi tempi accompagnare. I quali modi non sono difficili persuadere, quando vi si pensa assai ed entrasi per li debiti mezzi, ché in essi appare tanto la verità, che ogni comunale ingegno ne puote essere capace; la quale cosa chi ordina, pianta arbori sotto l'ombra de' quali si dimora piú felice e piú lieto che sotto questa' (*Arte della guerra*, 332–3; Gilbert, ii. 572).

2 *The Art of the State*

1. 'Pure, se io vi potessi parlare, non potre' fare che io non vi empiessi il capo di castellucci, perché la fortuna ha fatto che, non sapendo ragionare né dell'arte della seta e dell'arte della lana, né de' guadagni né delle perdite, e' mi conviene ragionare dello stato, e mi bisogna o botarmi di stare cheto, o ragionare di questo' (*Lettere*, 367; MF 225 (revised)).

2. 'e per questa cosa, quando la fussi letta, si vedrebbe che quindici anni che io sono stato a studio all'arte dello stato, non gl'ho né dormiti né giuocati; e doverebbe ciascheduno aver caro servirsi d'uno che alle spese d'altri fusse pieno di esperienzia' (*Lettere*, 428; MF 265). Some years earlier, during his mission at the court of the King of France, he was so bold about his own expertise that he replied to the powerful Cardinal of Rouen, minister of Louis XII—who had said that the Italians do not know of war—that the French 'did not know of the state [*dello stato*]', implying, of course, that he knew better than they did what was needed to preserve dominion over a foreign country. See *Il Principe*, ch. 3, and the letter of 21 Nov. 1500, in which he explains the general criterion to be used to preserve control over foreign countries, in *Legazioni*, i. 205.

3. 'Esaminate tutto, e vi conosco di tale ingegno, che, ancora che siano due anni passati vi levasti da bottega, non credo abbiate dimenticato l'arte' (*Lettere*, 467; MF 294).

4. I am borrowing this expression from Nicolai Rubinstein, 'Notes on the Word *stato* in Florence before Machiavelli', in J. G. Rowe and W. H. Stockdale (eds.), *Florilegium historiale: Essays Presented to Wallace K. Ferguson* (Toronto: University of Toronto Press, 1971), 321.

5. The expression 'government and public administration' ('governi publici') is in Guicciardin, *Dialogo del Reggimento di Firenze*; Eng. trans., *Dialogue on the Government of Florence*, ed. Alison Brown (Cambridge: Cambridge University Press, 1994), 1; 'the theory of the

best governments' is in Antonio Brucioli: *Gli otto libri della Republica che chiamono Politica di Aristotile* (Venice: Antonio Brucioli e i frategli, 1547), 3; 'the theory and practice of civil affairs' is in Donato Giannotti, *Discorso sopra il riordinare la repubblica di Siena*, in *Opere politiche*, ed. Furio Diaz (Milan: Marzoratri, 1974), 446.

6. 'Fu mondano uomo, ma di lui avemo fatta menzione, perch'egli fu cominciatore e maestro in digrossare i Fiorentini, e farli scorti di bene parlare, e in sapere guidare e reggere la nostra repubblica secondo la politica' (*Cronica* (Florence, 1845), 8. 10).

7. B. Latini, *Li livres dou tresor*, ed. F. J. Carmody (Berkeley: University of California Press, 1948), bk. I, 4.

8. 'Car se parleure ne fust cités ne serait, ne nus establissemens de justice ne de humaine compaignie' (*Li livres dou tresor*), bk. III, 1).

9. On the central role of rhetoric in the tracts on *podestà*-rule, see E. Artifoni, 'I podestà professionali e la fondazione retorica della politica comunale', *Quaderni storici*, 63 (1986), 687–719.

10. 'Et Tuilles dist que la plus haute science de cité governer si est rectorique, c'est à dire la science du parler' (*Li livres dou Tresor*, bk. III, 1).

11. 'son veg[n]uto per essere comunale e fare e mantíg[n]ere ad onne persona rasone' (Guido Faba, *Parlamenta et Epistole*, in *La Prosa del Duecento*, ed. C. Segre and M. Monti (Milan: Ricciardi, 1959), 15).

12. *Oculus pastoralis*, in D. Franceschi (ed.), *Memorie dell'Accademia delle Scienze di Torino*, 4/11 (1966), 66 ('Invectiva Iusticie contra rectores gentium'); see also D. Franceschi, 'L'*Oculus pastoralis* e la sua fortuna', *Atti dell'Accademia delle Scienze di Torino*, (Classe di Scienze Morali, Storiche e Filologiche, 99), 2 (1964–5), 206–61.

13. Cicero, *De finibus bonorum et malorum*, ed. H. Rackham (London: Harvard University Press, 1914), 304–5; Seneca also, referring again to the Peripatetic school, mentions 'civil philosophy' ('civilis philosophia') as a particular type of activity along with natural, moral, and rational philosophy (*Epistle* 89); I am quoting from Seneca, *Seneca ad Lucilium Epistulae Morales*, ed. R. M. Gummere (2 vols.; Cambridge, Mass.: Harvard University Press, 1958), 384–5.

14. See Joseph Canning, *The Political Thought of Baldus De Ubaldis* (Cambridge: Cambridge University Press, 1987), 159–69.

15. Coluccio Salutati, *De nobilitate legum et medicinae*, ed. E. Garin (Florence: Vallecchi, 1947), 168.

16. Ibid. 170.

17. Ibid. 18.

18. 'politicae rationis institutio atque preceptio' (ibid. 198).

19. 'Intendit politica conservationem humane societatis; hoc idem intendit

et lex. Vult politica civem bonum; et quid aliud latores legum suis institutionibus moliuntur?' (ibid. 170).

20. 'Nulla profecto convenientior discipline homini esse potest quae quid sit civitas et quod respublica intelligere et per que conservatur intereatque civilis societas non ignorare' (Leonardo Bruni, *In libros politicorum Aristotelis de greco in latini traducto prologus*, in *Leonardo Bruni Aretino, Humanistisch-philosophische Schriften*, ed. H. Baron (Wiesbaden: M. Sändig, 1969), 73).

21. 'Intentio igitur A. est ut post moralem et domesticam disciplinam civitatem constituat, et Rempublicam moderetur, in qua hominis, seu cives, quoad possint felicissime vivant' (Donati Acciaiuoli, *In Aristotelis libros octo Politicorum commentarii nunc primum in lucem editi . . .* (Venice: Vincentium Valgrisium 1566), 9).

22. 'excellentissima partium activarum scientia' (Donato Acciaiuoli Florentini, *Expositio super libros ethicarum Aristotelis in novam traductionem Iohannis Argyropyli Bizantii* (Florence: Sanctum Iacobum De Ripoli, 1478), fo. 9).

23. 'humano vivere et maxime politico et civile' (Alamanno Rinuccini, *Lettere ed orazioni*, ed. Vito Giustiniani (Florence: Olschki, 1953), 202); see also 191: 'Tacerommi di dire l'essersi per quello medesimo giorno corroborate et vivificate le vostre sacrosante et inviolabili leggi, nella cui observantia consiste il fondamento d' ogni buono et polytico viver.' For another example of the opposite of political life (*vivere politico*)— tyranny, see Giovanni Cavalcanti, *Istorie Fiorentine*, ed. Guido di Pino (Milan: Martello, 1945), v. 145.

24. Cf. Bernardo Machiavelli, *Libro di ricordi*, ed. Cesare Olschki (Florence: Le Monnier, 1954), 141.

25. *Discorsi*, bk. I, Proem.

26. *I primi scritti*, 516. Other examples are in the *Ritracto delle cose della Magna* (ibid. 530), and in *La cagione dell'ordinanza* (ibid. 433).

27. 'Come dimostrano tutti coloro che ragionano del vivere civile, e come ne è piena di esempli ogni istoria, è necessario a chi dispone una republica ed ordina leggi in quella presupporre tutti gli uomini rei, e che li abbiano sempre a usare la malignità dello animo loro qualunque volta ne abbiano libera occasione [. . .] Però si dice che la fame e la povertà fa gli uomini industriosi, e le leggi gli fanno buoni' (*Discorsi*, 1. 3).

28. *Discursus florentinarum rerum*, in *Arte della guerra*, 275–6. The idea that to write on public government is one of man's most noble occupations is also to be found in Guicciardini: 'How splendid and honourable it is to meditate on government and public administration, on which our well-being, our health and our life depend—as do all the notable deeds that are performed in this earthy life below! Quite apart from the useful and relevant material they provide for many aspects of our daily lives, the subject-matter is extremely worthy and worthwhile in itself' (Francesco

Guicciardini, *Dialogo del reggimento di firenze*, in *Opere*, ed. Emmanuella Lugnani Scarano (Turin: UTET, 1974), 299; Eng. trans. *Dialogue on the Government of Florence* ed. and trans. Alison Brown (Cambridge: Cambridge University Press, 1994).

29. See Cicero, *De officiis* 1. 34. 124, and Livy, *Ab urbe condita* 2. 3.

30. *Discorsi*, I. 10.

31. Ibid. III. 5; *Discourses*, 396.

32. *Discorsi*, III. 25.

33. The meaning of the word *stato* has been the subject of a vast scholarly literature. In contrast with the views of Francesco Ercole, *La politica di Machiavelli* (Rome: ARE, 1926), 123–42, Fredi Chiappelli pointed out that, in *Il Principe*, Machiavelli's genuine political treatise, the word *stato* denotes, with a few exceptions, the political organization of a people over a territory independent of the particular form of government or regime—that is, the modern abstract notion of the state; see *Studi sul linguaggio di Machiavelli* (Florence: Le Monnier, 1952), 59–68. An opposite view is suggested by Jack H. Hexter, who stressed that *Il Principe* does not contain the conception of the state as an abstract political body which transcends the individuals who compose or rule it; see *The Vision of Politics on the Eve of the Reformation: More, Machiavelli, and Seyssel* (New York: Basic Books, 1973), 150–78. See also Quentin Skinner, 'The State', in Terence Ball, James Farr, and Rusell L. Hanson (eds.) *Political Innovation and Conceptual Change* (Cambridge: Cambridge University Press, 1989), 90–131.

34. 'quelli che l'avevano rimesso e tanti ingiuriati cittadini pensarono senza alcuno rispetto d'assicurarsi dello stato loro' (*Istorie*, v. 4).

35. The disturbing features of the state were severely chastised by the Quattrocento humanists. See, for instance, Leon Battista Alberti, *I primi tre libri della famiglia* in *Opere Volgari*, ed. C. Greison (Bari: Laterza, 1966), 273; Poggio Bracciolini, *Secunda convivalis disceptatio*, in *La disputa delle arti nel Quattrocento*, ed. Eugenio Garin (Florence: Vallecchi, 1947), 29–30.

36. See Felix Gilbert, 'Florentine Political Assumptions in the Period of Savonarola and Soderini', *Journal of the Warburg and Courtauld Institutes*, 20 (1957), 208.

37. 'e così non si suole nelle cose delli stati' (ibid.).

38. Guicciardini, *Dialogue on the Government of Florence*, 159.

39. Ibid.

40. 'perché uno uomo, che voglia fare in tutte le parte professione di buono, conviene rovini infra tanti che non sono buoni. Onde è necessario a uno principe, volendosi mantenere, imparare a potere essere non buono, et usarlo e non usare secondo la necessità' (*Il Principe*, ch. 15; *The Prince* 54–5).

41. 'Et hassi ad intendere questo, che uno principe, e massime uno principe nuovo, non può osservare tutte quelle cose per le quali li uomini sono tenuti buoni, sendo spesso necessitato, per mantenere lo stato, operare contro alla fede, contro alla carità, contro alla umanità, contro alla religione' (*Il Principe*, ch. 18; *The Prince*, 62 (revised)).

42. 'se uno uomo di basso et infimo stato ardisce discorrere e regolare e' governi de' principi' (*Il Principe*, Dedicatory Letter; *The Prince*, 4).

43. 'non può osservare tutte quelle cose per le quali li uomini sono tenuti buoni' (*Il Principe*, ch. 18; *The Prince*, 62).

44. 'Quanto sia laudabile in uno principe mantenere la fede, e vivere con integrità e non con astuzia, ciascuno lo intende: non di manco si vede per esperienza, ne' nostri tempi, quelli principi avere fatto gran cose che della fede hanno tenuto poco conto, e che hanno saputo con l'astuzia aggirare e' cervelli delli uomini: et alla fine hanno superato quelli che si sono fondati in sulla lealtà' (*Il Principe*, ch. 18; *The Prince*, 61).

45. *Il Principe*, ch. 15; *The Prince*, 54.

46. See Q. Skinner, *The Foundations of Modern Political Thought* (2 vols.; Cambridge: Cambridge University Press, 1978) i. 128–38; see also Skinner, *Machiavelli*, (Oxford: Oxford University Press, 1981), 31–47.

47. *Il Principe*, ch. 18.

48. Cicero, *De officiis* 2. 7. 24.

49. *Il Principe*, ch. 17.

50. *Discorsi*, III. 40.

51. *Il Principe*, ch. 18.

52. See *Il Principe*, chs. 24 and 21; *The Prince*, 83, 79.

53. *Ai Palleschi. Notate bene questo scripto*, in *I primi scritti*, 533–5. In this text Machiavelli uses the word *stato* also in the sense of *political community* ('e' non gli muove el fare bene ad questo *stato*'); as *political regime* ('a me non pare che cosa alcuna, di che si truovi in colpa Piero Soderini, possa dare reputatione ad questo *stato* apresso al popolo: perché di quelle medesime cose di che potessi essere incolpato Piero, sempre questo *stato* ne sarà o incolpato o sospecto'); as *political power* ('stare uniti con lo *stato*').

54. 'Di qui nacque che in tanta varietà di fortuna, in sì varia città e volubile cittadinanza tenne uno stato XXXI anno; perchè sendo prudentissimo cognosceva i mali discosto, e perciò era a tempo o a non gli lasciar crescere, o a prepararsi in modo, che cresciuti non l'offendessero' (*Istorie*, VII. 5).

55. 'Li antecessori vostri, cominciandosi da Cosimo e venendo infino a Piero, usorno in tenere questo Stato piú industria che forza. A voi è necessario usare piú forza che industria, perché voi ci avete piú nimici e manco ordine a saddisfarli; però a voi bisogna, non ve li potendo riguadagnare,

che voi stiate ordinati che gli abbino paura a nuocervi' (Rudolf von Albertini, *Firenze dalla repubblica al principato* (Turin: Einaudi, 1970), 357).

56. 'tenere lo stato e governo della città di Firenze' (Francesco Guicciardini, *Delle condizioni in cui trovavansi le contrarie parti che dividevano la città per la mutazione dello Stato, e della difformità di pareri e d'intenti nel restringere il Governo*, ed. Guiseppe Canestrini, *Opere inedite di Francesco Guicciardini* (Florence: Barbera, 1858), ii. 316.

57. 'E questo interviene più oggi che mai, per essersi i cittadini nutriti e avvezzi dal 1494 sino al 1512 a uno modo di Governo popularissimo e liberissimo, e nel quale parendo loro essere tutti equali, con più difficultà si assettano a ricognoscere alcuno superiore, e massime vedendo uno solo tanto interamente assoluto arbitro e signore di ogni cosa' (ibid. 318).

58. 'la città voi non ve la potete riguadagnare' (*Ricordi di Paolo Vettori al cardinale de' Medici sopra le cose di Firenze*, in Rudolf von Albertini, *Firenze dalla repubblica al principato* (Turin: Einandi, 1970), 357).

59. Guicciardini, *Delle condizioni*, 320–1.

60. 'Perché li uomini sono molto piú presi dalle cose presenti che dalle passate, e quando nelle presenti truovono il bene, vi si godono e non cercano altro' (*Il Principe*, ch. 24; *The Prince*, 83).

61. 'con fatica e difficultà grande se li potrà mantenere amici' (*Il Principe*, ch. 20).

62. 'Quelli che si obbligano, e non sieno rapaci, si debbono onorare et amare; quelli che non si obbligano, si hanno ad esaminare in dua modi: o fanno questo per pusillanimità e defetto naturale d'animo: allora tu ti debbi servire di quelli massime che sono di buono consiglio, perché nelle prosperità te ne onori, e nelle avversità non hai da temerne. Ma, quando non si obbligano ad arte e per cagione ambiziosa, è segno che pensono piú a sé che a te; e da quelli si debbe el principe guardare, e temerli come se fussino scoperti inimici, perché sempre, nelle avversità, aiuteranno a ruinarlo' (*Il Principe*, ch. 9; *The Prince*, 35–6).

63. 'Concluderò solo che a uno principe è necessario avere el populo amico: altrimenti non ha nelle avversità remedio' (*Il Principe*, ch. 9; *The Prince*, 36).

64. 'Preterea, del populo inimico uno principe non si può mai assicurare, per esser troppi; de' grandi si può assicurare, per esser pochi' (*Il Principe*, ch. 9; *The Prince*, 35).

65. 'E' necessitato ancora el principe vivere sempre con quello medesimo populo; ma può ben fare sanza quelli medesimi grandi, potendo farne e disfarne ogni dí, e tòrre e dare, a sua posta, reputazione loro' (*Il Principe*, ch. 9, *The Prince*, 35).

66. 'perché questi principi, o comandano per loro medesimi, o per mezzo de' magistrati. Nell'ultimo caso, è piú debole e piú periculoso lo stare loro;

perché gli stanno al tutto con la volontà di quelli cittadini che sono preposti a' magistrati, li quali massime ne' tempi avversi, li possono tòrre con facilità grande lo stato, o con farli contro, o con non lo obedire. Et el principe non è a tempo ne' periculi a pigliare l'autorità assoluta; perchè li cittadini e sudditi, che sogliono avere e' comandamenti da' magistrati, non sono, in quelli frangenti, per obedire a' sua; et arà sempre, ne' tempi dubii, penuria di chi si possa fidare' (*Il Principe*, ch. 9; *The Prince*, 37).

67. 'perché le amicizie che si acquistono col prezzo e non con grandezza e nobiltà d'animo, si meritano, ma elle non si hanno, et a' tempi non si possono spendere' (*Il Principe*, ch. 17; *The Prince*, 59).

68. *Il Principe*, ch. 17; *The Prince*, 59.

69. 'perché sendo in quelli piú vedere e piú astuzia avanzono sempre tempo per salvarsi, e cercono gradi con quelli che sperano che vinca' (*Il Principe*, ch. 9; *The Prince*, 35).

70. *Il Principe*, ch. 14; *The Prince*, 51–2.

71. *Il Principe*, ch. 20; *The Prince*, 72.

72. 'Tucte le città, le quali mai per alcun tempo si son governate per principe soluto, per optimati, o per populo, come si governa questa, hanno auto per defensione loro le forze mescolate con la prudentia: perché questa non basta sola et quelle, o non conducono le cose, o conducte non le mantengano' (*Parole da dirle sopra la provisione del danaio, facto un poco di proemio et di scusa*, in *I primi scritti*, 412).

73. 'perché ognun sa che chi dice imperio, regno, principato, repubblica, chi dice uomini che comandano, cominciandosi dal primo grado et descendendo infino al padrone d'uno brigantino, dice iustitia et armi' (*La cagione dell'ordinanza. Dove la si truovi et quel che bisogni fare*, in *I primi scritti*, 432); see also the *Provisione della ordinanza*, in *I primi scritti*, 439.

74. See *The Prince*, ch. 18, 'Exhortation to Liberate Italy'.

75. Machiavelli, John M. Najemy has written recently, 'is uncompromising in his insistence that imagination and truth can indeed be differentiated, and that *he* will speak on the basis of truth alone'. The assessment of the intelligibility of political action is indeed one of the main divergencies between Machiavelli and Vettori: 'For Vettori, a rational, coherent interpretation of politics that corresponds to the essence or truth of things is not only difficult and inevitably a matter of imagination and *fantasia*; it is also "impossible", or nearly so, to translate such constructions into action, to use them to influence or shape events. Machiavelli's "verità effettuale" and his determination to write "cosa utile a chi la intende" are his answer to such pessimism' (*Between Friends: Discourse of Power and Desire in the Machiavelli–Vettori Letters of 1513–1515* (Princeton: Princeton University Press, 1993), 188, 191; but see also 58–71, and 185–201).

76. Ernst Cassirer, *The Myth of the State* (New Haven: Yale University Press, 1946), 130. A complete list of the scholars who have remarked on the scientific character of Machiavelli's style of thinking and writing about politics would be endless. I confine myself to quoting the more influential studies: Luigi Russo (*Machiavelli* (Bari: Laterza, 1949), 71): 'e si inaugura il ragionamento a catena, che sarà poi quello di Galilei e di tutta la prosa scientifica moderna. Iddio è disceso dai cieli, e anche l'arte ha scorciato le sue vie.'

77. 'Sogliono dire gli uomini prudenti, e non a caso né immeritatamente, che chi vuole vedere quello che ha a essere, consideri quello che è stato: perché tutte le cose del mondo in ogni tempo hanno il proprio riscontro con gli antichi tempi. Il che nasce perché essendo quelle operate dagli uomini che hanno ed ebbono sempre le medesime passioni, conviene di necessità che sortiscino il medesimo effetto' (*Discorsi*, iii. 43; *Discourses*, 517).

78. 'Vedi che, mutati solum e visi delli uomini et e colori estrinseci, le cose medesime tutte ritornano; né vediamo accidente alcuno che a altri tempi non sia stato veduto' (*Lettere*, 524; *MF* 339).

79. Francesco Guicciardini, *Ricordi*, in *Opere*, ed. Emmanuella Lugnani Scarano (Turin: UTET, 1974), 762.

80. 'Ma el mutare nomi e figure alle cose fa che soli e prudenti le riconoscono: e però è buona et utile la istoria, perché ti mette innanzi e ti fa riconoscere e rivedere quello che mai non avevi conosciuto né veduto' (*Lettere*, 524; *MF* 339).

81. 'Io credo che come la natura ha fatto a l'uomo diverso volto, così li abbi fatto diverso ingegno e diversa fantasia. Da questo nasce che ciascuno secondo lo ingegno e fantasia sua si governa' (*Lettere*, 244; *MF* 135).

82. *Il Principe*, ch. 18.

83. 'né potrei intorno ad questa cosa scrivere altro alle Signorie vostre, ma per tutto dí martedí prossimo si doverrà vedere che via piglia quest'acqua, e da quello principio si doverrà conietturare piú là qualcosa, perché per molti segni io veggio resoluto questo Signore di partirsi fra 3, o 4 dí . . . di che ne sarà piú vero iudice il tempo, che alcuna altra cosa che se ne dica al presente' (*Legazioni*, i. 466).

84. Ibid. ii. 706.

85. 'Di luogo autentico non si può trarre alcuna cosa che paia ad altrui ragionevole e io non ho mancato, per averne la verità, di quella diligenzia mi si conveniva' (ibid. i. 499).

86. Messer Rimirro questa mattina è stato trovato in dua pezzi in sulla piazza, dove è ancora: e tutto questo popolo lo ha possuto vedere: non si sa bene la cagione della sua morte, se non che li è piaciuto cosí al Principe, il quale mostra di saper fare e disfare li uomini ad sua posta, secondo e' meriti loro' (ibid. 503).

87. 'questo Signore è segretissimo, né credo quello si abbi ad fare, lo sappi

altro che lui: e questi suoi primi secretarii mi hanno piú volte attestato, che non comunica mai cosa alcuna se non quando e' la commette, e commettela quando la necessità strigne, e in sul fatto, e non altrimenti; donde io prego vostre Signorie mi scusino, né m'imputino ad negligenza quando io non satisfaccia alle Signorie vostre con gli avvisi, perché il piú delle volte io non satisfo *etiam* ad me medesimo' (ibid.).

88. The Emperor, he writes, 'è umano quando dà audienza, ma la vuol dare a sua posta, né vuole essere corteggiato dalli ambasciatori, se non quando egli manda per loro; è segretissimo; sta sempre in continue agitazioni d'animo e di corpo, ma spesso disfà la sera quello conclude la mattina. Questo fa difficili le legazioni appresso di lui, perché la piú importante parte che habbia uno oratore che sia fuori per un principe o republica, si è coniecturare bene le cose future, cosí delle pratiche come de' fatti: perché chi le coniettura saviamente et le fa intendere bene al suo superiore è cagione che il suo superiore si possa avanzare sempre con le cose sue et provvedersi ne' tempi debiti' (*Discorso sopra le cose della Magna e sopra l'imperatore*, in *I primi scritti*, 485).

89. 'E benché sua Eccellenza, come vedete, mostrasse di aver desiderio che l'accordo tra voi e lui si faccia presto, nondimeno, non ostante che io gli entrassi sotto per trarre da lui qualche particolare, sempre girò largo, né potei mai averne altro che quello ho scritto' (*Legazioni*, i. 342).

90. In the report from Urbino on 1 July 1502, for instance, we read that the Duke, invoking God as witness, declared that he had never wished, nor did he wish, anything but the friendship and the alliance with Florence: 'chiamando Dio in testimonio che mai aveva desiderato né desiderava altro che la amicizia e coniunzione di cotesta città, e ora piú che mai, per esservi a confine in tanti luoghi; discorrendo l'onore, l'utile e la securtà che glie ne risulterebbe e cosí il contrario' (*Legazioni*, i. 280).

91. 'non fece mai altro, non pensò mai ad altro che ad ingannare uomini, e sempre trovò subietto da poterlo fare. E non fu mai uomo che avessi maggiore efficacia in asseverare, e con maggiori giuramenti affermarsi una cosa, che l'osservassi meno; non di meno, sempre li succederono li inganni *ad votum*, perché conosceva bene questa parte del mondo' (*Il Principe*, ch. 18; *The Prince*, 62).

92. 'Alcuno principe de' presenti tempi, quale non è bene nominare, non predica mai altro che pace e fede, e dell'una e dell'altra è inimicissimo; e l'una e l'altra, quando e' l'avessi osservata, li arebbe piú volte tolto o la reputazione o lo stato' (*le Principe*, ch. 18; *The Prince*, 63).

93. 'Né crederrò mai che sotto questo partito ora da lui preso ci possa essere altro che quello che si vede, perché io non beo paesi, né voglio in queste cose mi muova veruna autorità sanza ragione' (*Lettere*, 379; *MF* 233).

94. Giovanni Bardazzi, 'Tecniche narrative nel Machiavelli scrittore di lettere', in *Annali della Scuola Normale Superiore di Pisa*, ser. III, v (1975), 1486–7.

95. 'Ancora che, come vi ho scritto, mi paia spesso che le cose non procedino con ragione, e per questo giudichi superfluo il parlarne, discorrerne e disputarne, nondimeno chi è assueto in un modo insino in 40 anni, mal volentieri si può ritrarre e ridurre a altri costumi, a altri ragionamenti e pensieri' (*Lettere*, 391–2; *MF* 241–2).

96. *Lettere*, 415; *MF* 257 (revised).

97. 'perché e populi vogliono quello che e re, et non e re quello ch'e populi' (*Lettere*, 470; *MF* 296).

98. 'Questo ha dato loro più nome, hagli fatti più audaci per aver considerato e conosciuto più provincie e più uomini; et ancora ha misso loro nell'animo uno spirito ambizioso et una volontà di volere militare per loro' (*Lettere*, 403–4; *MF* 249–50).

99. 'Noi abbiamo a pensare che ciascuno di questi nostri principi abbia un fine, e perché a noi è impossibile sapere il segreto loro, bisogna lo stimiamo dalle parole, dalle dimostrazioni, e qualche parte ne immaginiamo' (*Lettere*, 392; *MF* 242).

100. *Lettere*, 382; *MF* 235.

101. 'e la ragione vuole che faccino un secondo accordo fra loro'; 'et è ragionevole che Spagna vegga questi pericoli, e che gli voglia evitare in ogni modo' (*Lettere*, 402; *MF* 248).

102. *Lettere*, 385–6; *MF* 236–8.

103. 'Parevami infino ad qui avere scritto in modo, che recandosi vostre Signorie in mano le mie lettere, giudicavo vedessino una storia di tutte le cose di qua' (*Legazioni*, ii. 663–4).

104. 'Dubito che'l vostro non volere, et il mio volere non abbino uno medesimo fondamento d'una naturale affezione o passione, che facci a voi dire no et a me sì. Voi adonestate il vostro no col mostrare esserci più difficultà nel condurre la pace, quando il re abbi a tornare in Lombardia; io ho mostro, per adonestare il mio sì, non essere così la verità, e dipoi che la pace presa per quel verso che io dico, sarà più secura e più ferma' (*Lettere*, 399; *MF* 247).

105. 'Doppo questo, compare, vi voglio rispondere alla prima parte della lettera, nella quale voi mostrate dubitare che una naturale affezione o passione possa fare ingannare o voi o me. A che io vi rispondo che non ho affezione alcuna alla parte contro a Francia, né passione alcuna che mi muova' (*Lettere*, 408; *MF* 253).

106. *Lettere*, 419; *MF* 259–60.

107. *Lettere*, 426; *MF* 264.

108. *Lettere*, 401; *MF* 248.

109. 'questo Duca si cominci avvezzare ad tenersi delle voglie, e che conosca come la fortuna non liene dà tutte vinte' (*Legazioni*, i. 464).

110. 'Questo Signore è molto splendido et magnifico, et nelle armi è tanto

animoso, che non è sí gran cosa che non li paia piccola, et per gloria et per acquistare stato mai si riposa né conosce fatica o periculo: giugne prima in un luogo, che se ne possa intendere la partita donde si lieva; fassi ben volere a' suoi soldati; ha cappati e' migliori uomini d'Italia: le quali cose lo fanno vittorioso et formidabile, aggiunto con una perpetua fortuna' (*Legazioni*, i. 267–8).

111. See, for instance, the standard account given by Matteo Palmieri: 'Scientia è vera cognitione delle cose certe: certe sono solo le cose che altrimenti essere non possono; altrimenti essere non possono solo le cose eterne; è adunque scientia solo di cose eterne' (*La vita civile*, ed. Gino Belloni (Florence: Olschki, 1982), 66).

3 The Power of Words

1. Fredi Chiappelli, *Studi sul linguaggio di Machiavelli* (Florence, Le Monnier, 1952), 224.

2. Nancy S. Struever, *Theory as Practice: Ethical Inquiry in the Renaissance* (Chicago: University of Chicago Press, 1992), 151.

3. Thomas M. Greene, 'The End of Discourse in Machiavelli's *Prince*', in Patricia Parker and David Quint (eds.), *Literary Theory/Renaissance Texts* (Baltimore: Johns Hopkins University Press, 1986), 70, 75.

4. Eugene Garver, 'Machiavelli's *The Prince*: A Neglected Rhetorical Classic', *Philosophy and Rhetoric*, 13 (1980), 99–120.

5. Victoria Kahn, *Machiavellian Rhetoric: From Counter-Reformation to Milton* (Princeton: Princeton University Press, 1994), 8, 59. Harvey C. Mansfield and Nathan Tarcov notice, *en passant*, the 'presence of rhetoric' in the *Discourses*. They also remark that Machiavelli 'accuses both rhetoric and philosophy of attempting to rule deeds with words' (Niccolò Machiavelli, *Discourses on Livy*, ed. Harvey C. Mansfield and Nathan Tarcov (Chicago: University of Chicago Press, 1996), Introduction, pp. xviii–xix, xliii). Leaving aside the fact that nowhere does Machiavelli make such an accusation, why would a person write the *Discourses* (and *all* his works) rhetorically, if he did not believe that words do indeed govern deeds?

6. Quentin Skinner, *Reason and Rhetoric in the Philosophy of Hobbes* (Cambridge: Cambridge University Press, 1996), 170.

7. Emilio Santini, *Firenze e i suoi oratori nel Quattrocento* (Milan: Sandron, 1922), 67; see also Jerrold E. Seigel, *Rhetoric and Philosophy in Renaissance Humanism* (Princeton: Princeton University Press, 1968); Nancy S. Struever, *The Language of History in the Renaissance* (Princeton: University Press, 1970).

8. Angelo Poliziano, *Oratio super Fabio Quintiliano et Statii Sylvis*, in

Eugenio Garin (ed.), *Prosatori latini del Quattrocento* (Milan: Ricciardi, s.d), 883–5.

9. 'Ricordo come questo dí 16 di dicembre io ò renduto a Matteo Cartolaio la Rettorica Nuova di Tullio m'avea prestato più dì fa, e più ò renduto a Zanobi Cartolaio Tullio De Oratore m'avea prestato più dì fa' (Bernardo Machiavelli, *Libro di ricordi*, ed. Cesare Olschki (Florence: Le Monnier, 1954), 123.

10. 'deliberativum, quod positum in disceptatione civili habet in se sententiae dictionem' (*De inventione*, ed. H. M. Hubbel (Cambridge, Mass.: Harvard University Press, 1960), 1. 5. 7.

11. Cicero, *De inventione* 1. 7. 9. For an excellent account of the elements of classical rhetoric, see Skinner, *Reason and Rhetoric in the Philosophy of Hobbes*, 40–51.

12. *De inventione* 1. 15. 20.

13. Ibid. 1. 16. 22.

14. 'Attentos autem faciemus si demostrabimus ea quae dicturi erimus magna, nova, incredibilia esse, aut ad omnes aut ad eos qui audient, aut ad aliquos illustres homines aut ad deos immortales aut ad summam rem publicam pertinere' (ibid. 1. 16. 23).

15. 'Dociles auditores faciemus si aperte et breviter summam causae exponemus' (ibid. 1. 16. 23).

16. Cf. the letter of Agostino Vespucci to Machiavelli of 25 Aug. 1501: 'E non so come tam feliciter costui mai havessi potuto orare nisi imitatus sit Demosthenem, qui actionem solebat componere grande quoddam speculum intuens. E lassando la dottrina, la eloquenzia, i colori infiniti, molti flosculi et aculei quibus inspersa sua oratio est, illud, mehercule, prestitit, ut sibi conciliaret, persuaderet, moveret, ac denique delectaret' (*Lettere*, 112; MF 41–2).

17. A truly spectacular example of misunderstanding of the rhetorical meaning of the *Dedicatory Letter* and of *The Prince* as a whole is Thomas Green's essay 'The End of Discourse in Machiavelli's Prince', which contains, among others, the following claim: 'The dedicatory epistle repudiates rhetoric; the clipped opening chapter repudiates the graces of humanist elegance; from the beginning, the book refuses to be literature, the most refined corrupter of communal discipline' (p. 58).

18. 'la cognizione delle azioni delli uomini grandi, imparata con una lunga esperienza delle cose moderne et una continua lezione delle antique'; 'intendere tutto quello che io in tanti anni e con tanti mia disagi e periculi ho conosciuto' (*Il Principe*, Dedicatory Letter).

19. 'Né voglio sia reputata presunzione, se uno uomo di basso et infimo stato ardisce discorrere e regolare e' governi de' principi; perché, cosí come coloro che disegnono e' paesi si pongano bassi nel piano a considerare la natura de' monti e de' luoghi alti, e per considerare quella de' bassi si

pongano alto sopra monti, similmente a conoscere bene la natura de' populi bisogna esser principe, et a conoscere bene quella de' principi bisogna esser populare' (ibid).

20. Ibid.

21. See Quintilian, *Institutio oratoria* 2. 17. 39; *The Institutio Oratoria of Quintilian*, trans. H. E. Butler (Cambridge, Mass.: Harvard University Press, 1993), i. 343.

22. 'in qua rerum earum de quibus erimus dicturi breviter expositio ponitur distributa' (*De inventione* 1. 22. 31).

23. Ibid. 1. 52. 98–100.

24. On the central role of peroration to excite or calm down feelings, see Skinner, *Reason and Rhetoric in the Philosophy of Hobbes*, 121.

25. 'quod taetrum, crudele, nefarium, tyrannicum factum esse dicamus' (*De inventione* 1. 53. 102).

26. 'inopia, infirmitas, solitudo demonstratur' (ibid. 1. 55. 109).

27. *Il Principe*, ch.2; *The Prince*, 6.

28. 'Le cose soprascritte, osservate prudentemente, fanno parere uno principe nuovo antico, e lo rendono subito piú sicuro e piú fermo nello stato, che se vi fussi antiquato dentro' (*Il Principe*, ch. 24; *The Prince*, 83).

29. *Il Principe*, ch. 26; *The Prince*, 88.

30. When one misses the intended meaning of a text, anything is possible, even to say that 'chapter 26 is the final, brilliant example of Machiavelli's theatrical overshooting of the mark, of a rhetoric that is neither constrained by logic to represent the truth nor guided by practical reason in its achievement of ethical decorum but that rather aims to produce the effect of truth—and to achieve success' (Kahn, *Machiavellian Rhetoric*, 43) or that 'the typical reader's reaction to the last chapter should serve effectively to provoke questions of whether the abilities the prince can acquire in this way enable merely discursive success or practical power in a more general sense' (Eugene Garver, *Machiavelli and the History of Prudence* (Madison, Wis.: University of Wisconsin Press, 1987), 45).

31. 'Tota autem oratio simplex et gravis et sententiis debet ornatior esse quam verbis' (Cicero, *De partitione oratoriae* 27. 97); 'ita cum verba rebus aptentur, ipso materiae nitore clarescunt' (Quintilian, *Institutio oratoria* 3. 8. 61; Butler, i. 511).

32. 'Rem ornatiorem facit cum nullius rei nisi dignitatis causa sumitur; apertiorem, cum id quod sit obscurius magis dilucidum reddit; probabiliorem, cum magis veri similem facit; ante oculos ponit, cum exprimit omnia perspicue ut res prope dicam manu temptari possit' (*Ad Herennium* 4. 49. 62).

33. 'La quale opera io non ho ornata né ripiena di clausule ample, o di parole

ampullose e magnifiche, o di qualunque altro lenocinio o ornamento estrinseco, con li quali molti sogliono le loro cose descrivere et ornare; perché io ho voluto, o che veruna cosa la onori, o che solamente la varietà della materia e la gravità del subietto la facci grata' (*Il Principe*, Dedicatory Letter).

34. *Il Principe*, ch. 6; *The Prince*, 19. While it is true that Machiavelli's aim in the *Exhortatio* is to achieve success, he surely was not providing 'a divine justification of the Medici as the redeemers of Italy', as Victoria Kahn writes (*Machiavellian Rhetoric*, 43).

35. *Il Principe*, ch. 16; *The Prince*, 60.

36. On Machiavelli's use of examples, see Barbara Spackman, 'Machiavelli and Maxims', *Yale French Studies*, 77 (1990), 152, and John D. Lyons, *Exemplum: The Rhetoric of Example in Early Modern France and Italy* (Princeton: Princeton University Press, 1989), esp. 35–6, 49, 63–5.

37. See Skinner, *Reason and Rhetoric in the Philosophy of Hobbes*, 49–51.

38. 'Ma, sendo l'intento mio scrivere cosa utile a chi la intende, mi è parso piú conveniente andare drieto alla verità effettuale della cosa, che alla immaginazione di essa' (*le Principe*, ch. 15; *The Prince*, 54). The second translation is from Robert M. Adams, *The Prince* (New York: Norton, 1977).

39. In the oration he composed in March 1503 to persuade the Florentines to pay more taxes in order to levy a decent army, for instance, he writes: 'Tucte le città le quali mai per alcun tempo si son governate per principe soluto, per optimati, o per populo, come si governa questa, hanno hauto per defensione loro le forze mescolate con la prudentia; perché questa non basta sola, et quelle o non conducono le cose, o, conducte non le mantengano. Sono dunque queste due cose el nervo di tucte le signorie, che furno o che saranno mai al mondo: et chi ha observato le mutationi de' regni, le ruine delle provincie et delle città, non le ha vedute causare da altro che dal mancamento delle armi o del senno' (*I primi scritti*, 412). On the knowledge of truth to be attained through *sapientia*, as one of the fundamental qualities of the orator, seek Skinner, *Reason and Rhetoric in the Philosophy of Hobbes*, 74–84.

40. 'Per il che si ha a notare che li uomini si debbono o vezzeggiare o spegnere; perché si vendicano delle leggieri offese, delle gravi non possono; sí che l'offesa che si fa all'uomo debbe essere in modo che la non tema la vendetta' (*Il Principe*, ch. 3; *The Prince*, 9).

41. 'Di che si cava una regola generale, la quale mai o raro falla: che chi è cagione che uno diventi potente, ruina; perché quella potenzia è causata da colui o con industria o con forza, e l'una e l'altra di queste due è sospetta a chi è divenuto potente' (*Il Principe*, ch. 3; *The Prince*, 14).

42. 'Concludo, adunque, che, sanza avere arme proprie, nessuno principato è sicuro, anzi è tutto obbligato alla fortuna, non avendo virtú che nelle avversità lo difenda' (*Il Principe*, ch. 13; *The Prince*, 51).

43. *Institutio oratoria*, 3. 5. 12–15, Butler, i. 468–71.

44. 'Né creda mai alcuno stato potere sempre pigliare partiti securi, anzi pensi di avere a prenderli tutti dubii; perché si truova questo nell'ordine delle cose, che mai non si cerca fuggire uno inconveniente che non si incorra in uno altro; ma la prudenzia consiste in sapere conoscere le qualità delli inconvenienti, e pigliare el meno tristo per buono' (*Il Principe*, ch. 21; *The Prince*, 79).

45. 'Perché dall'uno e dall'altro di questi due modi possono nascere inconvenienti grandi, ed atti a fare rovinare uno principe: perché colui che troppo desidera essere amato, ogni poco che si parte dalla vera via diventa disprezzabile: quell'altro che desidera troppo di essere temuto, ogni poco ch'egli eccede il modo, diventa odioso' (*Discorsi*, III. 21). See also Lyons, *Exemplum*, 66.

46. 'in deliberationibus, ut nos arbitramur, quid honestum sit et quid utile' (*De inventione*, 2. 4. 12); 'In deliberativo autem Aristoteli placet utilitatem, nobis et honestatem et utilitatem' (ibid. 2. 51. 156).

47. 'Nam virtus est animi habitus naturae modo atque rationi consentaneus' (ibid. 2. 52. 159).

48. 'ut in re publica quaedam sunt quae, ut sic dicam, ad corpus pertinent civitatis, ut agri, portus, pecunia, classis, nautae, milites, socii, quibus rebus incolumitatem ac libertatem retinent civitates' (ibid. 2. 56. 168).

49. Ibid. 2. 66. 169.

50. 'Utilitas in duas partes in civili consultatione dividitur: tutam, honestam' (*Ad Herennium* 3. 2. 3).

51. Ibid. 3. 2. 3.

52. Ibid.

53. Ibid.

54. 'Laudabile est quod conficit honestam et praesentem et consequentem commemorationem' (ibid. 3. 4. 7).

55. *Institutio oratoria* 3. 8. 2–4; Butler, i. 465–7.

56. John F. Tinkler, 'Praise and Advice; Rhetorical Approaches in More's *Utopia* and Machiavelli's *The Prince*', *Sixteenth Century Journal*, 19 (1988), 198. Another passage from Tinkler's essay deserves quotation: 'Many indications suggest that Machiavelli knew precisely what he was doing in rhetorical terms: his plain style and rejection of superficial ornament: his insistence on his personal experience of politics; his rejection of flattery and mere praise; and, above all, his characteristically deliberative concern with advice that is *utile*, all suggest that he was conscious of replacing a demonstrative with a deliberative approach.' While I do not believe that Machiavelli was concerned with replacing the demonstrative or epideictic genre, the genre to be used when we speak to praise a person, with the deliberative approach, I

think that this passage illuminates very well the rhetorical nature of *The Prince*.

57. Kahn, *Machiavellian Rhetoric*, 9.

58. Skinner, *Reason and Rhetoric in the Philosophy of Hobbes*, 44.

59. *Il Principe*, ch. 3; *The Prince*, 7.

60. *Il Principe*, ch. 10; *The Prince*, 37–8.

61. *Il Principe*, ch. 18; *The Prince*, 56.

62. 'Ac summa quidem necessitudo videtur esse honestatis; huic proxima, incolumitatis; tertia ac levissima, commoditatis' (*De inventione* 2. 58. 173).

63. Ibid. 2. 58. 174.

64. 'Hoc genus in deliberationibus maxime versabitur, cum aliquid quod contra dicatur, aequum esse concedimus, sed id quod nos defendimus necessarium esse demostramus' (ibid. 1. 51. 96).

65. 'vere poterimus dicere nos honestatis rationem habere, quoniam sine incolumitate eam nullo tempore possumus adipisci' (ibid. 2. 58. 174).

66. 'Et quoniam non ad veritatem solum sed etiam ad opiniones eorum qui audiunt accomodanda est oratio, hoc primum intellegamus, hominum duo esse genera, alterum indoctum et agreste, quod anteferat semper utilitatem honestati, alterum humanum et politum, quod rebus omnibus dignitatem anteponat' (*De partitione oratoriae*, 25. 89–90).

67. *Ad Herennium* 3. 3. 6. On the techniques of redescription, see Skinner, *Reason and Rhetoric in the Philosophy of Hobbes*, 138–80.

68. 'honestum nihil oportere existimari quod non salutem pariat' (*Ad Herennium* 3. 5. 8).

69. 'Sed neque hic plane concedendum est esse id inhonestum' (*Institutio oratoria* 3. 8. 31; Butler, i. 495).

70. 'Haec autem, quae tantum inter se pugnant, plerumque nominibus deflecti solent' (ibid. 3. 8. 32; Butler, i. 491).

71. Ibid. 3. 8. 44–7; Butler, i. 501–3.

72. Ibid. 12. 1. 44; Butler, iii. 381.

73. Cicero, *De officiis* 2. 7. 34–8. 35.

74. 'Onde è necessario a uno principe, volendosi mantenere, imparare a potere essere non buono, et usarlo e non usare secondo la necessità' (*Il Principe*, ch. 15).

75. 'Et hassi ad intendere questo, che uno principe, e massime uno principe nuovo, non può osservare tutte quelle cose per le quali li uomini sono tenuti buoni, sendo spesso necessitato, per mantenere lo stato, operare contro alla fede, contro alla carità, contro alla umanità, contro alla relligione' (*Il Principe*, ch. 18). Necessity, as Cicero had explained, is 'something that no force can resist, ('*cui nulla vi resisti potest*'). To be in

a situation of necessity thereby means that we cannot accomplish some tasks that we would desire to accomplish or that we should try to accomplish. Necessity, however, has always to be qualified, as, for instance, in the following statement: it is necessary for the people of Casilinum to surrender to Hannibal 'unless they prefer to die of starvation'. When we use the word necessity we must therefore consider whether the qualification is 'advantageous or honourable' and keep in mind that 'the greatest necessity is that of doing what is honourable' and next comes the necessity of security (*incolumitas*) Cicero, *De inventione* 2. 57. 170–58. 175

76. *Discorsi*, III. 43; *Discourses*, 515 (revised).

77. 'Facci dunque uno principe di vincere e mantenere lo stato: e' mezzi saranno sempre iudicati onorevoli, e da ciascuno laudati' (*Il Principe*, ch. 18; *The Prince*, 63).

78. 'et ingegnarsi che nelle azioni sua si riconosca grandezza, animosità, gravità, fortezza' (*Il Principe*, ch. 19; *The Prince*, 64). 'E sopra tutto uno principe si debbe ingegnare di dare di sé in ogni sua azione fama di uomo grande e di nome eccellente' (*Il Principe*, ch. 21; *The Prince*, 77).

79. *Il Principe*, ch. 21; *The Prince*, 79.

80. See Skinner, *Reason and Rhetoric in the Philosophy of Hobbes*, 151–5.

81. *Il Principe*, ch. 15; *The Prince*, 55.

82. 'Credo che questo avvenga dalle crudeltà male usate o bene usate. Bene usate si possono chiamare quelle (se del male è licito dire bene') che si fanno ad un tratto, per necessità dello assicurarsi, e di poi non vi si insiste dentro, ma si convertiscono in più utilità de' sudditi che si può. Male usate sono quelle le quali, ancora che nel principio sieno poche, più tosto col tempo crescono che le si spenghino.' (*Il Principe*, ch. 8; *The Prince*, 33).

83. *Il Principe*, ch. 8.

84. 'By placing the struggle for power into the centre of all political action, and by praising the hour of war as the time in which the virtues of the citizens were truly vindicated', wrote Gerhard Ritter, 'he created the prototype for all modern political theory on the European continent— the theory, in fact, which has become notorious . . . [as] "militaristic"' (*Die Dämonie der Macht*, Munich: Leibniz Verlag, 1948), 46; Eng. trans., *The Corrupting Influence of Power* (Hadleigh, Essex: Tower Bridge Publications, 1952), 37).

85. *Ad Herennium* 3. 2. 3.

86. *Institutio oratoria* 6. 3. 85 and 9. 1. 29; Butler, iii. 365.

87. 'Ma è necessario questa natura saperla bene colorire, et essere gran simulatore e dissimulatore; e sono tanto semplici li uomini, e tanto obediscano alle necessità presenti, che colui che inganna troverrà sempre chi si lascerà ingannare' (*Il Principe*, ch. 18; *The Prince*, 62).

88. Benedetto Croce, *Elementi di politica* (Bari: Laterza, 1925), 60; see also Federico Chabod, *Machiavelli and the Renaissance*, (London, Bowes & Bowes, 1958), 116.

89. To claim that 'the humanist's assumption that *honestas* is compatible with *utilitas*, reflected in the maxim that the good orator is necessarily a good man, is politically useless to Machiavelli, however it is interpreted', as Victoria Kahn does (*Machiavellian Rhetoric*, 32), misrepresents the intended sense of Machiavelli's argument. Equally off the mark is the view that Machiavelli 'is not so much immoral as vicious, a discursive ruffian, breaking the peace (but not faith)' (Struever, *Theory as Practice*, 175).

90. See, for instance, Michael Walzer, 'Political Action: The Problem of Dirty Hands', in Marshall Cohen, Thomas Nagel, and Thomas Scanlon (eds.), *War and Moral Responsibility* (Princeton: Princeton University Press, 1974), 77.

91. 'essere tanto prudente, che sappi fuggire l'infamia di quelle che li torrebbano lo stato, e da quelle che non gnene tolgano guardarsi, se elli è possibile; ma, non possendo, vi si può con meno respetto lasciare andare' (*Il Principe*, ch. 15).

92. 'e nelle azioni di tutti li uomini, e massime de' principi, dove non è iudizio da reclamare, si guarda al fine' (ibid., ch. 18).

93. 'sempre propinquo al bene sia qualche male, il quale con quel bene sí facilmente nasca che pare impossibile potere mancare dell'uno volendo l'altro' (*Discorsi*, III. 37).

94. *Discorsi*, I. 9; *Discourses*, 134.

95. See Walzer, 'Political Action: The Problem of Dirty Hands', 66.

96. 'Historia vero testis temporum, lux veritatis, vita memoriae, magistra vitae, nuntia vetustatis, qua voce alia, nisi oratoris, immortalitati commendatur' (*De oratore* 2. 9. 36).

97. *Institutio oratoria* 3. 8. 66–7; Butler, i. 511–13.

98. Ibid. 12. 2. 29–31; Butler, iv. 339 (revised).

99. Leonardo Aretino, *Istoria Fiorentina*, tradotta in volgare da Donato Acciajuoli (Florence: Le Monnier, 1861), 3–4.

100. 'e per l'esempio degli uomini eccellenti accendere l'animo alla esercitazione della virtù' (ibid. 4).

101. 'Di che si può comprendere quanta utilità essa arrechi alla generazione humana, e quanto, volendo essere grata, gli sia obbligata; sendo sola custodia fedelissima dell' opere nostre, e quella, che sempre faccia presenti, e col suo mezzo riducendoci a memoria l'opere degli huomini singulari ci inviti a operare di farci immortali, e pe' progressi d'altri ci mostri la vita di ciascuno: e consigli nel deliberare, e partiti presi, e costumi delle republiche, e varietà grandi della fortuna, e varii eventi delle guerre, acciò che con l'esemplo d'altri possiamo eleggere quello sia

utile a Noi, e alla patria' (*Istoria di M. Poggio Fiorentino, tradotta di Latino in Volgare da Iacopo suo figliuolo* (Florence: Filippo Giunti, 1598), 1–2.

102. *Discorsi*, bk. I, Proem.

103. 'quello che [. . .] io iudicherò essere necessario per maggiore intelligenza di essi, a ciò che coloro che leggeranno queste mia declarazioni, possino più facilmente trarne quella utilità per la quale si debbe cercare la cognizione delle istorie' (ibid.).

104. Ibid. I. 10; *Discourses*, 138 (revised).

105. 'E sanza dubbio se e' sarà nato d'uomo, si sbigottirà da ogni imitazione de' tempi cattivi, ad accenderassi d'uno immenso desiderio di seguire i buoni' (*Discorsi*, I. 10; *Discourses*, 137–8).

106. *Discorsi*, I. 5.

107. 'Il che fu per un gran tempo sicuro, con somma gloria d'imperio e d'arme, e massime laude di costumi e di religione' (*Discorsi*, II. 4).

108. 'E se ogni esemplo di repubblica muove, quelli che si leggono della propria muovono molto più e molto più sono utili' (*Istorie*, bk. I, Proem; *FH* 6).

109. *Istorie*, v. 1; *FH* 186.

110. 'Perchè se niuna cosa diletta o insegna nella istoria, è quella che particularmente si descrive; se niuna lezione è utile a'cittadini che governano le repubbliche, è quella che dimostra le cagioni degli odj e delle divisioni della città, acciocchè possano, col pericolo d' altri diventati savj, mantenersi uniti' (*Istorie*, bk. I, Proem; *FH* 6).

111. 'Civilis quaedam ratio est, quae multis et magnis ex rebus constat. Eius quaedam magna et ampla pars est artificiosa eloquentia quam rhetoricam vocant' (*De inventione* I. 5. 6).

112. See the excellent essay by Brian Richardson, 'Notes on Machiavelli's Sources and his Treatment of the Rhetorical Tradition', *Italian Studies*, 36 (1971), 24–8.

113. *Istorie*, II. 34; *FH* 91–3 (revised).

114. Cicero, *De oratore* I. 34. 158; see also Quintilian, *Istitutio oratoria* 12. I. 35.

115. *Istorie*, II. 35; *FH* 93 (revised).

116. 'Però che a un popolo licenzioso e tumultuario gli può da un uomo buono essere parlato, e facilmente può essere ridotto nella via buona; a un principe cattivo non è alcuno che possa parlare né vi è altro rimedio che il ferro' (*Discorsi*, I. 58; *Discourses*, 256–7).

117. *Istorie*, III. 11; *FH* 119–20.

118. See *Institutio oratoria* 9. 2. 7–8; Butler, iii. 377–9.

119. *Istorie*, III. 11; *FH* 120.

120. *Istorie*, III. 11; *FH* 120.

121. 'Queste parole, perchè erano vere, commossero assai gli animi di quelli cittadini, e umanamente ringraziarono il Gonfaloniere di aver fatto l'ufficio con loro di buon signore e con la città di buon cittadino . . .' (*Istorie*, III. 11; *FH* 120).

122. See Quentin Skinner, 'Machiavelli's *Discorsi* and the Pre-Humanist Origins of Republican Ideas'; in Gisela Bock, Quentin Skinner, and Maurizio Viroli (eds.), *Machiavelli and Republicanism* (Cambridge: Cambridge University Press, 1990), 121–41.

123. *Istorie*, III. 13; *FH* 122.

124. *Istorie*, III. 13; 122–3.

125. *Istorie*, III. 13; *FH* 123.

126. 'Altre volte abbiamo discorso quanto sia utile alle umane azioni la necessità, ad a quale gloria siano sute condutte da quella e come da alcuni morali filosofi è stato scritto, le mani e la lingua degli uomini, duoi nobilissimi instrumenti a nobilitarlo, non arebbero operato perfettamente né condotte le opere umane a quella altezza si veggono condotte, se dalla necessità non fussoro spinte' (*Discorsi*, III. 12; *Discourses*, 440).

127. *Istorie*, III. 26; *FH* 141.

128. 'Le quali parole, ancorchè vere, non mossero in alcuna parte la moltitudine, o per timore, o perchè la morte di quelli due avesse fatti gli ucciditori odiosi' (*Istorie*, III. 27; *FH* 143).

129. 'quanto sia pericoloso voler far libero un popolo che voglia in ogni modo esser servo' (*Istorie*, III, 27; *FH* 143).

130. 'Adsecutus itaque est, ut aliquid eorum quoque causa videretur facere contra quos diceret' (*Institutio oratoria* 11. 1. 85).

131. 'se prima con qualche colore non si giustificasse la guerra' (*Istorie*, VI. 25; *FH* 258). See also *Istorie* VI. 26; *FH* 260: 'senza averne non che giusta, ma colorita cagione.'

132. *Istorie*, VI. 25; *FH* 259.

133. *Istorie*, III. 5; *FH* 110.

134. 'Mosso pertanto da queste passioni, pensò di adonestare con una onesta cagione la disonestà dell'animo suo' (*Istorie*, II. 21; *FH* 73).

135. 'Nam cum et nostrae rei publicae detrimenta considero et maximarum civitatum veteres animo calamitates colligo, non minimam video per disertissimos homines invectam partem incommodorum' (*De inventione* I. 1. 1).

136. 'multas urbes constitutas, plurima bella restincta, firmissimas societates, sanctissimas amicitias intellego cum animi ratione tum facilius eloquentia comparatas' (ibid.).

137. Cicero, *De oratore* I. 8. 30–4.

138. Ibid. 1. 9. 38.

139. *Institutio oratoria* 2. 16. 1–11; Butler, i. 319–23.

140. 'Di qui nacque che tutt'i profeti armati vinsono, e li disarmati ruino- rono. Perché oltra alle cose dette, la natura de'populi è varia; et è facile persuadere loro una cosa, ma è difficile fermarli in quella persuasione. E però conviene essere ordinato in modo, che quando non credono piú, si possa fare credere loro per forza . . . come ne' nostri tempi intervenne a fra' Girolamo Savonerola il quale ruinò ne' suoi ordini nuovi, come la moltitudine cominciò a non crederli; e lui non aveva modo a tenere fermi quelli che avevano creduto, né a far credere e discredenti' (*Il Principe*, ch. 6; *The Prince*, 21).

141. *Arte della guerra*, 518; Gilbert, ii. 724.

142. *Arte della guerra*, 440–1; Gilbert, ii. 661.

143. *Arte della guerra*, 440–1; Gilbert, ii. 661.

144. Along with religion, eloquence assists lawgivers who plan to introduce new orders: 'e veramente mai fu alcuno ordinatore di leggi straordinarie in uno popolo che non ricorresse a Dio, perché altrimenti non sarebbero accettate: perché sono molti i beni conosciuti da uno prudente, i quali non hanno in sé ragioni evidenti da poterli persuadere a altrui' (*Discorsi*, I. XI; *Discourses*, 141).

145. 'Poteva uno tribuno e qualunque altro cittadino proporre al Popolo una legge, sopra la quale ogni cittadino poteva parlare o in favore o incontro, innanzi che la si deliberasse' (*Discorsi*, I. 18; *Discourses*, 162).

146. 'Quanto al giudicare le cose, si vede radissime volte, quando egli ode duo concionanti che tendino in diverse parti, quando ei sono di equale virtú, che non pigli la opinione migliore, e che non sia capace di quella verità che egli ode' (*Discorsi*, I. 58; Discourses, 255).

147. *Discorsi*, I. 18; *Discourses*, 162.

148. Kahn, *Machiavellian Rhetoric*, 11.

149. Cicero, *De oratore* 3. 31. 122.

150. 'Perché gli è offizio di uomo buono, quel bene che per la malignità de' tempi e della fortuna tu non hai potuto operare, insegnarlo ad altri' (*Discorsi*, bk. II, Proem; *Discourses*, 268–9). Leo Strauss's remarks on Machiavelli as a 'teacher of evil' (*Thoughts on Machiavelli*, (Chicago: University of Chicago Press, 1978), 1) ought accordingly to be consid- ered a masterpiece in misinterpretation. Also Hanna Pitkin's comments on Machiavelli's 'foxiness' (*Fortune is a Woman*, 34–5) entirely misre- present the sense of Machiavelli's writing as an adviser on political matters.

151. *Arte della guerra*, 519; Gilbert, ii. 726 (revised).

4 The Theory of the Republic

1. Roberto Ridolfi, *The Life of Niccolò Machiavelli*, trans. Cecil Grayson (London: Routledge & Kegan Paul, 1963), 248.

2. 'Machiavellus Democratiae laudator et assertor acerrimus; natus, educatus, honoratus in eo reip: statu; tyrannidis summe inimicus. Itaque tyranno non favet; sui propositi non est, tyrannum instruere, sed arcanis Eius palam factis ipsum miseris populis nudum et conspicuum exibire . . . Hoc fuit viri omnium prudentissimi consilium, ut sub specie principalis eruditionis populos erudiret' (Alberico Gentili, *De legationibus*, (London: Thomas Vautrollarius, 1585), bk. III, ch. 9.

3. Benedict De Spinoza, *Tractatus politicus*, ch. V, 7, in *The Political Works*, ed. A. G. Wernham (Oxford: Clarendon Press, 1958), 313.

4. Pierre Bayle, *Dictionnaire historique et critique* 3 vols.; (2nd edn.; Rotterdam: Reiner Leers, 1702), article 'Machiavelli', note 'o'.

5. 'it was the fault of his contemporaries if they misunderstood what he was getting at: they took a satyre for a eulogy' (*Encyclopédie*, article 'Machiavelisme' (Neuchatel, 1765), ix. 793).

6. *Contrat social*, bk. III, ch. 6. In the 1782 edition was inserted the following note: 'Machiavelli was a decent man and a good citizen. But, being attached to the court of the Medicis, he could not help veiling his love of liberty in the midst of his country's oppression. The choice of his detestable hero, Caesar Borgia, clearly enough shows his hidden aim; and the contradiction between the teaching of *The Prince* and that of the *Discourses on Livy* and the *History of Florence* shows that this profound political thinker has so far been studied only by superficial or corrupt readers. The Court of Rome sternly prohibited his book. I can believe it; for it is that court it most clearly portrays.'

7. Friedrich Meinecke, *Machiavellism: The Doctrine of Raison d'état and its Place in Modern History*, trans. Douglas Scott (London: Routledge & Kegan Paul, 1957), 32–3.

8. Niccolò Machiavelli, *Discourses on Livy*, ed. Harvey C. Mansfield and Nathan Tarcov (Chicago: University of Chicago Press, 1996), Introduction, p. xxvi.

9. For John Pocock, Machiavelli's republicanism is above all a commitment to the ideal of the republic as 'a structure of virtue'. Machiavelli's popular republic, he stresses, is grounded upon the virtue of the citizen-soldiers—that is, a virtue which is at the same time civic and military, a devotion to the common good above personal and factional interests and valour in the battlefield. The ultimate reason for Machiavelli's preference of republics over monarchies was the fact that the former have greater capacity than the latter to mobilize and arouse virtue. The true subversive Machiavelli was, therefore, 'not a counsellor of tyrants, but a good citizen and a patriot' who was urging his fellow-citizens to retrieve

the virtue capable of ensuring the republic's vitality but above all the republi's capacity to conquer and expand (John Pocock, *The Machiavellian Moment: Florentine Political Thought and the Atlantic Republican Tradition* (Princeton: Princeton University Press, 1975), 183–218). Mark Hulliung claims that Machiavelli's republicanism is essentially 'predatory'. We should not be deceived, he warns us, by Machiavelli's talk on liberty and constitutional order. He was not 'a kindred spirit'; for him 'restoration of republican rule is not the end justifying the means; nor does the forcible unification of Italy, which was little more than an afterthought, play such a moral role in his writings. The end is greatness, and Italian unity is merely a possible by-product of the glorious, violent, and aggrandizing deeds that are better performed by republican citizens than monarchical subjects' (Mark Hulliung, *Citizen Machiavelli* (Princeton: Princeton University Press, 1983), 220). The interpretation of Machiavelli's republicanism both as a sort of monarchical or princely republicanism and as a commitment to civic virtue can be found in Hans Baron's essay 'Machiavelli the Republican Citizen and Author of *The Prince*', in Hans Baron, *In Search of Florentine Civic Humanism* (2 vols.; Princeton: Princeton University Press, 1988), ii. 146–7. The essay was first published in 1961.

10. Macrobius, *Commentary on the Dream of Scipio*, ed. W. H. Stahl (New York: Columbia University Press, 1952), 120. For the Latin text, I have used the *Commento al Somnium Scipionis*, ed. Mario Regali (Pisa: Giardinis 1983).

11. 'Por ce dist Tuilles ke cités est un assemblemens de gens a abiter un lieu et vivre a une loi' (B. Latini, *Li livres dou Tresor*, (Berkeley: University of California Press, 1948), bk. III, 73.3).

12. '*secundum aliquas leges et secundum aliquas laudabiles ordinationes*' (Aegidius Romanus) (Giles of Rome), *De regimine principum libri III*, (Aalen: Scientia, 1967; facsimile of edition of Rome, 1607), bk III, 1. 2.

13. See Joseph Canning, *The Political Thought of Baldus de Ubaldis* (Cambridge: Cambridge University Press, 1987), 159–169.

14. Ptolemy of Lucca, *De regimine principum ad Regem Cypri*, in R. Spiazzi (ed.), *Divi, Thomae Aquinatis Opuscule Philosophice* (Turin: Marietti, 1954), 11. 8.

15. 'Ubi vero leges principantur, est vera politia, et politicum est nisi quod bonum est' (Lorenzo de' Monaci, *Chronicon de rebus Venetiis*, in L. Muratori, *Rerum italicarum scriptores*, viii. Appendix (Venice, 1758), 276–7).

16. Coluccio Salutati, *De tyranno*, 1. 6; ed. Alfred v. Martin (Berlin: W. Rothschild, 1913); Eng. trans. in Ephraim Emerton (ed.), *Humanism and Tyranny* (Cambridge, Mass.: Harvard University Press, 1925), 77.

17. Giovanni Cavalcanti, *Istorie fiorentine* (Florence: Tipografia all' insegna di Dante, 1838–9), 11. 1.

18. Alamanno Rinuccini, *Lettere ed orazioni* ed. Vito R. Giustiniani (Florence: Olschki, 1953), 191.

19. Girolamo Savonarola, *Trattato circa il reggimento e il governo della città di Firenze*, in *Prediche sopra Aggeo*, ed. Luigi Firpo (Rome: Belardetti, 1965), 442. For Savonarola's intellectual debt to the Thomist theory as well as to the Florentine tradition, see Donald Weinstein, *Savonarola and Florence* (Princeton: Princeton University Press, 1970), 289–315.

20. See Canning, *Political Thought*, 113.

21. See ibid. 96.

22. Ibid.

23. The Latin expressions used to denote the status of the free person and the status of the slave were 'persona sui iuris' and 'alieni iuris' respectively; cf. C. Wirszubski, *Libertas as a Political Idea at Rome* (Cambridge: Cambridge University Press, 1950), 1–15.

24. Cf. Livy, *Ab urbe condita*, 37. 54. 26: 'Carthago libera cum suis legibus est'; and Livy, *Ab urbe condita*, 33. 32. 5: 'Liberos, immunes, suis legibus esse iubent Corinthios.'

25. 'Non in regno populum Romanum sed in libertate esse' (Livy, *Ab urbe condita*, 2. 15. 3).

26. 'Liberi iam hinc populi Romani res pace belloque gestas, annuos magistratus, imperiaque legum potentiora quam hominum peragam' (Livy, *Ab urbe condita* 2. 1. 1).

27. 'Nam quid a Pyrro, Hannibale, Philippoque et Antiocho defensum est aliud quam libertas et suae cuique sedes, neu cui nisi legibus pareremus?' Sallust, *Orationes et epistulae excertae de historiis* 4; Eng. trans. J. C. Rolfe, *Orations and Letters from the Histories*, in *Sallust* (Cambridge, Mass.: Harvard University Press, 1960), 386–7.

28. 'legum idcirco omnes servi sumus ut liberi esse possimus' (*Pro Cluentio* 146); Eng. trans. *The Speeches*, H. Grose Hodge (London: Loeb Classical Library, 1927), 379 (revised).

29. Letter to Niccolodio Bartolomei, Apr. 1369, in *Epistolario di Coluccio Salutati*, ed. Francesco Novati (4 vols., Rome: Forzani, 1891–1911), i. 90.

30. Cf. Nicolai Rubinstein, 'Florentine Constitutionalism and Medici Ascendancy in the Fifteenth Century', in N. Rubinstein (ed.), *Florentine Studies* (London: Faber 1968), 442–61, esp. 445.

31. Leonardo Bruni, *Historiarum florentini populi libri XII*, ed. E. Santini, 'Rerum Italicarum Scriptores', XIX, pt. 3, 82; see also Bruni, *Laudatio florentinae urbis*, in Hans Baron, *From Petrarch to Leonardo Bruni* (Chicago: University of Chicago Press, 1968), 259: 'Et iuris quidem gratia magistratus sunt constituti, iisque imperium datum est et in facinorosos homines animadversio, maximeque ut provideant ne cuius potentia plus valeat in civitate quam leges'; and 262: 'Nec est locus ullus in terris in

quo ius magis equum sit omnibus. Nusquam enim viget tanta Libertas et maiorum cum minoribus exequata condicio.'

32. *Ricordi storici di Filippo di Cino Rinuccini dal 1282 al 1460 colla continuazione di Alamanno e Neri suoi figli* ed. G. Aiazzi, (Florence: Piatti, 1840), 103.

33. Alamanno Rinuccini, *Dialogus de libertate*, in *Atti e memorie dell'Accademia Toscana di Scienze e Lettere 'La Colombaria'*, 22, (1957), 267–303.

34. 'Sed neque omnium rerum decernendarum hec tria collegia habent potestatem; sed pleraque, cum abillis approbata sunt, ad populare consilium communeque referuntur. Quod anim ad multos attinet, id non aliter quam multorum sententia decerni consentaneum iuri rationique iudicavit' (*Laudatio florentinae urbis*, 260). The source of this legal principle was the *Corpus iuris civilis, Codex* 5. 59. 5. 2: 'Quod omnes similiter tangit, ab omnibus comprobetur'.

35. As the Latin text shows, Poggio Bracciolini uses, however, the term 'aequo iure' rather then 'aequa libertas': 'Non enim unus, aut alter imperat, non optimatum, aut nobilium fastus regnat, sed populus aequo iure adiicitus ad munera civitatis: quo fit ut summi, infimi, nobiles ignobiles, divites, egeni communi studio conspirent in causam libertatis, propre ea conservanda nullos effugiant sumptus, nullos labores, nulla discrimina reformident' (*Epistolae*, ed. T. de' Tonelli (Florence: Marchini, 1859), ii. 183. Cf. Rubinstein, 'Florentine Constitutionalism', 448 n. 4.

36. 'Atque haec honorum adipiscendorum facultas potestasque libero populo . . . quantum valet ad ingegna civium excitanda . . .' 'Oratio in funere Jahannis Strozzae', in E. Baluze and G. Manzi, *Miscellanea novo ordine digesta . . . et aucta* (Lucca: V. Junctinium, 1764); Eng. trans. in G. Groffith, J. Hankins, and D. Thompson (eds.), *The Humanism of Leonardo Bruni* (Binghamton, NY: The Renaissance Society of America, 1987).

37. *Delizie degli eruditi toscani*, ed. Idelfonso di San Luigi (Florence: Gaetano Cambiagi, 1779), xii. 288.

38. 'ut eliciatur veritas' (see Rubinstein 'Florentine Constitutionalism', 458 n. 1).

39. *Dialogus de libertate* 283. A very useful summary of the Florentine interpretation of political liberty as being based on freedom of speech in deliberative bodies and in just distribution of public honours is to be found in the preamble to the text of the constitutional reform of 23 December 1494, which establishes the new republican government after the expulsion of the Medici: 'Intendendo e magnifici et excelsi signori . . . con tucto el loro ingegno et forza alla conservatione della libertà, lungo tenpo suta quasi occupata et nuovamente recuperata, et all'unione de' ciptadini, et di pensare a tucte le cose che riguardino el bene publico et universale; et conosciendo questo sommamente consistere nel consigliare, provedere et ordinare liberamente ne' casi publici et privati et

nella institutione delle optime et bene considerate provisioni et leggi et
nella giusta distributione degli honori et de' pesi che recha seco una bene
instituta republica . . . statuirono et ordinorono' (in Giorgio Cadoni (ed.),
Provvisioni concernenti l'ordinamento della Repubblica Fiorentina
1494–1512, i. (Rome: Istituto Storico Italiano per il Medio Evo, 1994), 40.

40. *Discorsi*, I. 25, I. 37.

41. *Istorie*, VIII. I. On the theme of civility, see Corrado Vivanti's Introduction to Niccolò Machiavelli, *Discorsi sopra la prima deca di Tito Livio*
(Turin: Einaudi, 1983), pp. xxiv–xxv.

42. *Discorsi*, III. 8.

43. *Discorsi*, I. 17; *Discourses*, 159.

44. 'non si truovano né leggi né ordini che bastino a frenare una universale
corruzione' (*Discorsi*, I. 18; *Discourses*, 160).

45. 'Però si dice che la fame e la povertà fa gli uomini industriosi, e le leggi gli
fanno buoni' (*Discorsi*, I. 3).

46. Ibid. I. 24.

47. 'perché ne nasceva offesa da privati a privati, la quale offesa genera paura,
la paura cerca difesa, per la difesa si procacciano partigiani, da' partigiani
nascono le parti nelle cittadi, dalle parti la rovina di quelle' (*Discorsi*, I. 7;
Discourses, 125–6).

48. 'Perché se ordinariamente uno cittadino è oppresso, ancora che li fusse
fatto torto, ne sèguita o poco o nissuno disordine in la republica; perché la
esecuzione si fa sanza forze private e sanza forze forestiere, che sono
quelle che rovinano il vivere libero; ma si fa con forze ed ordini publici,
che hanno i termini loro particulari, né trascendono a cosa che rovini la
republica' (*Discorsi*, I. 7; *Discourses*, 125).

49. 'perchè le leggi, gli statuti, gli ordini civili non secondo il viver libero, ma
secondo l'ambizione di quella parte che è rimasa superiore, si sono in
quella sempre ordinati e ordinano' (*Istorie*, III. 5; *FH* 110).

50. 'solo i potenti proponevano leggi, non per la comune libertà ma per la
potenza loro' (*Discorsi*, I. 18; *Discourses*, 162 (revised)).

51. 'e l'uno e l'altro ha avuto bisogno d'essere regolato dalle leggi: perché un
principe che può fare ciò ch'ei vuole è pazzo; un popolo che può fare ciò
che vuole non è savio' (*Discorsi*, I. 58).

52. 'dico come un popolo è piú prudente, piú stabile e di migliore giudizio che
un principe. E non sanza cagione si assomiglia la voce d'un popolo a
quella di Dio: perché si vede una opinione universale fare effetti mara-
vigliosi ne' pronostichi suoi; talché pare che per occulta virtú ei prevegga
il suo male ed il suo bene' (*Discorsi*, I. 58; *Discourses*, 255 (revised)).

53. 'E sanza dubbio questo bene comune non è osservato se non nelle republiche: perché tutto quello che fa a proposito suo si esequisce; e quantun-
que e' torni in danno di questo o di quello privato, e' sono tanti quegli per

chi detto bene fa, che lo possono tirare innanzi contro alla disposizione di quegli pochi che ne fussono oppressi' (*Discorsi*, II. 2; *Discourses*, 275).

54. On the theme of the guardianship of liberty, and more generally on the issue of legality within republican tradition, see the excellent essay by Riccardo Ferrante, *La difesa della legalità: I sindacatori della repubblica di Genova* (Turin: Giappichelli, 1995), 279–343.

55. *Discorsi*, I. 5; *Discourses*, 118.

56. Cicero, *De officiis* I. 142.

57. *Discorsi*, I. 2; *Discourses*, 118. Commenting upon this chapter of the *Discorsi*, Harvey Mansfield and Nathan Tarcov remark that 'In Aristotle the tyrannical element in a republic stands for its lapses from perfection, but in Machiavelli, tyranny is used precisely to the contrary—to make the republic perfect', and that 'in giving preference to Rome's accidental perfection because it is more flexible than that of Sparta's one-time classical legislator Lycurgus, he shows again that tyranny—the rule of *uno solo*—works well, or best, in the context of a republic' (Niccolò Machiavelli, *Discourses on Livy*, ed. Harvey C. Mansfield and Nathan Tarcov (Chicago: University of Chicago Press, 1996), Introduction, pp. xxvii–xxviii). Apart from the gross mistake of equating the rule of *uno solo*, as such, and particularly the rule of Romulus to tyranny, it is obvious that, for Machiavelli, Rome was not perfect because it allowed room for tyranny, but became perfect only when it gave itself a constitution in which 'all three kinds of government there had their part'.

58. 'il popolo non vi aveva dentro la parte sua' (*Discursus florentinarum rerum post mortem iunioris Laurentii Medices*, in *Arte della guerra*, 262).

59. 'dopo il quale, la città volle pigliare forma di repubblica, e non si appose ad appigliarla in modo che fussi durabile, perché quegli ordini non satisfacevano a tutti gli umori dei cittadini' (ibid. 263).

60. *Discorsi*, I. 37.

61. 'Essendo pertanto divenuta l'autorità tribunizia insolente e formidabile alla Nobilità e a tutta Roma, e' ne sarebbe nato qualche inconveniente dannoso alla libertà romana . . .' (*Discorsi*, III. 11).

62. *Istorie*, III. 1; *FH* 105.

63. Istorie, III. 1; *FH* 106. The result of the predominance of the nobility or of the populace is a restless oscillation between tyranny and licence, two forms of corrupt government that Machiavelli regards as equally pernicious. Cities, he writes in the Proem of book IV of the *Istorie Fiorentine*, 'e quelle massimamente che non sono bene ordinate, le quali sotto nome di repubblica si amministrano, variano spesso i governi e stati loro, non mediante la libertà e la servitù, come molti credono, ma mediante la servitù e la licenza'. Both are equally bad: 'l'uno non piace agli uomini buoni; l'altro dispiace ai savi; l'uno può fare male facilmente, l'altro con difficoltà può far bene; nell'uno hanno troppa autorità gli

uomini insolenti, nell'altro gli sciocchi.' He calls the 'popolani' 'ministers of licence' ('ministri della licenza') and the nobles 'ministers of servitude' ('quelli della servitù').

64. *Discorsi*, I. 4; *Discourses*, 113.

65. *Istorie*, I. I.

66. 'bisogna nello ordinare la republica pensare alla parte piú onorevole' *(Discorsi, I. 6)*.

67. Ibid.

68. Ibid. I. I.

69. Ibid. II. I.

70. *Il Principe*, ch. 5.

71. *Istorie*, III. 5.

72. 'una città non si poteva chiamare libera, dove era uno cittadino che fusse temuto dai magistrati' *(Discorsi, I. 29)*.

73. *Istorie*, bk. IV, Proem.

74. 'non serví mai umilmente né mai dominò superbamente; anzi con li suoi ordini e magistrati tenne il suo grado onorevolmente' *(Discorsi, I. 58; Discourses, 253* (revised))*.

75. 'in modo osservono le loro leggi che nessuno di fuori né di dentro ardisce occuparle' *(Discorsi, I. 55; Discourses, 244)*.

76. 'e' si comincia a corrompere una legge la quale è il nervo e la vita del vivere libero' *(Discorsi, I. 33; Discourses, 191* (revised))*.

77. *Discorsi*, I. 16; *Discourses*, 156–7.

78. *Discorsi*, II. 2; *Discourses*, 276 (revised). Harvey Mansfield and Nathan Tarcov refer to Machiavelli's claim that 'an important part of the reason why people love republics more than principalities is that all those who dwell in them can believe that their children can grow up to be princes through their virtue' as yet another evidence of 'the princely or tyrannical elements in his republicanism'. How can a passage in which Machiavelli praises republics because they permit the citizens to attain by their virtue the highest public honours support the view that Machiavelli's republicanism is tyrannical and princely is utterly unintellible—unless the two editors of the *Discourses* have made the mistake of taking the phrase 'diventare principi' to mean 'to become princes', as their translation reads, not in the sense of attaining the highest public honours, but in the sense of instituting a principality.

79. 'perché il vivere libero prepone onori e premii mediante alcune oneste e determinate cagioni, e fuora di quelle non premia né onora alcuno' *(Discorsi, I. 16; Discourses, 154)*.

80. *Discorsi*, I. 58.

81. Ibid. III. 25

82. *Discursus florentinarum rerum*, in *Arte della guerra*, 269. Republics can choose their leaders, their magistrates, and their commanders among many citizens with different qualities and appoint those who possess the qualities that are more suitable to face different circumstances. As a consequence, republics have longer life and enjoy good fortune for longer time than a principality. In sum, 'government by the people is better than government by princes' ('sono migliori governi quegli de' popoli che quegli de' principi') (*Discorsi*, I. 58).

83. Ibid. I. 18; *Discourses*, 162.

84. *Il Principe*, ch. 1.

85. *Discorsi*, I. 16; *Discourses*, 154 (revised).

86. 'come era il popolo romano, il quale, mentre durò la Republica incorrotta, non serví mai umilmente' (ibid. I. 58).

87. 'per altri modi si ha a cercare gloria in una città corrotta che in una che ancora viva politicamente' (ibid., III. 8).

88. Ibid. I. 55

89. 'le leggi bene ordinate non giovano' (ibid., I. 17; *Discourses*, 159 (revised)).

90. 'non si truovano né leggi né ordini che bastino a frenare una universale corruzione' (*Discorsi*, I. 18; *Discourses*, 160).

91. 'I giovani sono oziosi, i vecchi lascivi, e ogni sesso e ogni età è piena di brutti costumi; a che le leggi buone, per essere dalle cattive usanze guaste, non rimediano. Di qui nasce quella avarizia che si vede nei cittadini e quello appetito non di vera gloria, ma di vituperosi onori, dal quale dipendono gli odj, le inimicizie, i dispiaceri e le sètte, dalle quali nascono morti, esilj, afflizioni dei buoni, esaltazioni de'tristi' (*Istorie*, III. 5; *FH* 110).

92. *Istorie*, III. 5; *FH* 110.

93. 'Dipoi io mi meraviglio di te, che tu voglia, dove non si fa cosa alcuna laudabile o buona che vi si faccia questa: perché dove sono i costumi perversi conviene che il parlare sia perverso, et habbia in sé quello effemminato lascivo che hanno coloro che lo parlano' (*Discorso*, 54–5; see also the rich commentary for the classical sources of Machiavelli's analysis).

94. 'desolati gli antichi templi, corrotte le cerimonie' (*Discorsi*, I. 10; *Discourses*, 137).

95. 'in tutti la religione e il timor di Dio è spento' (*Istorie*, III. 5; *FH* 110).

96. 'dove manca il timore di Dio, conviene o che quel regno rovini o che sia sostenuto dal timore d'uno principe che sopperisca a' difetti della religione' (*Discorsi*, I. 11; *Discourses*, 141).

97. 'e volendolo ridurre nelle obedienze civili con le arti della pace, [Numa] si volse alla religione come cosa al tutto necessaria a volere mantenere una civiltà' (*Discorsi*, I. 11; *Discourses*, 139).

98. 'quelle città che hanno avuto il loro principio immediatamente servo abbino non che difficultà, ma impossibilità a ordinarsi mai in modo che le possino vivere civilmente e quietamente' (*Discorsi*, I. 49; *Discourses*, 231).

99. 'e cosí è ita maneggiandosi per dugento anni, che si ha di vera memoria, sanza avere mai avuto stato per il quale la possa veramente essere chiamata republica' (*Discorsi*, I. 49; *Discourses*, 231).

100. *Discorsi*, I. 16.

101. Ibid. I. 17; *Discourses*, 159.

102. *Discorsi*, I. 17; *Discourses*, 158.

103. Dependency and the habits of servility which ensue from it define for Machiavelli the social boundaries of citizenship, as he writes in a note whose date and context cannot be determined: 'Li uomini che nelle republiche servono alle arti meccaniche non possono sapere comandare come príncipi quando sono preposti a' magistrati, avendo imparato sempre a servire. E però si vuol tòrre per comadare di quelli che non hanno mai ubbidito se non a' re e alle leggi, come sono quelli che vivono delle entrate loro' (*Il teatro*, 223).

104. 'Né giova in questo caso che la materia non sia corrotta; perché una autorità assoluta in brevissimo tempo corrompe la materia e si fa amici e partigiani' (*Discorsi*, I. 35).

105. 'Le vie private sono, faccendo beneficio a questo ed a quello altro privato, col prestargli danari, maritargli le figliuole, difenderlo dai magistrati e faccendogli simili privati favori i quali si fanno li uomini partigiani e danno animo a chi è cosí favorito di potere corrompere il publico e sforzare le leggi' (*Discorsi*, III. 28; *Discourses*, 482).

106. 'oziosi vivono delle rendite delle loro possessioni abbondantemente, sanza avere cura alcuna o di coltivazione o di altra necessaria fatica a vivere' (*Discorsi*, I. 55; *Discourses*, 245–6).

107. *Discorsi*, I. 55; *Discourses*, 245–6.

108. 'nasce piú sanza dubbio dalla viltà degli uomini, che hanno interpretato la nostra religione secondo l'ozio e non secondo la virtú' (*Discorsi*, II. 2).

109. 'La nostra religione ha glorificato piú gli uomini umili e contemplativi che gli attivi. Ha dipoi posto il sommo bene nella umiltà, abiezione, e nel dispregio delle cose umane: quell'altra lo poneva nella grandezza dello animo, nella fortezza del corpo ed in tutte le altre cose atte a fare gli uomini fortissimi. E se la religione nostra richiede che tu abbi in te fortezza, vuole che tu sia atto a patire piú che a fare una cosa forte. Questo modo di vivere adunque pare che abbi renduto il mondo debole, e datolo in preda agli uomini scelerati, i quali sicuramente lo possono maneggiare, veggendo come l'università degli uomini per andare in Paradiso pensa piú a sopportare le sue battiture che a vendicarle' (*Discorsi*, II. 2. *Discourses*, 278).

110. *Discorsi*, I. 45; *Discourses*, 220.

111. 'et che si debbi prestare fede alla Signoria et che il volere certezza di ogni cosa è impossibile et che bisogna governarsi secondo li accidenti et non volere la città ruini per volere stare in sulla observanza delle leggi' (Lauro Martines, *Lawyers and Statecraft in Renaissance Florence* (Princeton: Princeton University Press, 1968), 426).

112. See ibid. 434.

113. See ibid. 441–5.

114. In a letter to a Chancellor of Lucca of early October 1500, he openly endorses the decision of the Republic's authorities and claims that Vitelli's conduct deserves 'infinite punishment' ('infinito castigo') (*Lettere*, 84–6; MF 22–3). In the *Decennale primo*, a historical poem composed in 1504, he speaks of Florence's 'full revenge' against Paolo Vitelli: 'Soon after, for the trick he played, you took revenge in full, | inflicting death on him who had caused you such great harm.' The Italian wording is 'vi vendicaste assai', which suggests that the revenge was excessive and unfair. See *Il teatro*, 244; Gilbert, iii. 1450.

115. *Discorsi*, III. 3.

116. Ibid. III. 22; *Discourses*, 469.

117. *Discorsi*, I. 55; *Discourses*, 244–5.

118. *Discorsi*, I. 12; *Discourses*, 143.

119. *Il Principe*, ch. 12; *The Prince*, 42–3 (revised)).

120. 'perché tutte l'arti che si ordinano in una civiltà per cagione del bene comune degli uomini, tutti gli ordini fatti in quella per vivere con timore delle leggi e d'Iddio, sarebbono vani, se non fussono preparate le difese loro; le quali, bene ordinate mantengono quegli, ancora che non bene ordinati. E cosí, per il contrario, i buoni ordini sanza il militare aiuto, non altrimenti si disordinano che l'abitazioni d'uno superbo e regale palazzo, ancora che ornate di gemme e d'oro, quando, sanza essere coperte, non avessono cosa che dalla pioggia le difendesse. (*Arte della guerra*, Proem, 325; Gilbert, ii. 566 (revised)).

121. 'mai alcuno cittadino grande non presunse, mediante tale esercizio, valersi nella pace, rompendo le leggi, spogliando le provincie, usurpando e tiranneggiando la patria e in ogni modo prevalendosi; né alcuno d'infima fortuna pensò di violare il sacramento, aderirsi agli uomini privati, non temere il senato, o seguire alcuno tirannico insulto per potere vivere, con l'arte della guerra, d'ogni tempo' (*Arte della guerra*, 337; Gilbert, ii. 575).

122. 'Debbe adunque una città bene ordinata volere che questo studio di guerra si usi ne' tempi di pace per esercizio e ne' tempi di guerra per necessità e per gloria' (*Arte della guerra*, 338; Gilbert, ii. 576).

123. 'L'arme in dosso a' suoi cittadini o sudditi, date dalle leggi, e dall'ordine non fecero mai danno, anzi sempre fanno utile e mantengonsi le città

piú tempo immaculate mediante queste armi che sanza' (*Arte della guerra*, 348; Gilbert, ii. 585). On the theme of the militia, see the excellent essay by Gennaro Sasso 'Machiavelli, Cesare Borgia, don Micheletto e la questione della milizia', in *Machiavelli e gli antichi e altri saggi* (3 vols.; Naples: Riccardo Ricciardi, 1987–8), ii. 57–117.

124. *Discorsi*, II. 4; *Discourses*, 283 (revised).

125. *Discorsi*, II. 21; *Discourses*, 341 (revised).

126. *Discorsi*, II. 21; *Discourses*, 226 (revised).

127. *Discorsi*, II. 21; *Discourses*, 343 (revised). See also *Discorsi*, III. 20: 'Here it is to be considered with this true example how much more a humane act full of charity is sometimes able to do in the spirits of men than a ferocious and violent act, and that often those provinces and those cities that arms, warlike instruments, and every other human force have not been able to open have been opened by one example of humanity, of mercy, of chastity or of liberality.'

128. *Istorie*, II. 38; *FH* 100 (revised).

129. *La cagione dell'ordinanza dove la si truovi et quel che bisogni fare*, in *I primi scritti*, 423.

130. In the *Storie Fiorentine*, Guicciardini does not absolve the Florentines' commissioners, nor Florence ('benchè e' commessari usassino ogni possibile diligenza che questo non seguissi, e molto dispiacessi alla città nostra'). He remarks only that the Florentines would have preferred to regain Volterra as rich and as neat as it was before the rebellion. See Francesco Guicciardini, *Storie Fiorentine*, in *Opere*, ed. Emanuella Lugnani Scarano (Turin: UTET, 1974), i. 86.

131. *Dell'asino d'oro*, in *Il teatro*, 287–8; Gilbert, ii. 762.

132. *Discorso sopra Pisa*, in *I primi scritti*, 403. In the Proem to the ordinances which institutes the Florentine militia, inspired by Machiavelli though not written by him, there is no mention at all of conquest or even expansion as the aims for which the militia is instituted, but only of the necessity to defend the republic from external aggressions ('per potersi difendere dalli inimici'), and the need to 'restrain and correct the subjects' ('raffrenare et correggere i subditi'), see *Militie Florentine Ordinatio*, in *I primi scritti*, 450. The peroration which ends the speech of 1503 is a most eloquent appeal to liberty as the overarching commitment which should guide the deliberations of Florentines: 'Il che io non posso credere che sia, veggiendovi Fiorentini liberi et essere nelle mani vostre la vostra libertà: alla quale credo che voi harete quelli respetti che ha hauto sempre chi è nato libero et desidera viver libero' (*Parole da dirle sopra la provisione del danaio, facto un poco di Proemio et di scusa*, in *I primi scritti*, 416).

133. 'perché ogni città, ogni stato, debbe reputare inimici tucti coloro che possono sperare di poterle occupare el suo et da chi lei non si può

difendere. Né fu mai né signore né repubblica savia che volessi tenere lo stato suo ad discretione d'altri o che, tenendolo, gliene paressi haver securo' (*Parole da dirle sopra la provisione del danaio*, in *I primi scritti*, 413).

134. *Discorsi*, I. 34.

135. 'Il quale rispetto era savio e buono: nondimeno e' non si debbe mai lasciare scorrere un male rispetto ad uno bene, quando quel bene facilmente possa essere da quel male oppressato' (ibid. III. 3).

136. 'Tanto che per non sapere somigliare Bruto, e' perdé insieme con la patria sua lo stato e la reputazione' (ibid. III. 3). For other important judgements on the conduct of Piero Soderini, cf. ibid. III. 9; and III. 30.

137. Ibid. I. 10; *Discourses*, 138 (revised).

138. *Discorsi*, I. 18.

139. *Istorie*, III. 5.

140. 'e veruna cosa fa tanto onore a uno uomo che di nuovo surga, quanto fa le nuove legge e li nuovi ordini trovati da lui. Queste cose, quando sono bene fondate et abbino in loro grandezza, lo fanno reverendo e mirabile' (*Il Principe*, ch. 26).

141. 'non è esaltato alcuno uomo tanto in alcuna sua azione, quanto sono quegli che hanno con leggi e con istituti reformato le repubbliche e i regni: questi sono, dopo quegli che sono stati Iddii, i primi laudati. E perché e' sono stati pochi che abbino avuto occasione di farlo, e pochissimi quelli che lo abbino saputo fare, sono piccolo numero quelli che lo abbino fatto: e è stimata tanto questa gloria dagli uomini che non hanno mai atteso ad altro che a gloria, che non avendo possuto fare una repubblica in atto, l'hanno fatta in iscritto; come Aristotile, Platone e molti altri: e' quali hanno voluto mostrare al mondo, che se, come Solone e Licurgo, non hanno potuto fondare un vivere civile, non è mancato dalla ignoranza loro, ma dalla impotenza di metterlo in atto' (*Discursus florentinarum rerum*, in *Arte della guerra*, 275–6; Gilbert, i. 115 (revised).

142. 'E quando pure la vi si avesse a creare o a mantenere, sarebbe necessario ridurla piú verso lo stato regio che verso lo stato popolare, acciocché quegli uomini i quali dalle leggi per la loro insolenzia non possono essere corretti, fussero da una podestà quasi regia in qualche modo frenati' (*Discorsi*, I. 18).

143. 'Nasce ancora questo ritiramento delle republiche verso il loro principio dalla semplice virtú d'un uomo, sanza dependere da alcuna legge che ti stimoli ad alcuna esecuzione' (ibid., III. 1; *Discourses*, 388).

144. 'I quali ordini hanno bisogno di essere fatti vivi dalla virtú d'uno cittadino, il quale animosamente concorra ad eseguirli contro alla potenza di quegli che gli trapassano' (ibid. III. 1). To reinforce his point that the institution of the rule of law often demands extraordinary means,

Machiavelli cites the Bible: 'E chi legge la Bibbia sensatamente vedrà Moisè essere stato forzato, a volere che le sue leggi e che li suoi ordini andassero innanzi, ad ammazzare infiniti uomini, i quali non mossi da altro che dalla invidia si opponevano a' disegni suoi' (ibid. III. 30).

145. 'Oltre a di questo, se uno è atto a ordinare, non è la cosa ordinata per durare molto quando la rimanga sopra le spalle d'uno, ma sí bene quando la rimane alla cura di molti, e che a molti stia il mantenerla' (ibid. I. 9). On the necessity to entrust the care of the republic in order to attain stability, see also the conclusion of the *Discursus florentinarum rerum*: 'Né ci è altra via da fuggire questi mali, che fare in modo che gli ordini della città per loro medesimi possino stare fermi; e staranno sempre fermi quando ciascheduno vi averà sopra le mani; e quando ciascuno saperrà quello ch'egli abbi a fare, e in che gli abbi a confidare; e che nessuno grado di cittadino, o per paura di sé o per ambizione, abbi a desiderare innovazione' (*Arte della guerra*, 277). In the *Ritracto delle cose della Magna*, however, Machiavelli remarks that matters which are committed to many are neglected: 'Et però, se si vede che in una ciptà le cose che apartengono a molti sono straccurate, tanto più debbe intervenire in una provincia' (*I primi scritti*, 530).

5 *The Passion of Liberty*

1. *The Miscellaneous Works of Lord Macaulay* (New York: Harper & Bros., 1899), i. 69, 71, 122.

2. See Carlo Curcio, *Machiavelli nel Risorgimento* (Milan: Giuffré, 1953), 22–3.

3. Luigi Russo, *Machiavelli* (Bari: Laterza, 1949), 227–39.

4. Cf. Maurizio Viroli, *For Love of Country* (Oxford: Oxford University Press, 1995).

5. 'pietas, per quam sanguine coniunctis patriaeque benivolum officium et diligens tribuitur cultus' (*De inventione* 2. 53. 161).

6. *De officiis* 1. 17. 57.

7. Ibid. 1. 17. 53.

8. *Ab urbe condita* 7. 40: 'Omnes caritate cives . . . complexus'; and 2. 2. 5: 'Invitum se dicere, hominis causa, Nec dicturum fuisse ni caritas reipublicae vinceret.'

9. Thomas Aquinas, *Summa Theologiae*, in *Sancti Thomae Aquinatis Opera Omnia* (Rome: Ex Typographia Polyglotte, 1897), 2a 2ae, CI, a.I, 368. The text of Cicero that Aquinas discusses is from *De inventione* 2. 53: 'Pietas, per quam sanguine coniuntis patriaeque benivolum officium et diligens tribuitur cultus.'

10. 'idem esse cum iustitia legali, quae respicit bonum commune' (*Summa Theologiae*, 2–2ae, CI, a.III, 370).

11. Ptolemy of Lucca, *De regimine principum*, in R. Spiazzi (ed.), *Divi Thomae Aquinatis opuscula philosophice* (Turin: Marietti, 1954), 299.

12. 'Magnificentius exprimi non potuit fortitudo charitatis, quam ut diceretur, *Valida est sicut mortis dilectio*. Quis enim resistit morti, fratres? Intendat Charitas vestra. Resistitur ignibus, undis, ferro; Resistitur potestatibus, Resistitur regibus: venit una mors, Quis ei resistit? Nihil illa fortius. Propterea viribus ejus Charitas comparata est, et dictum est, *Valida est sicut mors dilectio*. Et quia ipsa Charitas occidit quod fuimus, ut simus quod non eramus; facit in nobis quamdam mortem dilectio' (Augustin, *Enarratio in Psalmum CXXI*, in Jacques Paul Migne (ed.), *Patrologia Latina* (Paris: Garnier, 1845), XXXVII. 1627.

13. See Hans Baron, *In Search of Florentine Civic Humanism* (2 vols.; Princeton: Princeton University Press, 1988), i. 114.

14. Remigio de' Girolami, *Tractatus de bono communi*, in Maria C. De Matteis, *La teologia politica comunale di Remigio de' Girolami*, (Bologna: Pàtron, 1977), 8.

15. Remigio de' Girolami, *De bono pacis*, in C. T. Davis (ed.), *Remigio de'Girolami and Dante: A Comparison of their Conceptions of Peace*, in *Studi Danteschi*, 36 (1959), 128.

16. 'metterci l'avere e le persone, infine all'anima e a Dio' (see Giampaolo Tognetti, 'Amare la patria più che l'anima. Contributo circa la genesi di un atteggiamento religioso', in *Studi sul Medioevo cristiano offerti a Raffaello Morghen* (Rome: Istituto Storica Italiano per il Medio Evo, 1974), ii. 1014).

17. *Istoria di M. Poggio Fiorentino: Tradotta di Latino in Volgare da Iacopo suo figliuolo* (Florence: Filippo Giunti, 1598), 35.

18. 'Haec quidem docet sic diligere sanguinem, quod pro Christi nomine parum sit se ab omni necessitudinis illius complexibus liberari; sic monet amicitiam colere, quod animam suam, hoc est vitam transitoriam, pro eterna suorum amicorum salute, si tamen eterne se non perdat, exponat: sic imperat patriam rempublicamque defendi, ut civitates et omnes ad Dei gloriam conserventur' (Letter to Demetrio Cidonio, 18 (?) Feb. 1396, in *Epistolario di Coluccio Salutati*, ed. Francesco Novati (4 vols.; Rome: Forzani, 1891–1911), iii. 109.

19. 'Optime autem societas hominum coniunctioque servabitur, si, ut quisque erit coniunctissimus ita in eum benignitatis plurimum conferetur' (Cicero, *De officiis* 1. 16. 50).

20. 'debemus parentibus reverentiam, filiis dilectionem, fratribus equalitatem, cognatis amorem, prelatis obedientiam, uxori castitatem, et cunctis benivolentiam: patrie autem hec omnia et nosmetipsos debemus. Habet enim illa simul parentes, filios, fratres, agnatos, amicos, coniugem, socios et nos ipsos. Illa nos creavit, illa nos tuetur; ad illa, quod primum est, originem trahimus; qua re pre cunctis nobis esse cure debet' (*Epistolario Coluccio Salutati*, i. 26–7). 'Nulla enim caritas est qui sit cum caritate

patrie comparanda; parentes, filii, fratres, amici, agnati, affines et cetere necessitudines quedam singula sunt et simul omnia collata minus habent ipsa republica' (ibid. i. 21); 'caritas, que maior quam erga patriam esse non debet in terris' (ibid. ii. 87); 'patriam . . . cuius caritas non solum omnes necessitudines amplexa est, sed preterit et excedit' (ibid. iii. 638).

21. See Alfred von Martin, *Coluccio Salutati und das Humanistische Leben-sideal*, (Leipzig: Teubner, 1916), 128.

22. 'Thou knowest not how sweet is the *Amor patriae*: if such would be expedient for the fatherland's protection or enlargement [*sic*!] it would seem neither burdensome and difficult nor a crime to thrust the axe into one's father's head, to crush one's brothers, to deliver from the womb of ones' wife the premature child with the sword'. I am quoting from the translation by Ernst Kantorowicz, *The King's Two Bodies* (Princeton: Princeton University Press, 1957), 245.

23. 'Primum igitur omni cura provisum est ut ius in civitate sanctissimum habeatur, sine quo Nec civitas esse Nec nominari ulla potest; deinde ut sit libertas, sine qua nunquam hic populus vivendum sibi existimavit' (Leonardo Bruni, *Laudatio florentinae urbis*, in Hans Baron (ed.), *From Petrarch to Leonardo Bruni* (Chicago: University of Chicago Press, 1968), 259; Eng. trans. in G. Groffith, J. Hankins, and D. Thompson (eds.), *The Humanism of Leonardo Bruni* (Binghampton, NY: The Renaissance Society of America, 1987), 169.

24. *Laudatio florentinae urbis*, 262; *The Humanism of Leonardo Bruni*, 174 (revised).

25. 'ne quisquam patria se carere put donec Florentinarum superstit urbs' (*Laudatio florentinae urbis*, 251; *The Humanism of Leonardo Bruni*, 159).

26. 'Nam et ipsa urbs eiusmodi est ut nichil neque luculentius neque splen-didius in toto orbe terrarum inveniri possit' (*Laudatio florentinae urbis*, 232; *The Humanism of Leonardo Bruni*, 135).

27. 'sed potius sufficientem autument ad totius orbis dominium imperium-que adipiscendum' (*Laudatio florentinae urbis*, 239; *The Humanism of Leonardo Bruni*, 143).

28. *Laudatio florentinae urbis*, 248; *The Humanism of Leonardo Bruni*, 154.

29. 'Oratio in funere Jahannis Strozzae', in E. Baluze and G. Manzi, *Miscel-lanea novo ordine digesta . . . et aucta*, (Lucca: V. Junctinium, 1764), 3; *The Humanism of Leonardo Bruni*, 123.

30. 'Oratio in funere Jahannis Strozzae', 6; *The Humanism of Leonardo Bruni*, 124.

31. 'Non ti biasimerò se di te porgerai tanta virtù et fama che la patria ti riceva et impongati parte de' suoi incarichi, et chiamerò onore essere cosí pregiato da' tuoi cittadini' (Leon Battista Alberti, *I primi tre libri della famiglia* in *Opere volgari*, ed. C. Greison (Bari: Laterza, 1966), 277–8; Eng.

trans., Renée Neu Watkins, *The Family in Renaissance Florence* (Columbia, SC: University of South Carolina Press, 1969), 176.

32. 'Dicono e savi ch'e buoni cittadini debono traprendere la republica et soffrire le fatiche della patria, et non curare le ineptie degli uomini, per servire al publico otio et mantenere il bene di tutti i cittadini, et per non cedere luogo a viziosi, i quali per negligentia de' buoni et per loro improbità perverterebono ogni cosa, onde cose né publiche, né private più potrebono bene sostenersi' (Leon Battista Alberti, *I primi tre libri della famiglia*, 281; *The Family in Renaissance Florence*, 178).

33. 'Noi in questo mezo, Batista et tu Carlo, seguiamo con virtù, con ogni studio, con ogni arte a meritare lodo et fama, et cosí apparecchianci essere utili alla republica, alla patria nostra' (*I primi tre libri della famiglia*, 284; *The Family in Renaissance Florence*, 180).

34. *I primi tre libri della famiglia*, 283; *The Family in Renaissance Florence*, 179.

35. 'Da queste procede la pietà ne' padri, l'amore ne' figliuoli, la carità de' parenti, la difensione degli amici et ultimamente il publico governo et universale salute della civile unione et concordia' (Matteo Palmieri, *Vita civile*, ed. G. Belloni (Florence: Olschki, 1982), 52–3).

36. 'Le cose dunque che per loro medesime sono diricte et honeste, come è amare la virtù, difendere la patria, servare l'amicitia, in ogni modo si debbono fare, o comandilo il padre o no, et etiandio se il vietasse, ché sare' contro all'uficio del padre' (ibid. 56).

37. 'La pietà della patria condusse Oratio Clocles, nobilissimo cittadino romano, a sostenere in su il suo glorioso petto tutto l'empito de' potenti nemici . . . Per questa civile pietà Curtio con audace animo nella divoratrice voragine a certissima morte si gittò . . .' (ibid. 124–5).

38. 'Nulla opera fra gl'huomini può essere più optima che provedere alla salute della patria, conservare la città et mantenere l'unione et concordia delle bene ragunate multitudini' (ibid. 208).

39. 'L'honore l'utilità et la gloria publica non debbe mai essere postposta pe' privati commodi, né mai sarà utile quello che, giovando a pochi, nocerà a l'universale corpo della città. Molti sono gloriosi perchè non solo l'avere, ma ancora gli exili, il sangue et la propria vita hanno sprezato per salute commune della patria' (ibid. 124).

40. *Discorsi*, bk. I, Proem.

41. Ibid. III. 6. See on this issue the very pertinent observations of Elena Fasano Guarini, 'Congiure "contro alla patria" e congiure "contro ad uno principe" nell'opera di Niccolò Machiavelli', in Yves-Marie Bercé and Elena Fasano Guarini (eds.), *Complots et conjurations dans l'Europe moderne* (Rome: École Française de Rome, 1996), 22 and *passim*.

42. 'Eseguite che le sono, ancora non portano altri periculi che si porti la natura del principato in sé, perché divenuto che uno è tiranno, ha i suoi

naturali ed ordinari pericoli che gli arreca la tirannide, alli quali non ha altri rimedi che si siano sopra discorsi' (*Discorsi*, III. 6).

43. Ibid. I. 58.

44. Ibid. III. 46; *Discourses*, 523 (revised). In their translation of the *Discorsi* Mansfield and Tarcov completely alter the sense of Machiavelli's text. They render it as follows: 'Whoever reads the oration he made against Publius Sempronius, tribune of the plebs . . .', whereas Machiavelli refers to the oration made *by* Publius Sempronius: 'E chi leggerà la orazione che gli fece contro Publio Sempronio tribuno della plebe . . .'. The Walker translation is also mistaken.

45. 'ubi duae contariae leges sunt, semper antiquae obrogat nova'. 'An hoc dicis, Appi, non teneri Aemilia lege populum? an populum teneri, te unum exlegem esse?' (Livy, *Ab Urbe Condita* 9. 34).

46. *Discorsi*, III. 47.

47. 'A questa sì crudel sentenza data contra ad una sì nobile città non fu cittadino nè amico, eccetto che messer Farinata degli Uberti, che si opponesse; il quale apertamente e senza alcun rispetto la difese, dicendo non avere con tanta fatica corsi tanti pericoli, se non per potere nella sua patria abitare, e che non era allora per non volere quello che già aveva cerco' (*Istorie*, II. 7; *FH* 59).

48. 'Perché io non so quale cosa si fusse tanto sua (non eccettuando, non ch'altro, l'anima) che per gli amici volentieri da lui non fusse stata spesa; non so quale impresa lo avessa sbigottito, dove quello avesse conosciuto il bene della sua patria' (*Arte della guerra*, 328, Gilbert, ii. 568 (revised).

49. *Istorie*, III. 6; *FH* 112 (revised).

50. 'pensò di adonestare con una onesta cagione la disonestà dell'animo suo . . . Al che si aggiungeva l'ignoranza di molti altri, i quali credevano messer Corso per amor della patria muoversi' (ibid. II. 21; *FH* 73).

51. 'Si può dire più tosto che questi simili abbino fatto per amore della patria che della libertà; la patria abbraccia in sé tanti beni, tanti affetti dolci, che eziandio quegli che vivono sotto e' principi amano la patria, e se ne sono trovati molti che per lei si sono messi a pericoli' (Francesco Guicciardini, *Dialogo del reggimento di Firenze*, in *Opere*, ed. *Emmanuella Lugnani Scarano* (Turin: UTET, 1974), 39).

52. 'e veggiendo da l'altro canto le virtuosissime operazioni che le istorie ci mostrono, che sono state operate da regni e da republiche antique, dai re, capitani, cittadini, latori di leggi ed altri che si sono per la loro patria affaticati' (*Discorsi*, bk. I, Proem).

53. *Istorie*, VIII. 19.

54. 'Amo generalmente tutti gli uomini di quella, le leggi, li costumi, le mura, le case, le vie, le chiese et il contado, né posso avere il maggior dispiacere che pensare quella avere a tribolare e quelle cose, che di sopra

dico, avere andare in ruina' (Vettori to Machiavelli, 20 Aug. 1513, in *Lettere*, 408; *MF* 253).

55. 'E quando mai i padri non l'avessero ricordata, i palagi pubblici, i luoghi de' magistrati, l'insegne de' liberi ordini la ricordano; le quali cose conviene che sieno con grandissimo disiderio da' cittadini cognosciute. Quali opere volete voi che siano le vostre, che contrappesino alla dolcezza del vivere libero, o che faccino mancare gli uomini del disiderio delle presenti condizioni?' (*Istorie*, II. 34; *FH* 92).

56. 'Sempre ch' io ho potuto honorare la patria mia, etiamdio con mio carico et pericolo, l'ho fatto volentieri: perché l'huomo non ha maggiore obligo nella vita sua che con quella, dependendo prima da essa l'essere, et dipoi tutto quello che di buono la fortuna e la natura ci hanno conceduto; et tanto viene a essere maggiore in coloro che hanno sortito patria più nobile. Et veramente colui il quale con l'animo et con l' opera si fa nimico della sua patria, meritatamente si può chiamare parricida, ancora che da quella fussi suto offeso' (*Discorso*, 3–4). Gennaro Sasso has convincingly argued that Machiavelli's source is Plato's *Crito*, which had been translated into Latin by Leonardo Bruni and later by Marsilio Ficino. See Gennaro Sasso, 'Il "celebrato sogno" di Machiavelli', in *Machiavelli e gli antichi e altri saggi* (3 vols.; Naples: Riccardo Ricciardi, 1987–8), 286–94.

57. 'Niuno uomo buono riprenderà mai alcuno che cerchi difendere la patria sua, in qualunque modo se la difenda . . . perchè quella patria merita essere da tutti i cittadini amata, la quale ugualmente tutti i suoi cittadini ama; non quella che, posposti tutti gli altri, pochissimi n'adora' (*Istorie*, v. 8; *FH* 193–4).

58. 'Quale adunque può essere malattia maggiore a un corpo d'una Repubblica, che la servitù? Quale medicina è più da usare necessaria, che quella che da questa infermità la sollevi? Sono solamente quelle guerre giuste, che sono necessarie; e quelle armi sono pietose, dove non è alcuna speranza fuora di quelle. Io non so qual necessità sia maggiore che la nostra, o qual pietà possa superar quella, che tragga la patria sua di servitù' (*Istorie*, v. 8; *FH* 194).

59. As he did for all major figures of Florentine politics, Machiavelli appends a few words of comment upon Rinaldo, but his words are not at all condemnation: 'He was a man truly honoured in all fortune, but he would have been still more so if nature had had him born in a united city, because many of his qualities hurt him in a divided city that would have rewarded him in a united city.' (*Istorie*, v. 34).

60. 'le quali voci dettero materia ai nimici di calunniarlo, come uomo che amasse più sè medesimo che la patria, e più questo mondo che quell'altro' (*Istorie*, VII. 6; *FH* 283).

61. 'E quando era necessario commuoversi contro a un potente, lo faceva;

come si vide in Manlio, ne' Dieci ed in altri che cercorono opprimerla' (*Discorsi*, I. 58; *Discourses*, 253).

62. 'Perché tutte le terre e le provincie che vivono libere in ogni parte, come di sopra dissi, fanno profitti grandissimi. Perché quivi si vede maggiori popoli, per essere e' connubi piú liberi, piú desiderabili dagli uomini: perché ciascuno procrea volentieri quegli figliuoli che crede potere nutrire, non dubitando che il patrimonio gli sia tolto, e ch'ei si conosce non solamente che nascono liberi e non schiavi, ma ch'ei possono mediante la virtú loro diventare principi' (*Discorsi*, II. 2. *Discourses*, 280 (revised)).

63. 'E' si debbe molti di voi ricordare quando Gostantinopoli fu preso dal turcho. Quello imperadore previde la sua ruina, chiamò e' suoi cittadini, non potendo con le sue entrate ordinarie provedersi, expose loro e' periculi, monstrò loro e' rimedi: e' se ne feciono beffe. La obsedione venne. Quelli cittadini che haveno prima poco stimato e' ricordi del loro signore, come sentirno sonare le artiglierie nelle lor mura et fremere lo exercito de' nimici, corsono piangiendo allo 'mperadore co' grenbi pieni di danari; e' quali lui cacciò via, dicendo: "Andate ad morire con cotesti danari, poiché voi non havete voluto vivere sanza epsi"' (*Parole da dirle sopra la provisione del danaio*, in *I primi scritti*, 414–15).

64. *Discorsi*, I. 55; *Discourses*, 244–5.

65. 'Fanno adunque queste educazioni e sí false interpretazioni, che nel mondo non si vede tante republiche quante si vedeva anticamente; né per consequente si vede ne' popoli tanto amore alla libertà quanto allora' (*Discorsi*, II. 2; *Discourses*, 279).

66. 'E cosí quelli cittadini, i quali lo amore della patria le leggi di quella non ritenevano in Italia, vi furono ritenuti da un giuramento che furono forzati a pigliare' (*Discorsi*, I. 11; *Discourses*, 140).

67. 'Perché se considerassono come la ci permette la esaltazione e la difesa della patria, vedrebbono come la vuole che noi l'amiamo ed onoriamo, e prepariamoci a essere tali che noi la possiamo difendere' (*Discorsi*, II. 2; *Discourses*, 278–9).

68. *Istorie*, III. 7; *FH* 114.

69. *Discorsi*, III. 41; *Discourses*, 515 (revised).

70. *Istorie*, VII. 4.

71. 'la nacque sotto l'imperio romano, e ne' tempi dei primi imperadori cominciò dagli scrittori ad essere ricordata' (ibid. II. 2).

72. 'come si vede che è intervenuto alla città di Firenze, la quale per avere avuto il principio suo sottoposto allo imperio romano, ed essendo vivuta sempre sotto il governo d'altrui . . . ' (*Discorsi*, I. 49).

73. Ibid. I. 1.

74. 'Vero è che io so che io sono contrario, come in molte altre cose, all'oppinione di quelli cittadini . . . ' (Letter to Francesco Guicciardini, 17 May 1521, in *Lettere*, 520; *MF* 336).

75. 'e se questo modo si fusse trovato prima, non si sarebbe fatta la guerra contro il re Ladislao, nè ora si farebbe questa contro il duca Filippo; le quali si erano fatte per riempire i cittadini, e non per necessità' (*Istorie*, IV. 14).

76. Ibid. IV. 20; *FH* 166–7.

77. *Istorie*, VII. 30.

78. *Ritracto delle cose della Magna*, in *I primi scritti*, 25–6.

79. 'Intra regni bene ordinati e governati a' tempi nostri è quello di Francia; et in esso si truovano infinite costituzione buone donde depende la libertà e sicurtà del re' (*Il Principe*, ch. 19); 'In esemplo ci è il regno di Francia, il quale non vive sicuro per altro che per essersi quelli re obligati a infinite leggi, nelle quali si comprende la sicurtà di tutti i suoi popoli' (*Discorsi*, I. 16). See Giorgio Cadoni, *Machiavelli: Regno di Francia e "principato civile"* (Rome: Bulzoni, 1974).

80. *Discorso*, 4.

81. 'io non so quale repubblica o moderna o antica le fosse stata superiore; di tanta virtù d'arme e d'industria sarebbe stata ripiena' (*Istorie*, Preface, 7).

82. 'Oltra di questo, io voglio che tu consideri come le lingue non possono essere semplici, ma conviene che sieno miste con l'altre lingue. Ma quella lingua si chiama d'una patria, la quale convertisce i vocaboli ch'ella ha accattati da altri nell'uso suo, et è sì potente che i vocaboli accattati non la disordinano, ma ella disordina loro: perché quello ch'ella reca da altri lo tira a sé in modo che par suo. . . . E Romani, negl'exerciti loro, non havevono più che due legioni di romani, quali erono circa dodicimila persone, et dipoi vi havevono ventimila dell'altre nationi. Nondimeno, perché quelli erano con li loro capi il nervo dell'exercito, perché militavono tutti sotto l'ordine et disciplina romana, teneano quelli exerciti il nome, l'autorità et dignità romana' (*Discorso*, 50).

83. 'Et perché e' dicono che tutte le lingue patrie son brutte s'elle non hanno del misto (di modo che veruna sarebbe brutta), ma dico ancora che quello che ha di esser misto men bisogno è più laudabile, et senza dubbio ne ha men bisogno la fiorentina' (ibid. 57–9). For the Scholastic sources of this conception, see Paolo Trovato's commentary on p. 58.

84. Federico Chabod, *L'idea di nazione* (Bari: Laterza, 1962), 60.

85. '[German free cities] non hanno possuto pigliare i costumi né franciosi né spagnuoli né italiani; le quali nazioni tutte insieme sono la corruttela del mondo' (*Discorsi*, I. 55).

86. 'E veramente dove non è questa bontà non si può sperare nulla di bene; come non si può sperare nelle provincie che in questi tempi si veggono corrotte come è la Italia sopra tutte l'altre; ed ancora la Francia e la Spagna di tale corrozione ritengono parte' (ibid. I. 55).

87. 'Vero è che le sono le opere loro ora in questa provincia piú virtuose che in quella, ed in quella piú che in questa, secondo la forma della educa-

zione nella quale quegli popoli hanno preso il modo del vivere loro' (ibid. III. 43).

88. 'Dico per tanto che questi stati, quali acquistandosi si aggiungono a uno stato antiquo di quello che acquista, o sono della medesima provincia e della medesima lingua, o non sono. Quando e' sieno è facilità grande a tenerli, massime quando non sieno usi a vivere liberi . . . Ma quando si acquista stati in una provincia disforme di lingua, di costumi e di ordini, qui sono le difficultà' (*Il Principe*, ch. 3; *The Prince* 8).

89. 'Io amo messer Francesco Guicciardini, amo la patria mia più dell'anima; e vi dico questo per quella esperienza che mi hanna data sessanta anni, che io non credo che mai si travagliassino i più difficili articuli che questi, dove la pace è necessaria, e la guerra non si puote abbandonare, et avere alle mani un principe, che con fatica può supplire o alla pace sola o alla guerra sola' (*Lettere*, 629; *MF* 416 (revised)).

90. 'Era messer Benedetto uomo ricchissimo, umano, severo, amatore della libertà della patria sua, ed a cui dispiacevano assai i modi tirannici' (*Istorie*, III. 20).

91. 'Di me non m'incresce, perchè quelli onori che la patria libera mi ha dati, la serva non mi può tôrre; e sempre mi darà maggior piacere la memoria della passata vita mia, che non mi darà dispiacere quella infelicità che si tirerà dietro il mio esilio. Duolmi bene che la mia patria rimanga in preda di pochi, ed alla loro superbia ed avarizia sottoposta. Duolmi di voi, perchè io dubito che quelli mali che finiscono oggi in me, e cominciano in voi, con maggiori danni che non hanno perseguitato me non vi perseguitino. Confortovi adunque a fermare l'animo contro ad ogni infortunio, e portarvi in modo che se alcuna cosa avversa vi avviene, che ve ne avverranno molte, ciascuno cognosca, innocentemente e senza colpa vostra esservi avvenute' (*Istorie*, III. 23; *FH* 137–8 (revised)).

92. *Discorsi*, I. 36; *Discourses*, 199.

93. *Discorsi*, I. 36; *Discourses*, 199.

94. 'La quale cosa, quando fusse onorevole per il privato, è al tutto inutile per il pubblico' (*Discorsi*, I. 36; *Discourses*, 199).

95. 'Buon giudizio certo è stato quello de' nostri reverendi consoli dell'Arte della Lana avere commesso a voi la cura di eleggere un predicatore, non altrimenti che se a Pacchierotto, mentre viveva, fosse stato dato il carico o a ser Sano di trovare una bella e galante moglie a uno amico' (*Lettere*, 518; *MF* 335).

96. 'Io ero in sul cesso quando arrivò il vostro messo, e appunto pensavo alle stravaganze di questo mondo, e tutto ero volto a figurarmi un predicatore a mio modo per Firenze, e fosse tale quale piacesse a me, perché in questo voglio essere caparbio come nelle altre oppinioni mie. E perché io non mancai mai a quella repubblica, dove io ho possuto giovarle, che io non l'abbi fatto, se non con le opere, con le parole, se non con le parole, con i

cenni, io non intendo mancarle anco in questo' (Machiavelli to Guicciardini, 17 May 1521, in *Lettere*, 519–20; *MF* 336).

97. 'Quando io leggo e vostri titoli di oratore di Republica e di frati e considero con quanti re, duchi e principi voi avete altre volte negociato, mi ricordo di Lysandro, a chi doppo tante vittorie e trofei, fu dato la cura di distribuire la carne a quelli medesimi soldati a chi sì gloriosamente aveva comandato' (*Lettere*, 524; *MF* 338–9).

98. See the letter to Guicciardini of 18 May 1521, in *Lettere*, 525–7; *MF* 340–1.

99. On deceitfulness one must read the well-known lines from his letter to Guicciardini of 17 May 1521: 'Quanto alle bugie de' Carpigiani io ne vorrò misura con tutti loro, perché è un pezzo che io mi dottorai di qualità che io non vorrei Francesco Martelli per ragazzo; perché da un tempo in qua, io non dico mai quello che io credo, né credo mai quel che io dico, e se pure e' mi vien detto qualche volta il vero, io lo nascondo fra tante bugie, che è difficile a ritrovarlo' (*Lettere*, 522; *MF* 337).

100. *Il Principe*, ch. 26.

101. *Discursus florentinarum rerum*, in *Arte della guerra*, 275; Gilbert, i. 113–14.

102. *Lettere*, 244; *MF* 135.

103. *Lettere*, 437; *MF* 273 (revised).

Further Reading

Works of Machiavelli

Arte della guerra e scritti politici minori, ed. Sergio Bertelli (Milan: Feltrinelli, 1961).

Discorsi sopra la prima deca di Tito Livio, ed. Corrado Vivanti (Turin: Einaudi, 1983).

Discorso intorno alla nostra lingua, ed. Paolo Trovato (Padua: Editrice Antenore, 1982).

Istorie fiorentine (Florence: Le Monnier, 1990; repr. of 1857 edn.).

Legazioni e commissarie, ed. Sergio Bertelli (3 vols.; Milan: Feltrinelli, 1964).

Lettere, in *Opere di Niccolò Machiavelli*, iii, ed. Franco Gaeta (Turin: UTET, 1984).

I primi scritti politici (1499–1512), ed. Jean-Jacques Marchand (Padua: Editrice Antenore, 1975).

Il Principe e Discorsi sopra la prima deca di Tito Livio, ed. Sergio Bertelli (Milan: Feltrinelli, 1983).

Il teatro e tutti gli scritti letterari, ed. Franco Gaeta (Milan: Feltrinelli, 1965).

La vita di Castruccio Castracani da Lucca, ed. Riekie Brakkee, Introduction and commentary by Paolo Trovato (Naples: Liguori, 1986).

Biographical Works

Black, Robert, 'Machiavelli, Servant of the Florentine Republic', in Gisela Bock, Quentin Skinner, and Maurizio Viroli (eds.), *Machiavelli and Republicanism* (Cambridge: Cambridge University Press, 1990), 71–99.

De Grazia, Sebastian, *Machiavelli in Hell* (Princeton: Princeton University Press, 1989).

Ridolfi, Roberto, *The Life of Niccolò Machiavelli*, trans. Cecil Grayson (London: Routledge & Kegan Paul, 1963).

Rubinstein, Nicolai, 'The Beginnings of Political Thought in Florence', *Journal of the Warburg and Courtauld Institutes*, 5 (1942), 198–227.

—— 'Florence and the Despots: Some Aspects of Florentine Diplomacy in the Fourteenth Century', *Transactions of the Royal Historical Society*, ser. 5, 2 (1952), 21–45.

—— 'Politics and Constitutions in Florence at the End of the Fifteenth Century', in Ernest F. Jacob (ed.), *Italian Renaissance Studies* (London: Faber, 1960), 148–83.

—— 'Notes on the Word *stato* in Florence before Machiavelli', in John G. Rowe and William H. Stockdale (eds.), *Florilegium Historiale: Essays*

Presented to Wallace K. Ferguson (Toronto: University of Toronto Press, 1971), 313–26.

—— '"*Stato*" and Regime in Fifteenth-Century Florence', in *Per Federico Chabod* (Annali della Facoltà di Scienze Politiche; Perugia, 1980–1), i. 137–46.

Historical and Intellectual Background

Albertini, Rudolph von, *Firenze dalla Repubblica al Principato* (Turin: Einaudi, 1970).

Baron, Hans, *The Crisis of the Early Italian Renaissance* (2nd edn., Princeton: Princeton University Press, 1966).

—— *In Search of Florentine Civic Humanism* (2 vols.; Princeton: Princeton University Press, 1988).

Butters, Humfrey C., *Governors and Government in Early Sixteenth-Century Florence, 1502–1519* (Oxford: Oxford University Press, 1985).

Gilbert, Felix, 'Florentine Political Assumptions in the Period of Savonarola and Soderini', *Journal of the Warburg and Courtauld Institutes*, 20 (1957), 187–214.

Pieri, Piero, *Il Rinascimento e la crisi militare italiana* (Turin: Einaudi, 1952).

Pocock, John A. G., *The Machiavellian Moment: Florentine Political Thought and the Atlantic Republican Tradition* (Princeton: Princeton University Press, 1975).

Rubinstein, Nicolai, *The Government of Florence under the Medici 1434–1494* (Oxford: Oxford University Press, 1966).

Schmitt, Charles B., and Skinner, Quentin (eds.), *The Cambridge History of Renaissance Philosophy* (Cambridge: Cambridge University Press, 1988).

Skinner, Quentin, *The Foundations of Modern Political Thought* (2 vols.; Cambridge: Cambridge University Press, 1978).

Stephens, John N., *The Fall of the Florentine Republic 1512–1530* (Oxford: Oxford University Press, 1983).

Viroli, Maurizio, *From Politics to Reason of State* (Cambridge: Cambridge University Press, 1992).

On Machiavelli's Conception of Life

Chabod, Federico, *Scritti su Machiavelli* (Turin: Einaudi, 1964); Eng. trans. David Moore, *Machiavelli and the Renaissance*, with an Introduction by Alessandro Passerin d'Entreves (London: Bowes & Bowes, 1958).

Garin, Eugenio, 'Aspetti del pensiero di Machiavelli', in Garin, *Dal Rinascimento all'Illuminismo* (Pisa: Nistri-Lischi, 1970), 43–77.

—— *La cultura del Rinascimento* (Bari: Laterza, 1976).

Price, Russell, 'The Theme of Gloria in Machiavelli', *Renaissance Quarterly*, 30 (1977), 588–631.

Parel, Anthony, *The Machiavellian Cosmos* (New Haven: Yale University Press, 1992).

Sasso, Gennaro, *Machiavelli e gli antichi e altri saggi* (3 vols.; Naples: Riccardo Ricciardi, 1987–8).

On Machiavelli's Political Theory

Berlin, Isaiah, 'The Originality of Machiavelli', in Myron P. Gilmore (ed.), *Studies on Machiavelli* (Florence: Sansoni, 1972), 147–206.

Bock, Gisela, 'Civil Discord in Machiavelli's *Istorie Fiorentine*', in *Machiavelli and Republicanism* (Cambridge: Cambridge University Press, 1990), 181–201.

Colish, Marcia, 'The Idea of Liberty in Machiavelli', *Journal of History of Ideas*, 32 (1971), 323–51.

—— 'Cicero's *De Officiis* and Machiavelli's *Prince*', in *Sixteenth Century Journal*, 9 (1978), 81–93.

De Vries, Hans, *Essai sur la terminologie constitutionelle chez Machiavel* (Den Haag: Excelsior, 1957).

Gilbert, Allan H., *Machiavelli's 'Prince' and its Forerunners* (Durham, NC: Duke University Press, 1938).

Gilbert, Felix, 'The Humanist Concept of the Prince and *The Prince* of Machiavelli', *Journal of Modern History*, 11 (1939), 449–83.

—— *Machiavelli and Guicciardini: Politics and History in Sixteenth-Century Florence* (Princeton: Princeton University Press, 1965).

Mallet, Michael, 'The Theory and Practice of Warfare in Machiavelli's Republic', in *Machiavelli and Republicanism* (Cambridge: Cambridge University Press, 1990), 173–80.

Mansfield, Harvey C., *Machiavelli's Virtue* (Chicago: University of Chicago Press, 1996).

Najemy, John M., 'The Controversy Surrounding Machiavelli's Service to the Republic', in *Machiavelli and Republicanism* (Cambridge: Cambridge University Press, 1990), 101–17.

—— *Between Friends: Discourse of Power and Desire in the Machiavelli–Vettori Letters of 1513–1515* (Princeton: Princeton University Press, 1993).

Pocock, John G. A., *The Machiavellian Moment: Florentine Political Thought and the Atlantic Republican Tradition*, (Princeton: Princeton University Press, 1975).

Skinner, Quentin, *Machiavelli* (Oxford: Oxford University Press, 1981).

—— 'Machiavelli on the Maintenance of Liberty', *Politics*, 18 (1983), 3–15.

—— 'The State', in Terence Ball, James Farr, and Rusell L. Hanson (eds.), *Political Innovation and Conceptual Change* (New York: Cambridge University Press, 1989), 90–131.

—— 'Machiavelli's *Discorsi* and the Pre-Humanist Origins of Republican Ideas', in Gisela Bock, Quentin Skinner, and Maurizio Viroli, *Machiavelli and Republicanism* (Cambridge: Cambridge University Press, 1990), 121–41.

On Machiavelli's Rhetoric

Ascoli, Albert Russell, and Kahn, Victoria (eds.), *Machiavelli and the Discourse of Literature* (Ithaca, NY: Cornell University Press, 1993).

Bardazzi, Giovanni, 'Tecniche narrative nel Machiavelli scrittore di lettere', in *Annali della Scuola Normale Superiore di Pisa*, ser. III, V (1975), 1444–89.

Garver, Eugene, 'Marchiavelli's *The Prince*: A Neglected Rhetorical Classic', *Philosophy and Rhetoric*, 13 (1980), 99–120.

Gray, Hanna H., 'Renaissance Humanism: The Pursuit of Eloquence', *Journal of the History of Ideas*, 24 (1963), 497–514.

Kahn, Victoria, *Machiavellian Rhetoric: From Counter-Reformation to Milton* (Princeton: Princeton University Press, 1994).

Richardson, Brian, 'Notes on Machiavelli's Sources and his Treatment of the Rhetorical Tradition', *Italian Studies*, 26 (1971), 24–48.

Seigel, Jerrold E., *Rhetoric and Philosophy in Renaissance Humanism* (Princeton: Princeton University Press, 1968).

Struever, Nancy S., *The Language of History in the Renaissance* (Princeton: Princeton University Press, 1970).

Tinkler, John F., 'Praise and Advice: Rhetorical Approaches in More's *Utopia* and Machiavelli's *The Prince*', *Sixteenth Century Journal*, 19 (1988), 187–207.

On Machiavelli's Patriotism

Curcio, Carlo, *Machiavelli nel Risorgimento* (Milano: Giuffré, 1953).

Kantorowicz, Ernst H., *The King's Two Bodies: A Study in Medieval Political Theology* (Princeton: Princeton University Press, 1957).

Post, Gaines, 'Two Notes on Nationalism in the Middle Ages', *Tradition*, 9 (1953), 281–320.

Russo, Luigi, *Machiavelli* (Bari: Laterza, 1949).

Viroli, Maurizio, *For Love of Country* (Oxford: Oxford University Press, 1995).

INDEX